LEARNING HISTORY

LEARNING HISTORY

A.K.DICKINSON, P.J.LEE
and P.J.ROGERS

 HEINEMANN EDUCATIONAL BOOKS

Heinemann Educational Books Ltd
22 Bedford Square, London WC1B 3HH
LONDON   EDINBURGH   MELBOURNE   AUCKLAND
HONG KONG   SINGAPORE   KUALA LUMPUR   NEW DELHI
IBADAN   NAIROBI   JOHANNESBURG
EXETER (NH)   KINGSTON   PORT OF SPAIN

First published 1984

British Library Cataloguing in Publication Data
Learning History.
  1. History – Study and teaching
  I. Dickinson, A. K. II. Lee, P. J. II. Rogers, P. J.
  907'.1   LB 1581

  ISBN 0–435–80288–7
  ISBN 0–435–80289–5   Pbk

Printed in Great Britain by Biddles Ltd
Phototypesetting by Georgia Origination, Liverpool

Contents

Contributors

R. E. Aldrich: Senior Lecturer in History of Education
Institute of Education
University of London

A. K. Dickinson: Lecturer in Education with special reference
to the teaching of history
Institute of Education
University of London

P. J. Lee: Lecturer in Education with special reference
to the teaching of history
Institute of Education
University of London

P. J. Rogers: Senior Lecturer in Education
Department of Further Professional Studies in
Education
The Queen's University
Belfast

D. Shemilt: Senior Lecturer in Education
Trinity and All Saints Colleges, Leeds
and Director of the Schools Council Project
History 13–16, 1978–83

D. Thompson: Senior Lecturer in Education with special reference
to the teaching of history
Institute of Education
University of London

Acknowledgements

The editors and publishers wish to thank the following for permission to reproduce illustrations on the pages indicated:

Mary Evans Picture Library: p. 81.
Syndics of Cambridge University Library: p. 74.

They would also like to thank those who have given permission to reproduce extracts. Full details of the sources of copyright material are given in the Notes.

Preface

This book tackles two broad questions currently looming large in discussions of history teaching. Can history in schools be justified? And, if it is taught, how far can children cope with the thinking it demands of them?

Chapters 1 and 2 touch on some aspects of the first question, but from slightly different perspectives. Chapter 1 examines some reasons why history is worth learning, and argues that since we cannot escape assumptions of one sort or another about the past, we had better have the most rational knowledge we can get. Chapter 2 approaches the question from the other side, and considers why history should be taught, suggesting some specific benefits that accrue from school history. History may not be 'in danger' in quite the way it was in the 1960s, but perhaps there are new threats on the horizon. If there are, history teachers need to be more confident, and more aware of the possibilities as well as the problems of their discipline.

History teaching does seem to be changing: even a brief glance at the material offered by publishers for use in the classroom reveals the extent to which there is now at least face-value agreement that children ought in one way or another to have to *think* in history lessons. But what thinking it is reasonable to ask them to do, and how in fact they are likely to go about it, remain matters of dispute. Two sources of opinions in this area stand out. First, of course, there is the teacher's own experience. There is no question but that experience is enormously important because there is no set of rules that can be mechanically applied to produce effective teaching. Teachers just develop a 'nose' for things. The trouble is that different experiences can lead to very different views as to what children can do, and if there is no experience in common, there is some difficulty in assessing different claims. Secondly, there is the legacy of Piaget. It is hard not to feel that, for all his genius, the influence of Piaget in this country – at least on history teaching – has been malign. Teachers (perhaps especially history teachers) are often suspicious of theory, even if it is simply standing back and reflecting on their own practice. Yet somehow the one element of 'theory' that has passed into the everyday language of teaching is a notion of Piagetian stages as setting the limits of children's thinking. The gloom it has engendered has not been shared by everyone: many teachers have optimistically gone on insisting that children can do worthwhile things in history. None the less, even the publication of Margaret Donaldson's *Children's Minds* (Fontana, 1978) has not dispelled the view that history is fundamentally too difficult for children to tackle in any serious way until late adolescence. It is our hope that some of the contributions offered here provide grounds for a more sanguine assessment of what children can do in school history.

The central chapters of this book are concerned with children's thinking in history, their attempts to make sense of the past, and the assumptions they make in the process. The link between Chapters 3, 4 and 5 is to be found in a cluster of closely related concepts: empathy, imagination and understanding. Chapter 3 outlines an account of empathy in history, investigates adolescent constructions of empathy (with particular emphasis on intentional action) and sets out what is probably the first systematic analysis of 'empathetic' exercises. Chapter 4 provides an analysis of historical imagination, emphasizing its links with empathy and understanding, and concludes with a discussion of some recent psychological evidence. Chapter 5 reproduces detailed transcript material from pupils' attempts to sort out what seems to them strange behaviour in the distant past, and discusses its significance. The transcripts include substantial excerpts recording the efforts of primary as well as secondary schoolchildren. The next three chapters have a common concern with different ways of extending children's thinking in history. Chapter 6 emphasizes that visual representation offers an important – and under-estimated – way of simplifying and scaling down genuine historical inquiry for pupils, and demonstrates that it can enable teachers to do very valuable work with primary schoolchildren. In the seventh chapter some detailed examples of children's attempts to provide multi-causal explanations are set in the context of a wider discussion of the thinking and learning required by recent developments in history teaching. Chapter 8 outlines ways in which children cope with understanding certain kinds of historical actions, suggests how their understanding may be advanced in the light of clues given by the right kind of work, and discusses the implications of the possibilities raised here for examinations.

History teaching over the past two decades has been characterized by uncertainties and upheavals. These are not over, but it is harder now to divide school history into 'traditional' and 'new' approaches, or to label the attitudes of history teachers 'progressive' or 'reactionary'. The final chapter provides a sketch of the historical development of the ideas involved in the 'new' history, and their vicissitudes.

The warning was given in the late 1960s that history might be in danger, a warning that has frequently been repeated since. The time for this kind of defensiveness is past. Of course people should learn history, and of course it should be taught in schools – but only if it is worthy of the name history, and children's time is not wasted on mindless mechanical exercises requiring little more than recognition and recall. A wanton underestimation of children's ability must not be allowed to serve as an excuse for practices that put history in danger only by failing to teach history at all.

Our hope is that this book will be helpful to teachers who care about history teaching and are not content with easy certainties. That it has seen the light of day at all is in great part a result of the forbearance and encouragement of Janice Brown of Heinemann Educational Books, and especially to the energy and sheer professionalism of Fuz Bagum in the preparation of the manuscript. We owe them both our thanks and take this opportunity to express our gratitude.

1. Why Learn History?

P. J. LEE

I. THE PAST, HISTORICITY, AND HISTORY

There is no escape from the past. It is built into the concepts we employ to cope with the everyday physical and social world. Sometimes concepts encapsulate the past in the form of causal processes (e.g. 'tree', 'mother', 'bomb-crater'). Sometimes an institutional past is involved – in the case of (say) an illegal government or an illegitimate child, one in which certain legitimating criteria have not been met. But the grip of the past is often less formal. 'Science', 'communism', or 'nation-state' might be defined in a more or less atemporal way in the dictionaries. But communism is not just the name of a pattern of beliefs or attitudes, so that we can find out what it is in a dictionary definition or even a scholarly analysis of those beliefs or attitudes. Part of what communism is must be found in what communists have *done*. (And so also for liberalism, capitalism, and so on.) Similarly, our notion of science imports a conception of the kinds of activity that have counted as scientific in the past, and a picture of the changes that science has wrought in everyday life. And again, the view we take of nation-states is inevitably influenced by our understanding of their past. The past gives our concepts concrete content. If having a concept involves both knowing a rule and being able to pick out instances, in many areas of understanding it is the past that supplies the instances. Alternatively, where the question arises whether a rule of application has been satisfied (is this a *constitutional* government?) the past may be the only arbiter.

Concepts carry temporal luggage. But our world does not consist solely of instances of concepts. It is peopled also by individuals, particular things with particular pasts. The Common Market, Germany, or the Cold War in their different ways derive much of their substance from their temporal extension. The Common Market, for some people, is an institution that has put up food prices in the UK, and increased bureaucratic control over ordinary people's lives. It is the past that reveals the nature of the institution, and indeed an institution could hardly be conceived as instantaneous. In the same way Germany is less a geographical than a temporal entity, and is whatever its past reveals it to be.[1] The Cold War is the name of a particular series of events (and perhaps also of a certain kind of behaviour on the part of people, governments and states). Its lifespan is uncertain: it was recently thought to be dead, but the newspapers from time to time predict or announce its revival. Talk of such a resurrection is intelligible only as an invocation of the past.

Connections between past and present go beyond this. Actions are done for reasons, and people (as individuals or in social groups or institutions) have goals, finding or placing themselves in particular situations. These situations in turn are frequently understood in past-referring terms. An agent (or institution) sees himself (or itself) as having been threatened, or insulted, or undermined; a series of events is characterized in terms of a tradition, which prescribes not just how such events should be seen, but by the same token what sort of responses should be made. (Within Western diplomacy, trade unionism, politics and capitalist finance, for example, we might find events characterized or colligated as appeasement, a lock-out, democratization, or industrial growth.) Reasons for action are 'backward referencing', and so too must be understanding of those reasons. More generally, as Olafson has pointed out, 'our system of temporal distinctions is deployed by beings who are themselves in time, and . . . this being the case, there must be at least one feature of their present state that cannot be described without reference to any preceding state'.[2]

This 'historicity', or opening on the past and the future, is central to many of the concerns of this chapter. But historicity is one thing, and history another. To say that human beings are in time, and that actions refer to past events, or that particulars like 'Germany' or 'the Common Market' carry with them conceptions of their past, is to say nothing of what kind of past is at stake. Hence, the Cold War might be the name of a colligatory grouping of events and actions historically reconstructed, or it might be the name of an explanatory political, social and nationalist myth. We cannot escape *some* kind of past. But we may be in a position to choose what kind we shall have. J. H. Plumb offers us a choice between the mere past, which is 'always a created ideology with a purpose, designed to control individuals, or motivate societies, or inspire classes', and history, whose future is to 'cleanse the story of mankind from those deceiving visions of a purposeful past'.[3] Where the past has sanctioned authority or offered a guide to destiny, history 'by its very nature . . . dissolves those simple, structural generalizations by which our forefathers interpreted the purpose of life in historical terms'.[4] And so, Plumb concludes, the death of the past is upon us: 'History, which is so deeply concerned with the past, has, in a sense, helped to destroy it as a social force, as a synthesizing and comprehensive statement of human destiny.'[5] For Plumb, history is destructive, but it can 'still teach wisdom'. It offers a past in which mankind's condition has improved through the application of reason. What is not clear is whether this wisdom is substantive or formal. For while 'the greatest contribution that the historian can make is to teach all who are literate about the nature of social change' still, 'of course, there will not be agreement; historians will speak with different voices'.[6] There is, then, in Plumb's account, an ambiguity between history as on the one hand a formal, essentially negative instrument, and on the other a source of positive wisdom, giving knowledge of 'the mechanics of historical change', demonstrating the role of reason in man's success, and thus fulfilling at least some of the social purposes of the dead past.[7]

Another question raised by Plumb's account is whether his obituary for the dead past is not premature. Is the past really dead or dying? It is true that history destroys particular pasts 'like a woodworm working in the heart of a beam – always active, but rarely seen on the surface'.[8] But the destruction of particular pasts does not necessarily mean the end of the past. Writing two years before Plumb, Kitson Clark was less sanguine. He warned of the

> haphazard mass of misty knowledge, scraps of information, fiction in fancy dress and hardly conscious historical memories . . . woven [into] a network of historical associations which stretches over the whole field of human consciousness. Thus words are converted into spells, symbols are endowed with emotional force and stereotypes emerge which pretend to describe whole groups of people, and predict from their past their probable conduct in the future.[9]

There is on the face of it no reason why a past of this kind might not pretend to provide the sanctions and the keys to destiny which Plumb believed discredited by history. Has history then had no effect? Is the past a hydra-headed monster?

It is tempting to argue that if history cannot extirpate the past, it has indefinitely prolonged it, endowed it with a set of largely evolutionary processes, and turned it into a domain of fairly rapid and extensive change.

> The majority of men and women . . . realize that they are part of an historical process that has changed over the centuries . . . [and] that the process of change has accelerated and is accelerating so that they require to know what the nature of this process has been and is. They need an historical past, objective and true.[10]

No doubt history had a hand in this; but there seems little doubt that natural science and the social changes brought about by rapid industrial and urban development played at least an equal role.[11] None the less, for whatever reason, we inhabit a past long enough, complex and puzzling enough, and dynamic enough to reduce the power of any particular sanctions or destinies that may be sought in it, and one that appeals to history for its validation. The past still contains heroes and great men, moral examples and mythical golden-ages. 'Historic events' still roll glibly off the tongues of commentators and journalists. But the notion of a historic event is important: for all its connot-ations of cheap sensation and the *Guinness Book of Records* it carries with it the idea that lurking in the wings are the scribes of history, recording, analysing, weighing the significance of events. In principle the past is now the province of history, and despite the ambiguity of 'what history shows' it is the rational discipline of history that is recognized as the court of appeal, even if its procedures are little understood.[12]

If Plumb's division between the past and history does not go far enough, and his epitaph for the former is too hasty, Michael Oakeshott's distinction between history and the 'practical past' might be thought too radical.[13] We lapse from history into the practical past when 'the past is seen in a specific relation to the present', or is 'designed to justify . . . practical beliefs about the present and the future'.[14] It is the past employed by the lawyer, politician, or priest. Hence in the historical, as opposed to the practical past, there are 'no culminations, main movements, turning points or catastrophes: only a world of interrelated events'.[15] 'In "history" no man dies too soon by "accident"; .... Nothing is approved, there being no desired condition of things in relation to which approval can operate; and nothing is denounced.'[16] The practical past 'consists of happenings recognized to be contributory to a subsequent condition of things', whereas history represents 'an interest in past events ... in respect of their independence of subsequent or present events'.[17] It must be admitted that Oakeshott's analysis imposes impossible limits on history, and at the same time cuts it off from its roots – there is nothing wrong in principle with inquiry *starting* from current interests or practical problems.[18] But the strength of this account is that it allows us to distinguish between a lay past inhabited by heroes and depicted in moral tales, and the historical past that parallels it, not by prematurely interring the lay past now we have a historical past to replace it, but by recognizing different ways in which the past continues to be treated.[19]

The burden of what both Plumb and Oakeshott have to say is that without history there can be no rational past. Indeed, if in the absence of history the past is a merely practical one, it is hard to see how there could be an agreed conception of the past even in principle, unless there were agreement in practical life. (And for that condition to be met, the world would have to be very different from that which it currently is.)[20] Without history the past would merely serve practical interests, and so in an important sense we would be cut off from our own experience. For historical inquiry is simply the rational investigation of the past, and since we cannot escape the past, we had better seek the best knowledge of it we can get.[21] It is for this reason that it is odd to ask what use history has, or why it should be learnt. If our knowledge of the present world is never an 'instantaneous' knowledge, and brings with it willy-nilly some substantive conception of the past, then to be historically ignorant is just to be ignorant.

II. EVIDENCE

It has been asserted throughout section I that history supplies the only rational means of investigating the past. This claim is founded in part on history's developing concept of (and techniques for handling) evidence. There has been a great deal of discussion of historical evidence and its importance for history teaching in recent years, and I do not wish to discuss the strengths and weaknesses of particular classroom methods or syllabus arrangements here. What is important for the matter in hand is that if the use of evidence in certain ways is what makes a rational investigation of the past possible, then being able to use evidence in these ways is a valuable acquisition. But there are limits as to what can be claimed here. It cannot be assumed that the concept of historical evidence is co-extensive with the concept of evidence in general, and the way in which evidence is used in history is not necessarily the same as the way it is used in (say) natural science. The difference is partly one of techniques, but this is the result of more fundamental differences. The questions to be answered are different, and in consequence so is much of the evidential material. I cannot go into this properly here, but it is obvious that questions as to what was intended in certain actions do not arise in connection with the behaviour of inanimate objects, and that the meaning of a document or the significance of a social practice to those who participate in it have no counterpart as evidential problems in natural science.

It may seem that the price to be paid for distinguishing evidence in history from evidence in other empirical disciplines is high: learning to handle historical evidence may turn out to have no transfer value to other disciplines. If learning history is valuable, so too will be learning to use historical evidence, but the latter cannot give independent support to the former, since it derives from it. But this is not so restrictive as it seems, and certainly does not confine what is learnt in using historical evidence to a dim and dead past. We have already seen that the past cannot be neatly divided off from the present: understanding the one cannot be isolated from understanding the other. It is true that teaching children to use historical evidence may not be *ipso facto* equipping them to make effective use of the practical past; perhaps people more readily employ the past to solve their current problems when they are aware only of a practical past. Someone might even be found to argue that children need quick answers to practical problems, not history, which will bring merely paralysing academic doubts. But it would be difficult to take such a view seriously as a prescription for education, for it would amount to a denial of the importance of truth, and with it of all cognitive activity. (Perhaps the doctrines nearest to such a position in modern times would be Futurism and Fascism.) Less generally it would amount to a blessing on the uses of the past deplored by Plumb and so clearly exemplified in contemporary Northern Ireland. Learning to use historical evidence, and perhaps above all acquiring the 'rational passions' – concern for truth, objectivity and so on – that are essential to the operation of historical procedures is both one of the major reasons for learning history, and a central part of what learning history actually entails.

III. LAWS, LESSONS, AND GENERALIZATIONS

The relationship between the past and the present involves another aspect of history. Among academic historians perhaps one of the most discredited justifications for history is that it teaches 'lessons'. Politicians, journalists, and a great many others (including some professional historians) none the less persist in thinking that history does have lessons to teach. Munich, the experience of racial conflict in the USA, and the Industrial Revolution are put before us as examples of what can, might, or will happen if (respectively) the Nato powers try to 'appease' the USSR, inner urban decay and racial discrimination continue unchecked, or the silicon chip is not harnessed in the proper way. Unquestionably the past *can* be pressed into service in the advocacy of a course of action, at any rate as a practical past. But is there anything like this that may validly be sought in the historical past?

The 'lessons' of history are usually framed as generalizations of some sort, supporting predictions. The latter may be warnings of the way the world will 'run on' as it were by itself, if a particular course of action is not taken. Alternatively they may purport to demonstrate the likely (even 'inevitable') consequences of a particular action, emphasizing its desirability or undesirability. In natural science, of course, predictions are frequently based upon theories that embody statements of regularities or general laws, and specification of relevant initial conditions. And the application of science to practical problems has resulted in startling successes. It is tempting therefore to think that the generalizations that are, or form the basis of, 'lessons' of history are equivalent to the formally articulated theories of the scientific paradigm, only perhaps a little less precise. Such an assumption is dangerous. This is not the place to attempt a thorough examination of the possibility of or logical function of general laws in history, but some comments cannot be avoided. [22] There are clearly summative generalizations in history, which are explanatory in an everyday sense, but they make a weak basis for prediction. As Atkinson points out, 'One's surprise . . . that a particular Reformation Parliament was packed is undeniably diminished by the discovery that they all were.' [23] But unless we know why they were packed, we cannot employ the generalization in any useful way beyond the cases it summarizes. [24] So something more is needed: perhaps universal laws or statistical generalizations?

Doubtless it is in principle possible that universal laws or statistical generalizations may be discovered that are applicable to history. It may also be that in giving explanations historians necessarily commit themselves to the (implicit) assertion that *some* law covering that explanation exists, even if no one can formulate it. [25] But even were both these arguments accepted (and neither is without difficulties) they would offer little guidance on the issues central to this chapter. In the first place genuine universal laws applicable to history are likely to be of low probability, in the sense that the chances of their being true are small. It is difficult to think of a single example to which this does not apply. In the second place, statistical laws, which may have a better claim to truth, are applicable to a limited range of areas where there are large numbers of events that may be regarded as 'the same'; typically they are to be found in demographic (and some economic) history. Olafson has argued that 'the multiple routines by which the life of a human community is organized and stabilized' – ploughing a field, for instance – are 'resumed again and again without significant change', and any story of them would be 'a retelling of a story that has already been told countless times. Laid end to end these "stories" would [be] essentially self-contained and [could] be understood without reference to any particular past episode.' [26] For a *history* to be possible, events must be 'logically cumulative'. People describe events in ways that pick out (from the many possible descriptions available) certain features to which they will respond. These features will reflect the beliefs, expectations, intentions and purposes of whoever is responding, 'all of which presupposes a capacity to refer to events at prior or subsequent points in the time order. . . . Within a context of this kind the original event takes on a meaning – as a threat, for example, or as creating an opportunity – which gives it an orientation in time as blocking or facilitating other possible actions'. Thus an event initiates a sequence in which appropriate responses are made to past events seen in this way.[27] The recurring routines that are the typical domain of statistical laws (about, for example, the number of births per thousand under certain conditions) do not display this 'logically cumulative' character. Hence, such statistical laws as are currently to be found in history are mostly confined to certain specific kinds of historical analysis. Of course, over the long term, recurrent routines may produce changes (e.g. soil erosion, or a population explosion) that demand action outside the established repertory of such routines: but it is precisely changes of this kind that make the establishment of statistical laws transcending particular times and places very difficult. The point for this chapter is not that there are no candidates for the status of such laws, or that such laws are never presupposed in historical explanations, but that there are very few that could support predictions. And if it is hard to think of any statistical laws one would risk one's shirt on, it is harder still to find any well-supported *universal* laws.

There is an important reason for this. Just as there are not laws in physics about car radiators cracking that will explain why a particular radiator cracked, but instead laws relating changes in the pressure of liquids to their temperature and volume, so in history it is not to be expected that there will be laws about the overthrow of kings or the actions of foreign secretaries. But in history, unlike physics, there are as yet no sets of abstract concepts of the right kind. Even if such conceptual schemes were developed, there would be important problems about their employment in history. This is because many historical events are backward referencing and (in Olafson's sense) 'logically cumulative'. The conceptual framework in terms of which these events are picked out and understood by the agents involved is the everyday practical one, in which things are done for *reasons*. The significance of this is brought out by consideration of some points raised by Davidson.[28]

Causal claims, Davidson argues, entail laws only in the weak sense that 'A caused B' 'entails that there exists a causal law instantiated by some true descriptions of A and B'. We can give valid causal explanations without knowing the relevant predictive laws. Moreover,

> a generalization like 'Windows are fragile, and fragile things tend to break when struck hard enough, other conditions being right' is not a predictive law in the rough – the predictive law, if we had it, would be quantitative and would use very different concepts. The generalization, like our generalizations about behaviour, serves a very different function: it provides evidence for the existence of a causal law covering the case at hand.[29]

On this account, history can be explanatory without being predictive. In the case of human behaviour this is particularly important. If we wish to explain an action (characterized in everyday terms) we do not need (and cannot have) a law to the effect that people who believe so-and-so and want such-and-such will always act in a certain way. To be sure, the action will instantiate (under *some* true description) causal laws – so reasons are 'rational causes'. But these causal laws do not deal in the concepts in which rational explanation must deal (where notions such as *evidence*, *good reasons for believing*, and so on, must come in). The concepts required in the relevant causal laws, if we knew them, 'may even be neurological, chemical, or physical'.[30] Laws employing this sort of conceptual framework could not deal with events understood as reasons at all, let alone under the form of description so frequent in history, in which reasons are 'past-referencing'. A conceptual framework that bypassed reasons would bypass these reasons too, and would thus be unable to account for one central relationship between past and present. If Olafson is right, this would render much of history impossible.

Naturally there is much more to this argument.[31] What matters for this chapter, however, is that even on the most plausible analysis of reasons as causes, there remain serious difficulties for any claim that we can expect to achieve universal laws bearing on human action construed *as* action. We have in history few (if any) universal laws that could bear the weight of prediction. We perhaps could (in the future) have such laws, at the price of a new abstract conceptual framework. The price to be paid would be that we should be unable to explain reasons *as* reasons and actions *as* actions.

If the study of history offers no laws upon which predictions may be based, can it offer anything that will give us some purchase on the future? The first thing to notice is that in common sense and in science guarded and conditional predictions are possible without laws (something recognized in a qualified way by Hempel himself).[32] Once it is accepted that it is possible to give inductive support for assertions about the future independent of general laws, prediction based on historical knowledge is no longer in principle impermissible.[33] So long as it is recognized that all prediction is conditional (particularly in history, where other things often refuse to remain equal, but change instead), and that it is not the point of history to provide the basis for prediction (history – even Marxist history – is not organized in the requisite way) there is little harm in saying that historical knowledge may sometimes allow predictions to be made.[34] In the second place (without invoking general laws) explanations always have implications beyond the case in hand. If one cites A as an explanation of B, one can repudiate a similar explanation in another case only if there is a relevant difference between them. This does not justify either the assertion of 'Whenever *A* then *B*', or 'Only if *A* then *B*', but entails only 'that "because" always has a reference beyond the individual case in virtue of the generality of the descriptions under which the phenomena in question are explained'.[35] Concepts bring with them logical consequences that may be regarded (for some purposes) as sets of presuppositions about similar cases. If we are prepared to assert that the USSR sent troops into Czechoslovakia because its vital interests were threatened, then we must be prepared to show relevant differences if we wish to repudiate a similar explanation in apparently similar circumstances. The presupposition that great powers will protect their vital interests is loose and 'merely' suggestive, but not an empty truism or entirely formal, because built into the case that implies it (Czechoslovakia) are hints as to what sort of thing might be a vital interest. Even so, if circumstances are different, or other powers differ, or if they fail to recognize their interests, or if they have overriding considerations – the list is indefinitely long – the presupposition will fail.[36] Its *applicability* is always in question, because it will be a matter of judgement as to what is to count as 'the same', and what are the respects that are relevant to deciding this. How far do events in Poland have to go before the USSR's 'vital interests' impel intervention? The minimal generality implicit in the employment of one set of concepts rather than another in history records a historian's (often singular) judgement and indicates where he might look in other cases, rather than signifies the application of a law formulated independently or in advance. For this reason, if we choose to regard this implicit generality as more than formal, and so as supplying sets of presuppositions for other events, it is essential to realize that we are dealing with heuristic devices, whose role is to direct attention to certain elements in a situation as possibly important. The more explicit, precise, and law-like such presuppositions, the less likely it is that they will be relevant in that form to new situations. Atkinson has suggested an analogy here with canons of taste. 'It is widely recognized that such canons, if more than crutches for beginners or material for misguided textbook producers, are defensible only to the extent that they encourage one to see through them to the exemplary works, the subjects of comparison and contrast, which are the bases upon which they arise.'[37] Presuppositions and minimal implicit generalizations deriving from the concepts employed in explanation are seldom encountered as explicit statements in historical work, and then are usually rendered explicit in order to discount alternative sets of presuppositions. Where they do crop up is in school textbooks and in transcripts of teacher-talk in classroom interaction, or in popularizations of history.[38] This is important: 'crutches for beginners' is a little too dismissive – for someone *learning* history suggestive generalizations are valid and useful, so long as it is realized that they are not distillations of, or formal 'results' of, historical research. The point is not to apply them but to see beyond them.

Many of these presuppositions and implicit generalizations turn out to be similar to Dray's 'principles of action'. Hence Taylor glosses his generalization that 'suspicion is the normal relationship between great powers' with a schematic principle of action for military advisers. 'After all it is the job of generals and admirals and air marshals to prepare for wars. They can only prepare for war at all sensibly if they envisage an antagonist and when they cannot see an obvious antagonist then they find unlikely antagonists.'[39] Similarly, closely questioned by a pupil about French and Dutch caution during Marlborough's Blenheim campaign, a teacher responds 'Generals don't fight battles unless they think they're going to win them'. Taken as it stands, this latter statement is simply false. But as something like a principle of action for the relevant period, when training and maintaining professional troops was extremely expensive, and war was far from total, it draws attention to what is likely to be an important military premise. And it is used in the lesson both to show how most generals were likely to behave, and to indicate that Marlborough was different. A principle of action is defensible in individual cases without thereby being rendered worthless.

If so simplistic a distinction is permitted, it might be said that history is not a practical activity (i.e. it is a cognitive one), but that in important ways it is like practical activities. In it a mass of knowledge is produced, and this may be acquired by anyone who learns history. But this knowledge is not formalized or articulated in deductive schemas. And because it is not formalized, it cannot be *applied* to *instances* but only *employed* in *cases*.[40] Historical knowledge can be regarded as (among other things) vicarious experience: it points to what might be expected, while at the same time making it evident that what is expected is seldom exactly what happens. It gives some conception of the range of possibilities, and opens up the opportunity to hold this conception reflexively.

> A man's historical experience affects his sense of probability, his choice of the things he deems likely to happen because he believes they have happened before, or the motives which he believes are likely to be entertained because he thinks he knows that men have entertained them before. In all these matters it is important that men and women should realize what is likely to influence their way of thinking, because it is only if they do this they can bring such influences under some sort of control.[41]

Awareness of the basis of one's beliefs is only a necessary condition of bringing them under control, not a sufficient one. And of course a sense of the probable is not a touchstone of the possible: experience of this kind is disastrous if it is taken to be mechanically applicable to the future.

The notion of vicarious experience will be taken up in section IV, but there is one more way in which history may be given some purchase on the future, already hinted at in section I. Once again the central concepts are those of intentionality and historicity. Political action, institutional moves or developments, economic manipulation or forbearance, all make reference to conceptions of what is going on which are at the same time accounts of what has happened. This is particularly clear in the case of policies, which are necessarily temporally extended. Labour Party policy towards the EEC, for example, brings with it a certain understanding of what has been done by and happened to the UK in the past, and of what the EEC has been. Present circumstances are construed 'in terms of what they signify within the context of such a past'.[42] The same is true of (for example) Hitler's foreign policy, or the policy of 'Appeasement'. More generally, traditions of all kinds involve shared understandings, and although these

> can be represented in the form of general principles from which an application to present circumstances is then deductively derived, ... it is doubtful whether this is in fact the form in which the tradition would be understood by the people in question. The more plausible view is that this tradition is maintained in the more highly particularized and concrete form of an account of what society has done and suffered over the period of its existence.[43]

In so far as future action is a continuation of a policy (or tradition), historical knowledge may provide insights into the future by suggesting what moves might count as part of that policy. It does not ratify the account of the past enshrined in such policies or traditions, but creates the possibility of understanding and evaluating them.

Moreover, given that any action is taken within a situation conceived in a certain way, knowledge of the historical (backward referencing) elements in that situation will help in any assessment of what is likely to be done. Taylor, for example, drawing the attention of a lay audience to parts of the past he clearly thinks they are likely to know little of, declares:

> In fact Russia has been invaded by one European country or another five times since the beginning of the nineteenth century. By Napoleon in 1812, by the British and French in 1856, by the Germans in 1914 to 1917, by the British and French again in 1919 and by the Germans in 1941. Russia has never invaded Europe except in answer to the conqueror and one can say as a liberator.[44]

It is plain that if Taylor's assertion were accepted, it would lead to expectations as to Soviet behaviour in the future different from those that follow from a more cynical analysis of Soviet history. This is not because we are entitled to expect that the USSR will always do what it has done in the past, but because of our changed understanding of how those who control Soviet policies are likely to see things. The point is that to understand what the USSR is doing now, and to have a better chance to see what it may do next, it is necessary to know some history. Moreover historical knowledge may rule out certain conceptions of the past and so change our conceptions of the future – of what is possible and what is desirable.[45] History's hold on the future is not confined to assessments of probabilities as to what may happen to us (or in spite of us) but offers us some basis on which we can decide to act. And, of course, since what is attempted is seldom what is achieved, historical knowledge may (with the sort of qualifications raised throughout this section) indicate where to look in order to see what might have a bearing on events, regardless of what any historical agents think they are doing.

History is concerned with the study of the past, not the future. But *some* knowledge of that past gives us a purchase (however slight) on the future. That hold is not strengthened by trying to make history a source of quasi-scientific predictions: it only has something distinctive to offer when it remains itself.[46] It is not asserted here that historians and those who have studied history will be better at coping with the future than non-historians, because many things besides a knowledge of history enter into that. What is being claimed is that a man with a knowledge of history will be better placed, not than any other man who lacked that knowledge, but than he himself would be without it.

IV. VICARIOUS EXPERIENCE

History provides vicarious experience. But what is meant by that? 'Experience' is used here to indicate something personal (but not 'merely subjective'), and something accumulated as one becomes more *experienced*. What is acquired is not necessarily codifiable, and will not yield formulae, let alone recipes, for action. There are parallels here with art and craftwork, or with the practice of complex skills.[47] Someone who is experienced in the sense in question may be hard put to articulate even general principles, or, if he can, will feel that they are not applicable without experience on the part of whoever seeks to follow them. An experienced teacher is likely to see things an inexperienced one will miss, and will know what sort of situation he has to deal with. A seaman may know what weather is likely, without being able to explain how he knows. There is nothing mysterious here. Many things are involved: having the right concepts, recognizing instances, knowing principles, recognizing the conditions under which they are applicable, being able to spot countervailing tendencies, and so on. Given time, practice, patience, and a wide range of experience, most people can learn what is required. But without experience, even if general principles were found that could be set out in a formal way, they would be of little use. They could not be mechanically applied.

The experience gained in history is vicarious: in an obvious way it is second-hand. People who read about (or even research) different modes of life do not thereby live them, and following the progress of diplomatic negotiations is not engaging in diplomacy. But in coming to understand why people did as they did, and why diplomacy proceeded in just that way, one can extend the range of situations one is equipped to recognize, and the range of possibilities one is prepared to meet. Talk of 'recognizing' situations, and 'preparedness', might seem optimistic in view of what has been said above and in section III. But (again) it is not a matter of following a recipe or applying a formula. It is getting to know historical individuals (societies, nations, political parties, institutions) that are still with us, and have traditions and policies of a back-ward referencing kind. It is understanding systems of values and beliefs and the material conditions in which they are grounded.[48] It is knowing something of that immense variety of ways in which people have found it possible to act, and in which societies have been ordered. And it is recognizing 'the importance of contingencies – accidents, coincidences or other unforeseeable developments – in every human enterprise, relationship and institution'.[49] Such vicarious experience is only indirectly 'useful' in practical affairs – it opens up new ways of seeing things (and so, at one remove, new possibilities for action) rather than prescribing what must be done.

Experience of this sort will be of no value without a kind of openmindedness, which history cannot itself guarantee, but which is built into historical study. In so far as historical understanding requires the following of reasons, and the ability to see things from another point of view, it presupposes that people have reasons for doing things, and hence a minimal principle of rationality (as opposed, that is, to *a*rationality not to *ir*rationality). It is through this that something may be salvaged from the discredited claim that learning history develops tolerance. The 'tolerance' offered by history is not a vague feeling of sympathy and forgiveness, which condones everything on the basis of common humanity and generalized relativism. It is shown in a willingness and ability to entertain beliefs and values not necessarily found acceptable (let alone shared) for the purpose of understanding.[50] But understanding is not accepting, or even withholding criticism, either of the efficiency of means or the value of ends. A genuine historical tolerance must be well informed and critical. Too much must not be claimed here, however. We do not really know what effects particular ways of teaching history actually have, nor do we know what exactly has to be learnt for historical understanding and tolerance of this kind to be achieved.[51] Potentially, at any rate, the vicarious experience to be found in learning history is liberating. It can extend our conception of what 'man' is, by showing us what he has done, thought, and been, and how he has changed. More directly, it provides an immense range of concrete exemplifications of individual ideals, manifestations of the sort of life it is possible to lead. People may subscribe to different kinds of life (active, contemplative, practical, etc.), different goals (power, learning, wealth, etc.), different roles (scientist, soldier, etc.), and different styles of life ('responsible', iconoclastic, artistic, etc.). In so far as it makes sense to talk of people making choices here, history provides some concrete basis on which to make decisions. It also hints at possibilities that are not to be found exemplified in the contemporary world, or to which no attention is paid or the consequences of which have not yet been worked out in current terms. This is obviously of particular importance to children, who are constantly offered the individual ideals required by commercial interests in a capitalist industrial society, and by a relatively narrow spectrum of political opinion.[52]

For all these aspects of vicarious experience, imagination is central, both as an ingredient, and also as something that is itself to be developed. (The subject of historical imagination is taken up in detail in Chapter 4; here mention is made only of one or two general points relevant to this chapter.) In setting different scenarios for the investigation and imagination of possibilities, history encourages and demands imagination in two broad forms. It demands the imagining of different sorts of life, different beliefs and values, as part of historical understanding. This is a fundamental aspect of historical imagination, in which it is akin to *supposal*.[53] At the same time, in requiring assessments of significance, or in locating causes as necessary conditions, history encourages the imagination of alternative actions, events, and outcomes. Here the events imagined are *imaginary*, but not unfettered products of fancy.[54]

The vicarious experience that is acquired in learning history stimulates imagination and extends the learner's conception of what it is to be human, and therefore of what he or she is and might become. In this, as in everything discussed in this chapter, the claim is that someone who has learnt some history (taken here to include both substantive and procedural knowledge) will be better equipped to cope with the world than he would have been had he not learnt it. It is not asserted that someone who has studied history will *ipso facto* be a better politician, industrialist, citizen or teacher than someone who has not. Such becoming modesty, however, may seem to offer too many hostages to utility. Time for education is limited (and not just in schools). Some history may be better than none – but how can history compete for time with other disciplines? After all, it is plainly not so *useful* as science or mathematics. The weakness of this objection is in its crude conception of what is useful. The useful is often set against the intrinsically valuable, and there is some sense in such a juxtaposition. But something that expands one's conception of the world does not fall exactly into either category. At the same time it would be odd to assert that whatever produced such an expansion is *useless* even if it is not applicable to a specific goal on the model of technology. It is often forgotten that the greatest achievements of science have been of this wider, non-technological kind. Activities like this are *valuable*, both intrinsically and as means to ends. Of course something useful (as means) in the narrow sense may fit many ends, and so there is often wide agreement that it is useful (even between people with conflicting goals). On the other hand there are obvious wide differences as to ends, and so it is harder to achieve agreement about what is valuable in a non-technological sense. But in the end there must be some valuable things, or nothing can be useful as means. The object of this chapter is to have argued that history is valuable in just this non-technological way.

NOTES

1. As usual Kitson Clark gets to the heart of the matter: 'The words *German, Catholic,* and *Jew* stand respectively for a nation, a Church, and a race. They are used to describe things which exist in the world today, and therefore men's reaction to them should presumably be conditioned by what they are now. In fact, however, in each case men's reactions are largely affected by memories of history, or what passes for history, which seems to disclose the nature of Germans, or Jews, or Roman Catholics in their actions' (Kitson Clark, G., *The Critical Historian*, Heinemann Educational Books, 1967, p. 6).

   Two comments might be made on this. First, less dramatic examples are equally significant. Secondly, Kitson Clark's mild surprise that people do not take things as they are now is perhaps unjustified. For the whole point is that in so far as we can speak of 'great historic entities' (or lesser ones for that matter), they are not a series of disconnected present moments, but temporal entities, which carry their pasts with them as habits, beliefs, rules, policies, and continuing social relations. Even where there has been a major 'break with the past' (for example in Germany in 1945, where institutions, public morality and political philosophy underwent 'sudden' changes) the past is still inescapable; for questions still arise as to how deep that break goes, and in virtue of what it *is* a break. 'What a German is now' could not be answered without reference to the past even if all Germans completed questionnaires for sociologists and political scientists, for the past would be embedded in the answers. 'The past and the present and the future form a single domain of reference . . . within which the present has only a very qualified kind of priority. . . . In Heidegger's parlance, a human life "stretches itself along" ' (Olafson, F. A., *The Dialectic of Action*, University of Chicago Press, 1979, p. 97).

2. Olafson, op. cit., p. 150 and p. 94.
3. Plumb, J. H., *The Death of the Past*, Macmillan, 1969, p. 17.
4. ibid., p. 14.
5. ibid., p. 136. But Plumb does not give history the sole credit for this. See ibid., p. 14.
6. ibid., pp. 142–3.
7. ibid., p. 144.
8. ibid., p. 123.
9. Kitson Clark, op. cit., p. 7. The basis of this past, Kitson Clark believes, is 'confusedly remembered lessons learnt at school', 'the re-iterated assertions of politicians', 'misty recollections of newspaper controversies', 'scraps of special information or of personal experience, or the stories of chance acquaintances', and 'clear pictures of historical situations or of characters provided by historical novels or films'.
10. Plumb, op. cit., p. 16.
11. See Toulmin, S., and Goodfield, J., *The Discovery of Time*, Hutchinson, 1965.
12. This concept of 'the court of history', in which historians are something between judges and (in Bierce's words) 'broad gauge gossips' making and breaking reputations, straddles a range of notions of history and the past. Fundamentally it belongs to the 'practical past' (see

p. 3), but in recognizing that historians employ evidence according to certain more or less agreed procedures, it admits that history is a rational discipline in which the past is something to be *investigated*, and that the conclusions of historians are themselves subject to criticism.

13. Although there are some problems in *The death of the past*, it is one of the few accounts of history and its development which in general rises above a Whig interpretation of historiography. Paradoxically, Herbert Butterfield's *Man on his Past* (Cambridge University Press, 1969) is radically infected by such an interpretation, in which the history of history is seen as a kind of confused struggle to answer modern problems, which could only be successfully accomplished by modern critical methods: other interests in the past tend to be dismissed as primitive or simply a bad attempt at history. A similar approach is found in parts of Denys Hay's *Annalists and Historians* (Methuen, 1977). Plumb makes one or two uncharacteristic remarks (for example in his comments on the debate over the longevity of the patriarchs, p. 122) but in general takes a wider view, examining different concepts of the past in their own terms as well as charting the growth of critical history. Of course there *is* a legitimate sense in which the development of a rational concept of history may be charted, and Collingwood provided in *The Idea of History* an unfinished sketch of how it could be done. But such an account is the story of the progressive working out of sets of presuppositions, and is as much philosophical as historical. The history of our understanding of the past is in many ways almost in the same sad position as history of science thirty years ago. History of science has got beyond cataloguing the linear development of a current conception of the natural world, and is beginning to elucidate the historical origins and rationale of other conceptions. The history of the past awaits similar treatment.

14. Oakeshott, M., *Experience and Its Modes*, Cambridge University Press, 1933, p. 105.

15. Dray, W. H., 'Michael Oakeshott's theory of history', in Parekh, B. C., and King, P. T. (eds), *Politics and Experience*, Cambridge University Press, 1968, p. 32.

16. Oakeshott, M., 'The activity of being an historian', in his *Rationalism and Politics*, Methuen, 1962, p. 148.

17. ibid., pp. 153 and 155.

18. The impossible limits referred to here are inherent in the extended sense Oakeshott gives to 'practical' in his juxtaposition of the historical and practical pasts. It is difficult (for example) to see why a *historical* treatment of the Treaty of Versailles should exclude consideration of its connections with 'subsequent events' in Germany, and there seems a strong prima facie case for distinguishing this kind of treatment from one that seeks simply to exhibit the Treaty as a justification for the destruction of the Weimar Republic, or examines only those aspects of it held to be the 'origins' of some part of the present. For discussion of Oakeshott's view of history see the paper by Dray referred to above (note 15) and also in the same anthology, Walsh, W. H., 'The practical and historical past'.

19. There is no intention here to imply by '*the* past treated in different ways' that there are not questions about whether the past is 'discovered' or 'constituted'. Oakeshott in any case regards the past as the present seen in a particular way. But this is not the place to discuss the matter.

20. It would have to be a world without moral, religious or legal disputes, and without clashes of material interest. Perhaps a pre-Freudian conception of a socialist society as understood by Marx might get somewhere near what would be required? But left like this my account is too simple. There are limits to historical objectivity, but it may be that the basis of our assessment of what is relevant to an inquiry or (more widely) what is important in history, in so far as it is not settled in advance by the question asked, or by a theory of some sort, is to be found in a shared form of life. Agreement on the relative importance of massive changes in the kind of life possible for vast numbers of people, of longer life expectancy, and of freedom of various kinds, is perhaps to be traced to some basic agreement in physiological

needs, perceptual apparatus and so on. (Some sort of case could no doubt be made out along Wittgensteinian lines, but there are ambiguities in Wittgenstein's remarks on 'forms of life' which add to the difficulties.) (See also note 21.)

21. Everything said in this chapter plainly implies a 'form of knowledge' justification for history, and with it an emphasis in schools upon the acquisition of knowledge of a *discipline*. There remains the embarrassing question as to what substantive history ought to be taught: an issue largely ducked in the last fifteen years by invoking the pedagogical criterion that anything may be taught which exemplifies the discipline – sometimes the 'skills' – of history. This will not do: first, because within the paradigm-periods selected a choice must still be made as to what is important and what is not; and secondly, because learning a discipline also involves learning its criteria of importance. What these are is a question that must still be tackled. There is no space in this chapter to make a serious attempt to sort this out, but one or two tentative comments might be worth risking. It is impossible to provide children with a catalogue of 'everything you need to know' in advance of questions or interests. Practical interests in any case cannot *organize* the past in history teaching, or the practical past will replace history. But given that we are the kind of people we are, leading the life we do, we are likely to have an interest more in some passages of the past than in others. It has already been argued in the previous note that as human beings we share a common form of life at some level that might allow us the possibility of intersubjective agreement as to what is *humanly* important. If this step is taken, perhaps a (minimal) foot-hold can be gained for the concept of intrinsic importance in history. There might also be an argument from the nature of history itself. The activity of history presupposes at least a concern for freedom to assert what the evidence leads us to believe (for ourselves, and for others); and also a conception of man as rational (as opposed to *a*rational). It presupposes equality of treatment of, and respect for, persons as sources of arguments. In these circumstances it seems hardly reasonable without powerful countervailing arguments (and the onus is on those who would disagree to produce such arguments) to deny that past changes in the fortunes of freedom, equality, respect for persons, and the development of rationality in human societies is of intrinsic historical importance. Unquestionably all this involves appeal to some conception of human interests, and perhaps also to criteria implicit in education; but the historical and the educational are not in conflict here. Even the narrowest historian needs some idea of the range of human life, and of what it is open to man to be and do. Historical importance depends on a conception of human interests, and history enables us to hold that conception critically.

22. Discussion of 'laws' and 'generalizations' in history is often made harder through failure to distinguish the different types involved. A simplified list might look like this:

   (a) *generalizations* summing up a finite number of known cases;
   (b) *generalizations about an individual*;
   (c) *universal laws*, whether 'confirmed' or merely 'probable' – that is, 'probably true', which involves a different sense of probability from that which follows in (d);
   (d) *statistical laws*, asserting numerical probabilities – that is, of events of a certain type occurring in a population of events of another type;
   (e) *normic laws*, describing the tendencies of *things* (see Bhaskar, R., *A Realist Theory of Science*, Harvester, 1978);
   (f) *truisms* (see Scriven, M., 'Truisms as the grounds for historical explanations', in Gardiner, P. (ed.), *Theories of History*, Free Press, 1959);
   (g) *heuristic 'laws'* or *generalizations*;
   (h) *principles of action*.

   Given the concerns of this chapter, discussion will focus on (a), (c), and (d), but brief reference will also be made to (g) and (h).

23. Atkinson, R. F., *Knowledge and Explanation in History*, Macmillan, 1978, p. 111.

24. Except as a heuristic device. See below, pp. 8–10.
25. See White, M., *Foundations of Historical Knowledge*, Harper & Row, pp. 14–104.
26. Olafson, op. cit., pp. 115–17. See also pp. 100–1.
27. ibid., pp. 100–1. Cf. G. H. von Wright's discussion of 'quasi-causal chains' in *Explanation and Understanding*, Routledge & Kegan Paul, 1971, pp. 139–43.
28. There is not room here to discuss the possibility of a historical sociology investigating changing *structures* in society. Marxists have sometimes argued for something close to this, and Marxist concepts have a prima facie claim to the necessary level of abstraction. But the kind of study usually envisaged by Marxists would not employ laws of the kind envisaged by (say) Hempel. (See Bhaskar, op. cit., and his *The Possibility of Naturalism*, Harvester, 1979; also Cohen, G. A., *Karl Marx's Theory of History, a Defence*, Oxford University Press, 1979.)
29. Davidson, D., 'Actions, reasons and causes', in White, A. R. (ed.), *The Philosophy of Action*, Oxford University Press, 1968, pp. 91–2.
30. ibid., p. 93. Davidson's argument might (crudely) be summarized like this:

(i) If desire and belief are to explain action in the right way they must *cause* it in the right way: perhaps through a chain of reasoning meeting standards of rationality.

(ii) We cannot distinguish the right sort of causal processes without giving an account of how a decision is reached in the light of conflicting evidence and conflicting desires; this means we must use notions of *evidence, good reasons for believing*, and so on.

Therefore

(iii) We cannot give necessary and sufficient conditions for acting on a reason, if we only use concepts such as belief, desire and cause.

(iv) For the same reasons we cannot give serious laws connecting reasons and actions. *If* we had sufficient conditions we could say, 'Whenever a man has such and such beliefs and desires, and such and such further conditions are satisfied, he will act in such and such a way.'

There are no serious laws like this (i.e. with fixed probabilities springing from the nature of a theory, and where it is possible to determine in advance whether the conditions of application are satisfied).
In 'Psychology as philosophy' (in Glover, J. (ed.), *The Philosophy of Mind*, Oxford University Press, 1976) Davidson concludes that attitudes, beliefs, desires, etc. 'are not, even in theory, amenable to precise prediction or subsumption under deterministic laws. The limit thus placed on the social sciences is set not by nature, but by us when we decide to view men as rational agents with goals and purposes, and as subject to moral evaluation' (pp. 109–10).
31. For further detailed argument see Pears, D., *Questions in the Philosophy of Mind*, Duckworth, 1975, especially ch. 5: 'Sketch for a causal theory of wanting and doing'; Mackie, J. L., *The Cement of the Universe*, Oxford University Press, 1974, ch. 11: 'Teleology'; Davidson, D., 'Psychology as philosophy', in Glover (ed.), op. cit.; and Olafson, op. cit., pp. 175–88.
32. See Nell, E. J., Review Essay (of C. G. Hempel's *Aspects of Scientific Explanation*), *History and Theory*, vol. 7, no. 2, pp. 224–40.
33. ibid., *passim*. There are of course severe *general* problems connected with induction, but these are scarcely to be solved by the concept of 'general law'.
34. In the following chapter of this book Peter Rogers takes a more sanguine view of prediction in history. But see also note 36.
35. Atkinson, op. cit., p. 112. A similar point is made by Nell, op. cit., p. 230. The traditional claim that history is concerned with understanding particular events rather than subsuming them under general laws is not thereby falsified. The fact that we employ concepts in any

cognitive enterprise (to put it no stronger) no more commits historians to seeking or employing general laws than it does (say) art critics. The object of comparisons and contrasts beyond the case in hand may still be 'the enlarging of one's understanding of the individual case and not its assimilation to other cases by subsuming it with them under a law' (Atkinson, op. cit., p. 113).

36. Peter Rogers argues in the next chapter that these presuppositions are filled out in history into 'inductively elaborated generalizations', reducing their formality still further. I agree that this happens, and that we seldom have anything *better* to work with, but take a more pessimistic view of predictions based upon them. One difficulty here might be illustrated by comparing (say) Gladstone's and Disraeli's conceptions of 'vital interests'. But I agree with Peter Rogers that as heuristic devices such generalizations are of immense importance in history *teaching*.

37. Atkinson, op. cit., p. 114.

38. See, for example, Taylor, A. J. P., *How Wars Begin*, Book Club Associates, 1979, p. 158: '. . . suspicion is the normal relationship between great powers'.

39. ibid.

40. Reference to 'cases' here is meant to indicate a very loose analogy with clinical practice, but it still implies something too close to 'instances'.

41. Kitson Clark, op. cit., p. 197.

42. Olafson, op. cit., p. 148.

43. Loc. cit.

44. Taylor, op. cit., p. 170.

45. That historical investigation would rule out some conceptions of the Irish past held by participants in the struggle in Ireland, and hence some conceptions of possible action, does *not* mean that to provide people with new, more accurate information will stop them holding the views they do. People may have other reasons for holding such views. If we could substitute knowledge and understanding of the past, then *ex hypothesi* the views would change. But this is merely a conceptual point, and is of course too weak to affect the substantive questions: (i) whether this is possible in current economic circumstances, and (ii) how it could be attempted.

46. There is a danger here of saying 'History gives one the ability to do *A, B*, and *C*. So instead of worrying about getting the facts right, or thinking too much about the past in a substantive way, let's teach *A, B*, and *C*.' If this were simply a warning against handing on sterile information – sterile because there is no understanding – it would be harmless enough. But it can lead to confusion as to what there is in history to be learnt. This is perhaps evident in Connel-Smith, G., and Lloyd, H. A., *The Relevance of History*, Heinemann Educational Books, 1972, in which 'an exact knowledge of past events' is contrasted unfavourably with, for example, 'habits of judgement and capacity for action' (p. 28), and an approach advocated that 'elevates the practical needs of living people above theoretical obligations to "the past" and to "posterity" – or even to that most elusive of concepts, "objective truth" ' (p. 85). It is simply *assumed* that 'an exact knowledge of past events' can have no connection (apart from a malign one) with 'habits of judgement and capacity for action'; and that 'theoretical obligations to the past' can have nothing to do with 'the practical needs of living people', who presumably have no need of 'objective truth' for their mundane and everyday purposes! (See the discussion in section II of this chapter, pp. 4–5.

47. None of this is meant to deny that there may be principles or even rules operating in aesthetics.

48. I will not attempt to clarify *how* they might be grounded: that is a task both beyond this chapter and my competence.

49. Gallie, W. B., *Philosophy and Historical Understanding*, Chatto & Windus, 1964, p. 133. Gallie argues that history 'can and does assist us to achieve a "masterful manipulation of the

unforeseen" '. He admits that it would be an absurd paradox to expect history to help us to anticipate or forestall 'specifically predicted developments', but argues that it can, in a manner analogous to practice in games of skill, prepare one 'for whatever shall happen'. He develops the analogy in terms of 'form' – 'an all-round readiness, quickness and flexibility of responses' – and formulates two quasi-principles whose (odd) function it is to cover just those situations that escape the net of all our other principles and categories. These he calls 'the principle of the reserve' and 'the all-or-nothing principle'. It seems to me that Gallie has isolated something important in practical affairs, but which stands in need of much further analysis. It is true that 'form' in games is not simply a physical matter, but the analogy has limited scope, because experience in history remains *vicarious* – it is in a sense 'spectator' experience.

50. See Lee, P. J., 'Explanation and understanding in history', in Dickinson, A. K., and Lee, P. J. (eds), *History Teaching and Historical Understanding*, Heinemann Educational Books, 1978.
51. But see the companion chapter to this by Peter Rogers.
52. I am not, of course, advocating the teaching of history through biography as a series of moral lessons to be learnt from the lives of 'great men'.
53. See chapter 4 of this volume p. 86.
54. Even if one took at face value the declarations of some historians to the effect that they are not interested in what *might* have happened, and therefore concluded that this is not strictly historical, imagination of this kind may have an important place in the *learning* of history. (This is discussed further in chapter 4 of this volume, pp. 101–4.)

2. Why Teach History?

P. J. ROGERS

I. MYTHOLOGY AND HISTORY – POISON AND ANTIDOTE?

Like the poor, the past is always with us; not because we choose to tolerate it (as we do poverty) but because we cannot escape it. *Experientia docet* because, as beings endowed with memory, we cannot have a perception of the present that is not strongly influenced by a version of the past – some sort of version – which we have internalized in the course of growing up, and articulated in our adult lives. Such versions vary and *matter* because they determine how we understand and behave towards events that occur in our own present world. If, for example, one believes that since the Balfour Declaration the UK, and latterly other Western powers, have used Zionism and Jewish immigration into Palestine as an imperialist device for controlling the Arabs, one's view of the current Middle East problem will be very different from what it will be if one views the West as under intolerable pressure to allow a refuge to the survivors of Nazi death camps. According to whether one believes that Palestinian Arabs vacated their lands on the instructions of the Arab League, or were terrorized into leaving them by Israeli massacres, so one's perspective will differ – and so, accordingly, will one's classification of *present* events. Again, one's expectations, and, hence, conduct, cannot but vary according to whether or not one believes that the USSR 'rescued' the Arabs after the 1967 war and would do so again.

A dozen other examples could be chosen without even leaving the Middle East; but the point is that only through the historical record can the accuracy or adequacy of these alternative views and the aptness and relevance of their underpinning assumptions be checked. Such assumptions form the frame of reference within which current events are perceived and in terms of which sense is made of them, and an inappropriate frame will result in their disastrous misinterpretation. Without wishing to appear to take sides, it is difficult to escape the impression that the wave of pro-Israeli feeling that swept the West in 1967 had little to do with any dispassionate objective review of the merits of the case, because it lacked any reference to the relevant past. It seemed to stem from two main sources (apart from the foolish and threatening rhetoric of some Arab leaders): a most naïve conceptualization of the David Israel assaulted by the Arab Goliath, and a vague sense of uncomprehending resentment of Arab 'intransigence' – uncomprehending precisely because the past that explains the 'intransigence' was not known.

History thus has a crucial specific role to play because it is scarcely possible to understand a practical present problem without a sound knowledge of its background and development. But while true, this view is too limited. What is at stake is not just a few individual events that need scrutiny against the historical record as they happen to impinge upon present adult experience. This need only arises because the whole frame of reference within which the present is perceived has been drawn from an image of the past that is not the outcome of historical study and is therefore more or less seriously inadequate.[1] It is this that indicates the importance of history in education. A version of the past – some sort of version – has already affected every child by the time he enters school. Without historical education there will be nothing to monitor the development of the framework within which he will come (largely) to see the world, and the problem of adult misconception will be perpetuated. In particular, the occasional tendency in schools to eschew historical content that has implications for present controversial issues achieves nothing except the removal of any possibility of their rational scrutiny. It may *evade* them: it does not *avoid* them. Because conceptual frames are necessarily backward-referencing, both sides to any dispute almost invariably present their cases, at least in part, in terms of their versions of history, and there is no way in which their conflicting claims can be appraised except by a person with adequate *historical* knowledge to assess the claims critically. In the absence of the relevant knowledge the only alternatives are outraged rejection or gullible acceptance; contemporary events in Ireland demonstrate the consequences.[2] As one authority has recently observed, the way in which teaching Irish history was discouraged in the past simply handed over the field to the demagogue.

> Mythology took the place of history, with the result that political and religious demagogues fabricated a purely fanciful past that appeared to give credibility and justification for present attitudes. History was part of the armoury of politics, and references to the massacres of 1641 or Drogheda, to William of Orange or Robert Emmet raised dangerous emotions in people who had only the vaguest idea of the circumstances in which these occurrences took place or in which these men lived .... The Irish, despite what outsiders believe, are not preoccupied with history but obsessed with divisive and largely sectarian mythologies, acquired largely outside school.[3]

The fact that *some* version of the past is incorporated in such dangerous polemics as these indicates the first and most obvious role for historical education. The 'facts' cited in support of versions of the past, and the assumptions that underpin them, need critical and astringent review to see whether the facts *really* justify one's view of Catholics or Protestants or coloureds or whites, etc. and it is submitted that in so far as such attitudes involve an image of the past only history can supply the needed check. By no means is it claimed that there exists 'one right version' of past events into conformity with which all other versions must be brought by historical education. History deals largely with matters that are essentially contested and to look for unanimity among historical accounts is simply to misunderstand the nature of historical knowledge. But to repudiate 'one right version' as a feasible objective gives no sanction whatever to the polemical and uninformed accounts of the past criticized above. There is, after all, such a thing as a judicious and well-informed opinion as opposed to a silly, ignorant and prejudiced one. What is at stake is the sort of *ground* for a valid knowledge claim, and history provides much more reliable grounds for such claims about the past because it embodies and employs the techniques and procedures for identifying and handling evidence that have been refined over time into the best available – and that are still, of course, in the process of further development.

A short chapter on the subject of 'Why teach history?' cannot undertake a lengthy account of what the procedures of historical inquiry are.[4] But in view of the superiority claimed for accounts of the past that embody those procedures, something may be said on two cardinal points. First, the historian's knowledge encompasses not only the events of the past but their consequences. What enables him to discriminate an event as important is largely his *hindsight*, his knowledge of *which* events were fecund with important consequence. Not all, nor even many, of the facts about the past are of interest to historians.[5] Important *historical* facts are those with consequences, and only historical study can reliably isolate these.

But what is involved is not just the *fact* of 'consequences' as if one thing just happened to follow another. To discriminate an event as important because of its consequences includes coming to see *why* it had those consequences, and protracted experience of this kind is what largely gives a sense of cause and effect – of what *sort* of consequences are likely to follow from particular circumstances.[6]

And this fact compounds the weakness and inadequacy of any account not based upon *historical* procedures. Not only are events themselves often wrongly discriminated because imperfectly known and described; this distortion necessarily clouds the discrimination of consequences, and the true significance of events is lost. But to say that is of course to say that the possibility of forming reliable and valid frames of reference is, at the least, gravely compromised; and the way is left clear for polemic and prejudice to determine present perceptions and behaviour. The only remedy is that offered by *historical* procedures to which informed hindsight is central.

Secondly, it is important that history is an *ópen* inquiry, by which is meant that historians make up a community of scholars of widely different views whose standards and expertise constitute a built-in collective check upon the work of each individual member. Hexter amusingly makes clear what is meant. He describes the criteria of historical scholarship as 'commandments' vested in, and exercised by, the community of scholars:

> The commandments are counsels of perfection, but they are not merely that; they are enforced by sanctions, both external and internal. The serried array of historical trade journals equipped with extensive book-review columns provides the most powerful external sanction. The columns are often at the disposal of cantankerous cranks ever ready to expose to obloquy

'pamphleteers' who think that Clio is an 'easy bought mistress bound to suit her ways to the intellectual appetites of the current customer'. On more than one occasion I have been a cantankerous crank. When I write about the period between 1450 and 1650 I am well aware of a desire to give unto others no occasion to do unto me as I have done unto some of them.[7]

Thus paradoxically the feature of historical knowledge that at first sight makes one uncertain of its trustworthiness is in fact just what gives it objectivity. The fact that historians disagree is exactly what makes historical knowledge reputable by providing the most rigorous check upon its provenance and content.

These, briefly, are two of the main grounds for believing that the outcomes of historical inquiry are the best we can do with the past. To refuse to prefer those outcomes to the kind of account criticized at the beginning of this chapter is almost to reject the concept of rationality itself. To quote one authority, 'a reasoned hypothesis based on a careful consideration of evidence which has been tested critically and systematically might be considered to have a claim to be called "scientific". Indeed, it seems possible that much historical work has a better title to that question-begging adjective than much theorising that assumes it as a matter of right.'[8]

But this argument cannot be confined to the mere checking of particulars, and confronting polemical accounts with facts incongruous or incompatible with them. For, even given the superiority of scholarly historical accounts, because of the rigorous procedures of which they are the outcome, it is still true that 'the facts of the case' are not, except in the broadest sense, *given*: they have to be selected and interpreted by the historian not only by means of hindsight but also because of their *relevance* to a general frame of reference in terms of which the explanation is to be given. And the ubiquity of frames of reference in historical explanation is due to a fundamental feature of historical knowledge; it is isomorphic in character. To explain what is meant, a resumé of Dr Kitson Clark's admirable discussion of the point may be given.

II. THE PLACE AND POWER OF HISTORY – ANALOGY, EXPLANATION AND PREDICTION

Dr Kitson Clark points out how in history it is very rarely possible to impose a 'decisive negative test' of the kind commonplace in science. 'What is often done, therefore, is to judge not by law but by analogy' (p. 28). Knowledge-claims and explanations tend to be accepted or rejected according to how far they correspond with, or are different from, the ordinary experience of life. This

closely resembles the kind of test that most people, historians as well as others, apply all their lives both to descriptions of actions in which they are interested, and to any explanation of the motives of the actors involved. The questions: 'Is that action probable? Could it have happened like that?', or 'Does that motive ring true?' are very unconsciously translated in the mind into the questions: 'Does that action, as reported, remotely resemble any other actions of which I have reliable knowledge?', or 'Does the suggested motive correspond with human motives as I have known them in myself or other people?' Very often the whole process is more or less unconscious – only very simple people say, 'They never heard the like', and that possibly most often in works of fiction, but that sentiment is often the true meaning of more sophisticated expressions of disbelief.[9]

Dr Kitson Clark's account and the subsequent discussion show why the commonly held view that history is the study of unique events will not do. For if events really were *unique* – each utterly unlike every other in all important respects – the whole process of understanding and explaining by analogy would be impossible. But this would abolish the possibility of historical explanation altogether. Professor Elton puts the matter directly when he writes:

> As for history's preoccupation with the particular, that must be seen in its proper light. It is often asserted that the special distinction of the historical method is to treat the fact or event as unique. But frequent assertion does not create truth, and this statement is not true. No historian really treats all facts as unique; he treats them as particular. He cannot – no one can – deal in the unique fact, because facts and events require reference to common experience, to conventional frameworks, to (in short) the general before they acquire meaning. The unique event is a freak and a frustration; if it is really unique – can never recur in meaning or implication – it lacks every measurable dimension and cannot be assessed. But to the historian, facts and events (and people) must be individual and particular: *like* other entities of a similar kind, but never entirely identical with them. That is to say, they are to be treated as peculiar to themselves and not as indistinguishable statistical units or elements in an equation; but they are linked and rendered comprehensible by kinship, by common possessions, by universal qualities present in differing proportions and arrangements.[10]

The 'unique event', then, is a myth. Events are not *unique* but *particular* and are to be understood by analogy. It is now claimed that this reasoning by analogy described by Dr Kitson Clark is the source of the 'frames of reference' briefly mentioned above. To bring out what is meant consider how one might set about explaining the Soviet intervention in Czechoslovakia. Why did the USSR intervene? 'Because', the political commentator will reply, 'it feared the ideological consequences of Czech "liberalization" upon the other satellite countries, and, indeed, within the USSR itself; because, having many different nationalities, it feared the disruptive force of growing nationalism among its satellites; because the extreme strategic importance of Czechoslovakia made the possibility, though disavowed, that it might drift out of the Warsaw Pact militarily intolerable; because Western, and more particularly, German, activity in Eastern Europe, both diplomatic and economic, was, in the USSR's eyes, reaching dangerous proportions', and so on. But, of course, all these explanations involve unspoken assumptions about how states behave, about the nature of national interests, and the mainsprings of foreign policy –

assumptions that historians take for granted their readers share (or at least understand) and that make such explanations explanatory. But where do these assumptions come from? They are, of course, the outcome of the process of analogy that Dr Kitson Clark describes and the capacity to draw such analogies has, it is submitted, to be gradually acquired over time by experience of many events that come to be perceived as isomorphic. (More is said in section III about how this occurs.)

Such events must lie in the past, not only because (by definition) the bulk of experience does, but, even more important, only past events can have been discriminated with the help of hindsight and have therefore been really *explained*. The point about hindsight is that it shows the consequences, and, hence, the significance, of the component particulars of a past event and thus makes its identity and classification clear in a way that can never be true of a comtemporary, continuing event, the significance of whose particulars is, by definition, as yet unclear. (Some will not yet even have occurred.) It is, therefore, with past experience and from the study of history that analogies must be drawn.

As an example of this use of analogy, compare the Soviet intervention in Czechoslovakia just discussed with that of England in Ulster in the 1590s. The events in question are separated by nearly 400 years and, manifestly, not a single *particular* event is common to them. Yet, it is submitted, they are isomorphic. To the list of reasons for the Soviet intervention given above a corresponding list might run somewhat as follows:

> Spanish power never looked more formidable than in the early 1590s. The defeat of the Armada was rightly attributed by the English as much to the weather as to their own naval prowess and staved off, without removing, the Spanish threat. Indeed, the total failure of the Portugal expedition of 1589 and, especially, the failure to finish off the crippled Spanish fleet in Santander, left Spain able to intervene forcefully in the French Civil War using the Catholic League as puppet and bidding fair to secure domination of the whole of France. Immediately, the danger was acute enough. With Spanish naval power recovered, the invasion of Brittany posed a mortal threat to England and the Low Countries. Against this background there was simply no way in which the strategic implications of Ireland's position could be altered or ignored, and the threat was sharpened by religion, which provided an ideological basis for Spanish intervention, as promptly solicited by the Irish against the heretic English.

It is suggested that the two interventions, Soviet and English, although utterly dissimilar in their particulars, share a common rationale, and that the frame of reference necessary to understand them comes from the study of analogous instances in history.

It must be emphasized that in the stress upon frames of reference and argument by analogy the fundamental and equal importance of particulars must not be overlooked. Both are equally important and, indeed, inseparable. In trying to understand the Soviet invasion we have to pick out numerous specific events and factors that presuppose and activate the relevant generalization and conceptual frame – that embody them in this instance, as it were. To try to give an explanation in terms of the concepts and generalizations alone would reduce one to saying, 'It was in the USSR's self-interest to do so, or at least its rulers thought so'. But that would obviously be no explanation at all because it would lack any particulars of the events that took place. To try to explain without a conceptual frame in some sense shared, on the other hand, is equally impossible. The problem would then be that the proferred explanation made no contact with the reader's sense of probability, of how things hang together, and the task is to shape and form that sense of probability by the study of history – so that the particulars of the present case, as far as they are known, are seen as constituting an event isomorphic with some event (or class of events) already studied and explained.

The argument of this section really involves the status of historical knowledge and the logic of historical explanation. This chapter cannot cover the large issues involved – especially the role and status of 'laws' and generalizations in history.[11] Briefly, it is suggested that the frequent attempt to deal with historical explanation in terms of strict deduction from validated laws is mistaken because it overlooks the isomorphic nature of historical knowledge. What is fundamentally at stake is not deduction, but recognition. How far *any* deductive system, at least when applied to empirical knowledge, can be logically watertight is debatable;[12] in history the very possibility does not arise because the prerequisite 'laws' cannot, in principle, be formulated – if we really mean *laws* (i.e. rules that accurately describe the invariant behaviour of stereotyped phenomena under circumstances that actually occur). The reason is that the data with which history is concerned – human behaviour – simply do not possess the degree of regularity that would be necessary for rigorous lawful classification. But by no means does this imply that human conduct is random or ruleless. Given that *laws* are unattainable in any future that is foreseeable, the conceptual frameworks inductively elaborated by drawing analogies and identifying isomorphs in the course of historical study provide the best tools we can have for handling important areas of experience. The justification of this claim is that explaining an historical event and understanding a contemporary one (with the possibility of exerting benign influence over its course and outcome) are operations essentially similar in kind. The second may thus be learned from the first.

What is really involved in this is that *explanation* of historical events is linked in a non-trivial, though strictly limited, sense to prediction. The nature and extent of this asserted linkage must be clearly established.

Some authorities argue that prediction is essentially the same process as explanation, and this argument has been applied to history. For, it could be held, in constructing an explanatory account of (say) Bismarck's foreign policy, an historian in effect 'predicts'. In showing how one step was followed by another he takes it for granted that this is not just a fortuitous succession, but that given the first, the second could be predicted as 'likely'. If this is not so, then he has failed to establish connection between the events, and has explained nothing.

But, of course, there is a crucial difference between this sense of 'prediction' and that – surely the normal sense – which refers to a future that has not yet occurred. By definition (normal) prediction cannot encompass so extensive a set of particulars as can explanation of events now lying in the past. For it refers to a *future* state and some particulars (which will or may eventually prove relevant) will be events that have not yet occurred and that cannot therefore be taken into consideration. The same, of course, is true of weighing the *significance* of even those events that have occurred. The 'hindsight' which is so important a feature of historians' explanations is available only in attenuated form for predictions because many of the particulars whose consequences will in fact prove to be important will be very recent, and there will not have been time for their consequences to have become clear and to have been assessed. Hindsight is not only, necessarily, retrospective but, *de facto*, often long term. So, compared to what is the case for explanation, the array of particulars and their consequences available to underpin a prediction is amorphous and, hence, the generalizations that can be activated are relatively uncertain.

But while this importantly limits comparison between explanation and prediction it does seem to represent a difference in degree, rather than in kind. For it would be a mistake to imagine that explanation rests upon – or, at least, can be *known* to rest upon – the review of a *complete* set of particulars. For what would such a set be? It is impossible, even in giving the most (seemingly) convincing explanations of the (apparently) best-attested past events, ever to be certain that *all* relevant particulars have been identified and assessed – and that, consequently, the analogous linkages and isomorphic relationships in which the explanations are given are *undoubtedly* apt. That explanation, for the reasons already given, is more reliable than prediction is not doubted, but this does not mean that the latter cannot reasonably be made at all. The frames of expectation that the study of history leads us to entertain and the discrimination among particulars of a continuing *contemporary* event which they cause us inferentially to make, cannot but represent an extrapolation from a previous experience to an ongoing present one that appears analogous to us, and, hence, leads us to a tentative prediction of its likely outcome shaped by the previous (explained) events with which our present event is perceived as isomorphic. But this extrapolation and drawing of analogy is essentially the same process as that which generates explanation. The difference between the two is important, but contingent, not intrinsic, and to rule out prediction *tout court* is to disparage historical *explanation* as well. To understand the English invasion of Ulster *ex post facto*, and to predict as 'likely' the Soviet intervention in Czechoslovakia prior to its occurrence one has to do much the same thing. In both cases what is crucial is the 'facts of the case' without which, manifestly, no reconstruction is possible. Yet in discriminating the facts we select from others that we do not, we have also already made judgements concerning *which* particulars (from among a vastly greater number) deserve to be attended to, and this amounts to acknowledging the central importance of an organizing frame of reference with which such judgements can be made.

III.   EDUCATION. BUILDING FRAMES OF REFERENCE – PIAGET AND BRUNER

There is, of course, something of a 'chicken and egg' situation in the account given here of the relationship between particulars and frames of reference. The latter are said to be of prime importance in interpreting and selecting from among the particulars of the case – which particulars, it is claimed, determine the frames of reference that are discriminated as appropriate. But this circularity, if it is such, is not vicious. It is true of all forms of empirical knowledge.[13] What is needed is an account of the learning process that will resolve the seeming tension between particulars and frames and it is suggested that Piaget's model of 'assimilation/accommodation' provides a helpful starting point. The very young child, Piaget holds, is equipped with a bundle of reflexes that prompt certain stereotyped responses to encountered stimuli. The varied nature of these gradually produces modification and differentiation of the responses in accordance with how far, and in what ways, the stimuli are experienced as analogous or different. This is a continuous and very long-term process. It is how, at bottom, we orient ourselves to the world – either by straightforward recognition or, more importantly (and increasingly often as experience increases and is disciplined by education), by spotting and articulating analogies and isomorphs between and within invisible structural relationships among the stimuli that are encountered. The refining and deepening of our filing system, so to speak, is the result of continuing dialogue between the existing (provisional) frame of reference so far built by encounters with experience and the new data which it classifies and by which it may be modified even as classification takes place. A key element in this process is the articulation of the like/unlike concept, gradually refined and deepened. This is no one-way process. There is no conceptual oblivion until an adequate range of data is amassed, after which point the fully formed concept springs to life like Athena from the head of Zeus: for what could be the definitive criteria for 'adequate' or 'fully formed'? The process is two-way, where even the most preliminary adumbration of a concept is actively *employed* in the attempt to classify new experience, and is modified and enlarged in the process. The classifying process is (or should be) continuous and the task of education is to make it so.

This aspect of Piaget's overall description of the course of cognitive growth is convincing and provides a resolution to the problem of seeming circularity mentioned above. But two crucial aspects of his account call for further comment. He has been criticized for his seeming assumptions that the process of mental growth is one of maturation and that what is involved is the development of mental powers that are general. Whatever stage of development a child is in, it is alleged that he will have a particular intellectual style (say, formal operations) that is indifferent to variations of content. What matters, according to Piaget, is the logical structure of the operations which characterize his whole mental stance and determine the strategies his brain-processes embody, regardless of differences of *content* between different problems he may face.

Such a view is implicitly different from the position developed in this chapter with its stress on a distinctive and particular mode of inquiry (historical)[14] which produces versions of the past superior to any others, and which has to be *learned* – it does not just develop automatically because, even if Piaget's account of mental development is correct, more is involved than the growth of general logical processes. Like all other modes of inquiry – the scientific, for example – historical inquiry embodies a distinctive adaptation of such fundamental processes shaped by the particular nature and demands of the area of experience and type of problem it exists to confront. Consider, for example, what would be involved in testing these two knowledge-claims:

I know that these ruins are those of a Roman villa.
I know that the oxides of non-metals are acidic.

It is surely obvious that the two inquiries would have scarcely one important feature in common. What the inquirers would actually do, and what would count as evidence, would be quite different. It is true that both, in their respective ways, embody logical processes – but this is just the point; their *respective* embodiments – the various forms in which logic is experienced – are *different*, and to assume competence in one type of inquiry because of demon-strated competence in the other is to embrace the old error of transfer of training between discrepant – not merely separate – materials.[15] What is needed is to learn over time the various frames of reference and relevance that grow from the application of logical processes to *particular* types of knowledge and problem-areas, and which give to those processes the idiosyncratic twists and adaptations that bring them to life and make them practically useful.

If we wish children gradually to come to reason in a fully mature way then they must be given extended experience not just of logical operations as such, nor of those operations as met with in a narrow range of knowledge areas. They must be experienced as variously embedded and embodied in all the various forms of intellectual content that we wish the pupils to master. The criteria for choosing these are exactly what curriculum theory should be concerned with and, as such, lie beyond the scope of this chapter. But that such (justified) criteria must be evolved is certain. Piaget has nothing to say about this, and Bruner, among others, has criticized him for his non-interventionist stance. It is only fair to point out, of course, that Piaget is not primarily an educationalist and that he has been concerned to map the course of cognitive growth – to describe what naturally occurs – rather than to devise or suggest strategies to facilitate or accelerate growth. But Bruner points out that assimilation and accommodation are, for education, mere 'portmanteau' terms unless *what* is to be assimilated, the *nature* of the accommodation(s) that are desired, and the means by which that can be done, are specified. In Bruner's words, 'A theory of development [which is what Piaget really offers us] must be linked both to a theory of instruction and a theory of knowledge, or be doomed to triviality.'[16]

In other words, the stimuli to be provided by schooling must be prescribed and controlled; a main purpose of such education is to provide learning experi-ences that are not haphazard and that cannot be relied upon to occur by chance. Why, after all, do we have schools at all? The first thing to say about schooling is that it is highly unnatural. In its universal and compulsory form it has existed for only a tiny fragment of human history. Why is it a phenomenon of the last 100 years or so? It is submitted that life in modern societies is so complex that vast amounts of knowledge and understanding are required for effective living and that these cannot simply be acquired in the process of ordinary life. That history is, pre-eminently, a prime ingredient of such 'enabling knowledge' should be clear from the opening, and the concluding, sections of this chapter; and the point of teaching history well exemplifies the point of education itself. From his encounter with (carefully chosen) experiences the child inductively elaborates the whole conceptual system within which he can conceive of the world in an educated way.

This is clearly both a long-term process and dependent upon a skilled instructor for its accomplishment.[17] Applied to history, for example, the required and relevant concepts and principles (such as those immanent within the Czech and Irish cases described above) have to be discriminated and then represented at different levels of complexity in a continuously linked experience. The alert reader will see that this virtually specifies the first two elements of Bruner's theory of instruction – the related need for structural analysis of content to discriminate its fundamental principles, and the use of the spiral curriculum continuously to communicate to the children the principles that analysis reveals as crucial.[18] The isomorphic nature of historical knowledge means that what is fundamentally at stake is more and more complex but continuously connected discriminations of 'like/unlike' on relevant content. This is the task of the history teacher – to provide a continuously stretching treatment of content identified as crucial, such that understanding is constantly deepened into wider and more sophisticated frames of reference.

IV. EDUCATION. BUILDING FRAMES OF REFERENCE – THE IMPORTANCE OF CONTEXT

Not enough has been said about what is involved in 'spotting isomorphs'. To bring out the isomorphic nature of historical knowledge and explanation it was necessary to concentrate first upon an example of different events that were fundamentally similar. It is now imperative to stress that in other cases the reverse may be true – the seeming similarity between two events may prove, on examination, to be trivial and the differences to be fundamental. The operative phrase is, of course, 'on examination' and this reinforces the emphasis already placed on the importance of closely studying particulars as a check upon seeming similarity. But there is a further point – the importance of *context*. Historical explanation is given not only by a *conceptual* frame of reference, as already explained, but also by a *contextual* frame given by the mores and assumptions of the time and society to which a study relates. In order to understand a policy or action and to decide whether or not it should be classified with one from another period and place to which, at first sight, it may seem similar, it has to be understood in terms of the perspective and assumptions of *both* periods, which may be significantly dissimilar from one another – and also from one's own.

But of course the contextual frame is not *'given'* by the 'mores and assumptions of the time'; it has to be *constructed from* them. And how are these assumptions to be known? The answer once again is through detailed study of, and hence informed inference from, the *particulars* of the case. To assess Cromwell's Irish campaign (to take a highly emotive example) one has, as far as possible, mentally to reconstruct the situation as he perceived it and this includes not only the constant long-term considerations related to Ireland's strategic importance, but the sharpened context of 1649–50 – the insecurity of the revolution just after the King's execution and the still greater danger brewing in Scotland that made a quick end to the Irish campaign seem imperative. And behind such specific considerations lies the whole contextual frame of circumstance and assumption provided by (for example) the norms of seventeenth-century warfare, the bitter 'memories' of the 1641 rising – contemporaries did not, of course, know that the tales of massacre were greatly exaggerated – and the position of Cromwell as a Puritan (with all that that implies) living in the distinctive emotional and intellectual climate of seventeenth-century England. (As one authority once remarked, 'Cromwell lived closer to the fires of Smithfield than we do'. To work out the meaning and implications of that statement would be an invaluable exercise for secondary pupils in constructing an explanatory context.)

Nevertheless Cromwell's actions are fairly readily explicable because to construct the context within which they may be understood is relatively straightforward. With the partial exception of the religious facet of his motivation, little inferential reasoning from particulars whose appearance is strange and mystifying is required. On the contrary their study builds fairly directly into a context familiar to sophisticated students because it is highly consistent with their knowledge of how states and statesmen behave under the perception of threat, and of what sort of thing is so perceived.[19] Isomorphism is readily grasped by such students because they see the situation as structurally similar to many others that they understand and Cromwell's actions as functionally equivalent to those of other agents similarly placed.

But to establish a context adequate for full understanding – and, hence, appropriate classification – is not always straightforward, because particulars often do not so readily build into such a context. Far more inferential reasoning may be needed, and if this is overlooked then either the event will be wrongly classified because a mistaken and inadequate underpinning for the contextual frame is provided, or it will be inexplicable because the particulars remain dumb and inert so that no explanatory context can be built at all. It must be stressed that it is not necessarily the explanatory contexts themselves but the handling of particulars needed to build them that are more complex, and an excellent example is provided by R. W. Southern's discussion of serfdom and liberty.[20] A source is identified (records of the monastery of Marmoutier), its typicality is shown, and a significant section is quoted. This deals with the common practice, even among men of substance, of voluntarily entering into a state of serfdom, and even committing their descendants to the same status for ever. Few things, on the face of it, could surprise us more; Southern sets out to explain the matter by setting it in its contemporary context. He concentrates first on drawing out the particulars stressed in the document, and then, in two lengthy paragraphs, reconstructs the eleventh-century reality by the discussion of them. He shows how in that context, the symbolic acts mentioned in the document, so strange from our modern standpoint, are in fact significant. Their joint purpose, he shows, was to establish, for a largely illiterate age in which 'the gradations of society were infinite and there was no close relation between status and wealth', a clear and simple demarcation line between 'free' and 'unfree' (p. 98).

The same section of Southern's book is useful for bringing out the relationship between contextual and general frames of reference. Rarely does the contextual frame stop short of a fully intelligible linkage with our *general* frame of reference. Its function is normally to show that appearances are misleading if they give us the impression that past events are very puzzling. Once we see them whole and in context they fall into an intelligible pattern because we see that they are only superficially incongruous with *reasonable expectations*. Explanation is, after all, a matter of connecting some unfamiliar event to our general frame of expectation (and, perhaps, modifying the latter) and this is the role of the contextual frame.

One qualification of this position must be made – namely that the link with general conceptual frames is not always direct or simple. For, of course, general frames of expectation themselves must be *built*, and built from just the assemblages that contextual frames (themselves resting on particulars) are concerned to give. They are provisional and developing. It follows – and this is a point of great importance – that they are always open to, and are developed by, modifications caused by the assimilation of new data. The conscious process of education is largely concerned with bringing about just such development by regularly provoking appropriate modifications with well-chosen new data, and the relationship between contextual and general frames is thus reciprocal. A good historical example of this is provided by Southern's account of the feudal view of 'liberty'. He shows that the crucial distinction for 'liberty' was not between restraint and its absence but between contrasting forms of restraint, between the predicament of men who were restrained by *law* (free men) and those restrained solely by arbitrary *will* (serfs).

> The higher one rose towards liberty, the more the area of action was covered by law, the less it was subject to will. The knight did not obey fewer laws than the ordinary freeman, but very many more; the freeman was not less restricted than the serf, but he was restricted in a different, more rational way. Law was not the enemy of freedom; on the contrary, the outline of liberty was traced by the bewildering variety of law which was slowly evolved during our period. The irksome rules and tedious gradations of society did not appear, as they did to a later age, as so many strangle-holds on liberty. . . . . The most highly privileged communities were those with the most laws.[21]

What this explanation provides is not a straightforward linkage to an existing and static general frame of reference that itself remains unchanged. By showing the rationale of a different concept of 'liberty', it modifies and extends that general frame.

The other important feature of the relationship between contextual and general conceptual frames is that a contextual frame may activate more, or less, complex general conceptual frames in different cases. Another way of putting the point is to say that the general conceptual frames activated may sometimes be trivial. An excellent example is afforded by the remainder of Southern's discussion of serfdom (pp. 98–9). As we saw, he has already established, by a reconstruction of context through particular evidence, the function of the symbolic acts of serfdom; but that only explains the function of the relationship once established, not why men were prepared voluntarily to enter into it. *Why* was serfdom a status acceptable to even quite prosperous free men? '*Why* were landlords . . . willing to make bargains which were, in effect, costly purchases of a man's liberty?' By establishing the context – built, of course, from particulars – Southern makes the whole matter directly intelligible. In the eleventh century, he shows, 'land was plentiful and labourers were comparatively few . . . . Landlords were not above competing for labour. The condition of serfdom, though it did not take away a man's property, prevented him from moving elsewhere . . . henceforth the lord was assured of their continual service – and would pay a price for this assurance'. Southern goes on to illustrate how the serf could drive a very good bargain, and he has previously shown how in the eleventh century (though not later) to accept serfdom entailed almost no practical disadvantage. 'No new or burdensome services followed in the wake of the new status . . . and, conversely, a man who held land by the most onerous services might be by status a free man.' (By this seeming paradox we are prepared for the later explanation of 'liberty' already discussed.) Southern summarizes the whole matter by a helpful analogy. He shows that labourer and landlord acted in just the same way as the modern skilled worker and his employer when the latter offers, and the former accepts, a substantial payment in return for an undertaking that the worker will not move elsewhere.

This hasty résumé does no real justice to Southern's account, but it may serve to make the point at stake. The puzzle is the consequence of our ignorance. It is our concept of 'serfdom' that is at fault, and once it is corrected by an adequate contextual frame (built from particular knowledge) the whole puzzle dissolves. *Of course* the landlord must secure a reliable and adequate labour force; *of course* the labourer would be willing to strike a bargain that he could make so advantageous. But 'of course' does not mean that there is *no* linkage with our general sense of probability of 'how things are'; it simply means that the covering generalizations are, in this case, so obvious and trivial as to be part of everyone's everyday experience. No modification is needed to assimilate the explanation and, consequently, none is provoked by its assimilation.

But if the frames of reference activated by particulars are regularly as trivial as this example suggests surely they amount to mere common-sense or general knowledge and do not need to be *learned* from history or from anything else. As soon as the relevant particulars have been identified, everything falls into place.

Popper's statement of this argument is particularly unambiguous. He argues that

> these laws (as he calls the frames of reference) may be so trivial, so much part of our common knowledge, that we need not mention them and rarely notice them. If we say that the cause of death of Giordano Bruno was being burnt at the stake, we do not need to mention the universal law that all living things die when exposed to intense heat. But such a law was tacitly assumed in our causal explanation.[22]

Popper's argument is in any case flawed by his assumption that historical explanation is a matter of deduction from general laws – the position shown to be erroneous above – but apart from this his procedure seems highly suspect. It involves an attempted *reductio ad absurdum* of the opposing argument by means of a specially chosen example; in fact, of course, it is not true that the 'laws' underlying historical accounts are always so platitudinous. But Popper's error is more fundamental than this. By the example he chooses, he implies what he does not prove – that this sort of trivial 'law' is peculiar to history. In fact, of course, exactly because it is part and parcel of commonplace knowledge, it is common to all modes of discourse. Hence (unsurprisingly) it appears in history; but to conclude, as Popper does, that it is therefore *typical* of history (still less peculiar to it) is to use the selected example not to penetrate, but to sidestep, the very question that is crucial – namely the possibility that there may be other sorts of 'law-like generalizations' used by historians which are not universal commonplaces and which are to be learned from the study of history itself.

The two claims – on the one hand that the 'frames of reference' needed for understanding are trivial and immediately accessible to common-sense and general experience, and, on the other, that they are sophisticated and available as the result of protracted study of history – can, surely, be tested, and an attempt to do so may be described.

In October 1968 176 Honours graduates representing a wide spread of academic disciplines, all of whom were undergoing a postgraduate course in teacher training, were asked to answer a test on the Soviet intervention in Czechoslovakia. The test asked for responses to questions based on a leading article in *The Times* upon which the graduates were asked to comment. The criteria against which their responses were scored were obtained from content analysis of both a scholarly Western explanation[23] and a Soviet account of the intervention,[24] together with a set of criteria provided by a specialist in international affairs (who knew nothing of the purpose of the experiment) after he had read through the test. The criteria so obtained were highly uniform and are certainly examples of the sort of assumptions that underlie historical accounts of inter-state conflicts. If, then, they are trivial or obvious, or merely general knowledge, then certainly these very highly educated subjects should be fully familiar with them, and should have no difficulty with the test. If, on the other hand, the (tacit) generalizations are learned from history, one might expect the history graduates to surpass the others in test performance.

The results were interesting. Very briefly, they lent no support whatever to the claim that the relevant concepts are trivial and readily available.[25] The graduates' scores can only be described as calamitous. With a possible maximum of 50, the mean score returned was 5.9. Even more significant than the scores was the number of graduates (nearly one-quarter of the sample) who did not really attempt the test, entering some response to the effect that they knew nothing of the matter, and felt unable to comment. This response was particularly common among science graduates, one of whom wrote 'Your test is hardly designed for the scientifically minded'. In view of the massive coverage by all the media of the Czech crisis in the middle and late summer of 1968, it is inconceivable that highly educated people could have been actually ignorant of what had been going on during those months. What was lacking – and the scripts of many respondents made this clear – was not sufficient factual information but any significant idea of *where to look* among the mass of information with which they had been bombarded. But that is to say that they lacked just the conceptual frame of reference necessary to discriminate among, and make sense of, the mass of particulars.

It is this that makes the historians' performance interesting, for there was a highly significant difference between their mean score and that of the other subject specialists, whether these were treated as one group, or whether individual subject groups were compared with the historians (in fact no subject group other than historians returned a mean score of more than 6.5). It is true that other variables (such as reading the 'Quality' newspapers, or listening/viewing serious news programmes) correlated significantly with test performance; but such effects seemed clearly subordinate to subject specialism. Thus the historian who read (say) *The Times* or *Observer* would much more frequently than not surpass in test performance a reader of such papers from any other group. And the same was true of radio and television programmes.[26]

These findings, it is submitted, lend modest empirical support to the claim that it is the study of history that is important for forming the frames of reference relevant to understanding contemporary political events.

V. THE GENERAL ROLE OF HISTORY IN THE CURRICULUM

The discussion so far may seem to imply that the contribution of history is only to political knowledge and understanding. In fact, there may well be a case for believing that history may have a further general role to play in education. The suggestion is that all existing structures of knowledge are the products of development over time and, to be fully understood, they need to be placed, and viewed, in the historical perspective of that development. The possibility is thus strong that history may have a second major educational role in addition to its contribution to correctly understanding political issues. The possibility cannot be explored in this short chapter but its shape and nature may be glimpsed. First, it is likely that if a subject – and particularly its 'know how' – is really to be understood then case studies from its historical development may have a most valuable part to play.[27] The second possibility is even more interesting. To understand a body of knowledge may require not only some study of its own development, but of the connections between that development and other aspects of contemporary society. It is not possible, for example, fully to understand Impressionist painting or Cubism without a knowledge of scientific developments in the understanding of vision and of new theories of the mind. In short, *context* is crucial, and this, no less than the process of the subjects' own development, is exactly what the complete historical record of a period should reveal.

On the other hand, the various subject specialists will not usually view the examination of context as the main objective – if indeed it is one at all – and they will not, therefore, find it appropriate to explore the whole – or even nearly the whole – range of connections between their subjects, other subjects and the general social context. This indicates a possible *general* curricular role for history. At a time when there is a marked trend towards 'breaking down subject barriers' and 'integrating' the curriculum – with a resulting proliferation of rather shallow and artificial schemes based on little more than casual association of content[28] – history may provide a reasoned basis for binding together the curriculum. That basis may consist of the network of connections among the subjects of the curriculum that the historical record reveals, and the historical element in their study that all should variously employ.

But – and this is absolutely crucial – history will only make these posited contributions, whether to political understanding, the mastery of other subjects and their modes of thought, or to 'integration', if what is taught (and, thus, experienced by the pupils) is *genuine* history. What has been outlined is the *potential* contribution of history, not what it will necessarily contribute to understanding, however experienced. The remaining crucial question is, therefore, 'What is it to teach history?' A good deal of what is at stake may be inferred from the foregoing discussion. A more detailed and systematic answer has been attempted elsewhere.[29]

NOTES

1. Something is said below (pp. 22–3) as to *why* a version of the past that is the outcome of history is preferable to any other. See also the previous chapter in this book.

2. See note 45 to the previous chapter. I agree that teaching children history will not *necessarily* supply the required corrective; but nothing *else* will, because of the image of the past by which attitudes are so largely sustained. There may be pupils whose prejudices seem immune from *any* educational approach: the danger is that because such pupils present a particularly intractable problem, the problem presented by pupils in general is deemed intractable. As always in education, success is neither 'all' nor 'nothing'. Colloquially, you win some and you lose some; and how many you win is powerfully affected by how skilfully the teaching is done.

3. Magee, J., 'Are there any remedies?', in *Irish History – Fact or Fiction?*, NI Churches Central Committee for Community Work, 1976.

4. For some discussion see Rogers, P.J., *The New History – Theory into Practice*, Historical Association, 1979, especially chs 1, 2 and 3.

5. See Carr, E. H., *What is History?*, Penguin, 1964, p. 12. Carr's argument has been strongly attacked by G. R. Elton in *The Practice of History*, Fontana, 1969, pp. 75ff. It is not possible to go into the matter in detail here. Essentially, however, Carr's point seems to hold. For an amusing, and most telling, discussion see Danto, A., *Analytical Philosophy of History*, Cambridge University Press, 1968, p. 131.

6. For further discussion and elucidation of this claim, see pp. 24–5 of this chapter.

7. Hexter, J. H., *Reappraisals in History*, Longman, 1961, p. 8.

8. Kitson Clark, G., *The Critical Historian*, Heinemann Educational Books, 1967, p. 27.

9. ibid., p. 29. Of course (as Dr Kitson Clark states) *all* explanations, including the sort of polemic criticized here, use analogy, conscious or unconscious. What is different about scholarly historical explanations is that the analogies are drawn between events whose identity has been determined by the most stringent processes available for investigating the past with all that this entails for the aptness and delimitation of the analogies themselves.

10. Elton, op. cit., p. 23.

11. For some discussion, see the previous chapter; for a full account of the present writer's view see also Rogers in Dixon, K. (ed.), *Philosophy of Education and the Curriculum*, Pergamon Press, 1972, pp. 75–133.

12. Gödel, K., 'On formally undecidable propositions of *Principia Mathematica* and related systems', (1931) discussed in Nagel, E. and Newman, J. R., *Gödel's Proof*, Routledge & Kegan Paul, 1959.

13. In science, for example, Kuhn has shown the importance of 'paradigms' – ultimately constraining sets of assumptions that cause thought to flow in certain channels, and experience to be viewed in certain ways, but that can, none the less, be disrupted by emergent facts discrepant with them.

14. For a fuller description with regard to history, see Rogers, *The New History*, op. cit., especially ch. 1, and 'Some thoughts on the textbook', *Teaching History*, no. 31, 1981. For an outstanding account of the general issue see Hirst, P. H., 'Liberal education and the nature of knowledge', in Archambault, R. D. (ed.), *Philosophical Analysis and Education*, Routledge, 1965.

15. For evidence and argument in support of this assertion see pp. 34–5.

16. Bruner, J. S., *Towards a Theory of Instruction*, Harvard University Press, 1966, p. 21.

17. The stress on *education* should make clear that such 'inductive elaboration' is in no way solo or private. Concepts are public and social achievements.

18. This short chapter cannot go into detail. For a full account, with examples, of Bruner's theory applied to the teaching of history, see Rogers, *The New History*, op. cit., especially chs. 2, 4 and 5.

19. The context is, of course, *only* explanatory for the mature student. The frame of reference that makes *this* event familiar to him is the fruit of his study. It is just what education should enable pupils to learn in the manner outlined in section III above, and Cromwell's intervention in Ireland is an excellent example of the sort of event that could help to articulate and build the appropriate conceptual frame.

20. Southern, R. W., *The Making of the Middle Ages*, Hutchinson's University Press, 1953, pp. 96–105.

21. ibid., p. 105.

22. Popper, K. R., *The Poverty of Historicism*, Routledge, 1957, p. 145.

23. Burnham, C. G., *Yearbook of World Affairs*, October 1969, pp. 53–81.

24. 'On events in Czechoslovakia', anonymous, Moscow, 1969.

25. They also support the criticism of Piaget's assumption of the general applicability of mental operations in any stage of development (see note 15 above). Obviously all the graduates would be well within the 'formal operations' stage in their own subject areas. How, then, can the very marked differences of performance on this *specific* test be accounted for on

Piaget's assumption? It is submitted that they cannot, and that the argument for *specific* enabling knowledge and conceptual frames is supported.

26. For full details and discussion of this experiment, including the highly significant similarity between the criteria employed by the Western and Soviet sources, and the specialist in international affairs, see Rogers, P.J., 'History and political education', *Teaching Politics*, vol. 8, no. 2, pp. 153-69.

27. For this argument related to science, see Conant, J. B., *On Understanding Science*, Mentor Books, 1951; and Hutten, E. H., *The Ideas of Physics*, Oliver & Boyd, 1967. The views of these writers, who recommend a historical approach to science teaching, are discussed by the present author in Dixon (ed.), op. cit., pp. 75-85, where the same historical approach is applied to the teaching of art.

28. For the permanent danger that this may happen if the logic of disciplines is not respected, see Stenhouse, L., 'The humanities curriculum project', *Journal of Curriculum Studies*, vol. 1, no. 1, November 1968. For the theoretical and conceptual difficulties in 'integration', see Pring, R., 'Curriculum integration', in Peters, R. S. (ed.), *The Philosophy of Education*, Oxford University Press, 1973, pp. 123-49. The present writer hopes to develop the 'history and integration' point on a subsequent occasion.

29. Rogers, *The New History*, op. cit.

3. Beauty and the Philosopher: Empathy in History and Classroom

D. SHEMILT

'The contest is unequal between a beautiful woman and a beginner in philosophy'. (Epictetes)

Like any beautiful woman, the theory of 'empathetic reconstruction' excites the devotion of some and the censure of others. Many teachers see in 'empathy' the essence of the historian's craft, the divine wind that breathes life into the dry bones of the past, turns dust to flesh, and inspires pupils to commune with their predecessors. More sceptical teachers scorn the currently fashionable projective approaches to empathy as unhistorical at best and fraudulent at worst. And, in truth, the stock empathetic question is readily parodied: 'Imagine you are John Wilkes at a party thrown by Jemmy Twitcher; describe your hopes for the present and fears for the future.' Worse still: 'Imagine you are about to be defenestrated: predict the causes of the Thirty Years War.'

Empathy, its critics contend, has caught on because it savours of profundity without demanding much thought, and intimates a methodology that looks historical but is susceptible to no rational analysis.

Such mockery is not altogether undeserved. Teachers who consider the development of 'empathetic awareness' to be an indefeasible aim of school history, find it difficult to agree a definition of empathy applicable to the written work produced by adolescents. Empathy is variously defined as

an attitude or disposition comparable to 'tolerance' and 'sympathy for others';
a mental faculty akin to imagination and creativity;
an interpersonal skill possessed by social workers and confidence tricksters;
a methodological procedure or technique, cf. 'scientific method';
a set of propositions about people in the past.

Teachers also disagree as to why empathy should be taught. For some, it is a socially useful skill or attitude of mind that history helps develop and which, thereby, justifies the subject's retention on the school curriculum. There is something in this. If it can be shown, first, that what is taught in school history transfers to life at large, and second, that adolescents high on empathy are low on interpersonal brutishness, then the lady's beauty may prove more marketable than the philosopher's scruples. Unfortunately, this is difficult to demonstrate. An alternative argument starts from the premise that the study of history is good for pupils and that empathetic reconstruction is a part of this study. If he who loves truth must first love beauty, the lady is a worthy sophist. But in arguing this second justification we must return to the question of what empathy is in history, what it may be in the minds of adolescent students, and whether or not it can be effectively taught and assessed. These questions will be addressed in turn.

1.   EMPATHY AND HISTORY

What is empathy?

In common parlance empathy is taken to refer to 'the ability to put oneself in someone else's shoes' or, more formally, to 'reciprocate positions' (i.e. (a) to view the world from the situation of another person; and (b) to conceive how he would see things were he in your shoes). In history the term is usually associated with Collingwood's dictum that 'all history is the history of thought'. The historian penetrates past 'thought' by re-enacting experience, by rethinking ideas:

> Historical knowledge is the knowledge of what mind has done in the past, and at the same time it is the redoing of this, the perpetuation of past acts in the present. Its object is therefore not a mere object, something outside the mind which knows it; it is an activity of thought, which can be known only in so far as the knowing mind re-enacts it and knows itself as so doing. To the historian, the activities whose history he is studying are not spectacles to be watched, but experiences to be lived through in his own mind.[1]

What does Collingwood mean? Is he an idealist advocating mystic communion with the past? Gardiner, for one, thinks so:

> If an historian is said to understand why Caesar crossed the Rubicon he becomes Caesar and intuitively rethinks in his own mind thoughts which are literally identical with Caesar's thoughts on the occasion in question.[2]

Other commentators demur. For Rex Martin, empathetic re-enactment

> derives its explanatory force . . . from the investigator's calculation, from his supposal of alternative courses of action and his deliberative consideration of plausibilities. Contrary to the interpretation of Collingwood as an intuitionist, I do not think that, for Collingwood, an explanation of an action is ever warranted by appealing to a 'literal identity' between the agent's thought and the investigator's interpretative re-creation of that thought.[3]

Exegesis of Collingwood's *The Idea of History* must remain in dispute. For present purposes it is sufficient to outline three competing portraits of Collingwood's empathizing historian.

(a) The thoroughgoing idealist sees the historian as a 'psyche-snatcher', a 'stealer of souls' who literally relives the thoughts and feelings of his subjects. It follows that the historian's descriptions of thought and feeling are part of, or at least on a par with, the factual record.

In some cases, the empathizing historian (as 'psyche-snatcher') may be obliged to improve upon the factual record and attempt more than a literal audit of past minds. Rather than simply re-enact Caesar's thoughts on crossing the Rubicon, the 'psyche-snatcher' may choose to exercise his prerogative as Caesar – or, rather, as Caesar's mind – and tell us what the great man would have thought had he had occasion to rehearse formally his reasons or to explain himself after the event. And, in truth, there is little chance of any historian saying, 'Although this was the decisive moment in Caesar's career, I'm afraid his mind was a blank at the time.'

This view of empathetic reconstruction has profound philosophical implications. For example, it may entail our abandoning the convenient distinction between ideas and thoughts, since if the latter are detachable from a particular agency at a given point in time they become indistinguishable from the former. Also, the claim to articulate 'potential' and 'implicit' thought implies the dissolution of boundaries between minds, hence between present and past realities and, thereby, between action within the present and re-enactment of the past.

More serious, however, is the affront to common-sense. Can the reader re-live my toothache or re-enact my motives for writing this chapter? And if the reader can do so, in what sense may toothache or motives be considered mine rather than his? Or may they not more properly be thought the property of all in the same way that objects of perceptual experience – trees, flowers, record offices – are the shared furniture of a known-in-common world? And even supposing we grant the premise, how may we be sure that re-enactment has focused upon *my* toothache or motives and not upon those of the cat next door? After all, two men beholding a forest may find it impossible to focus attention upon the *same* tree! Should the historian make too many empathetic errors, history would be in danger of becoming, in Voltaire's phrase, 'a joke which the living play upon the dead'.

(b) A second interpretation of Collingwood involves viewing the empathizing historian as a 'time-traveller' projecting his own psyche into the past and mentally reliving events from the situation, though not necessarily from the standpoint, of the other. This brand of empathy rests upon detailed academic knowledge of times past without demanding privileged access to other minds. More important, unlike the radical claim to a literal correspondence of thought and psyche, the products of the hypothetical reciprocation of positions have the status of *rational* explanation, not intuited fact. Given access to other minds, the 'stealer of souls' has no need to argue a persuasive connection between reasons and actions since this connection is, in fact, intuited. In his capacity as 'time-traveller', however, the historian – who, despite asking questions of the form 'What would I do? Think? Feel?' is not writing a speculative autobiography – must argue first, that Everyman, or someone like his historical subject, P_1, in situation S_1 would have feelings, ideas and goals, $x_1 \ldots x_n$ rather than any others; and second, that the known action A_1 may be reasonably inferred from the feelings, ideas and goals, empathetically imputed. Empathy thus involves the hypothetical rehearsal of mental events linking situation and action such as to show that, given this situation S_1 action A_1 may be reasonably expected to follow. The literal truth of the reconstruction is probable yet not certain; that is, within limits set by our less than perfect knowledge of action and situation, on the one hand, and by our knowledge of human nature and, in particular, of what passes for rational action, on the other, the historian may regard an empathetic reconstruction as a fair approximation to reality.

One problem with this view of empathetic reconstruction is its pre-supposition of a science of human nature validating claims of the form, 'In situation S_1, an ambitious, strong and self-confident man like Caesar would perceive his situation so . . ., feel so . . ., think so . . . and intend so . . .'[4] The science that would allow the historian to arbitrate among the plethora of mental states and events that can be posited as connecting situation to behaviour, just does not exist.[5] The problem is that it is all too easy to empathize and rather difficult to say why one empathetic reconstruction should be preferred to another. It is possible to think of many reasons for Caesar crossing the Rubicon, or for Nixon leaving the tapes running, but difficult to say which is correct.

A second problem is that for arguments of the form: 'In situation S_1 *someone like* Caesar would think and feel $x_1 \ldots x_n$' it must, in principle, be possible to transfer the empathetic generalization to others *like* Caesar in *similar* situations, to Hitler on the eve of Operation Barbarossa, for example. But suppose the case does not fit. What does this prove? That the empathetic generalization does not hold for Hitler and thus for Caesar neither, or simply that Caesar is not so very like Hitler after all? If the generalization does not hold, then differ-ences between Caesar and Hitler are deemed significant; if it does hold, the conclusion follows that such differences are peripheral to the case in point. In short, nothing can be tested and nothing proved.

A final problem attaches to what Rex Martin terms 'transhistorical general-izations'.[6] For a reconstruction of Caesar's reasons for crossing the Rubicon to hold good for similar people in similar situations across time, we must also suppose values, mores, beliefs and forms of reasoning to hold good across time. This is a debatable assumption and is, in fact, questioned by no less authority than Collingwood:

> Types of behaviour do, no doubt, recur, so long as minds of the same kind are placed in the same kind of situations. The behaviour patterns character-istic of a feudal baron are no doubt fairly constant so long as there were feudal barons living in a feudal society. But they will be sought in vain (except by an inquirer content with the loosest and most fanciful analogies) in a world whose social structure is of another kind.[7]

(c) The third and final interpretation of Collingwood portrays the empathizing historian as a 'necromancer' conjuring apparitions of, but not from, the past to appear and address the present in the language of the present. As the 'necromancer' conceit suggests, the historian hides his epistemological machinery behind a persuasive illusion. Yet no charlatanism is involved for the pleasingness and persuasiveness of the illusion is the measure of the machinery.

Instead of lending dead souls the use of his mouth or formulating some para-syllogistic relation between situation and action, the historian as 'necromancer' conjures a vision of past action that a contemporary audience will find recognizable, intelligible and plausible. What he does not do is to play the antiquarian psychologist and seek to make action accountable as behaviour (= a series of events in space and time).

It is useful to conceive of the empathetic crux as a black-box problem. The inputs, those aspects of a situation of which an historical subject is likely to be aware, are known; as are the outputs, his actions. The unknowns are the contents of his mind – the black box.

Situation ⟶ ▨ ⟶ Action

The 'psyche-snatcher' purports to solve this problem by 'becoming the black box' and flipping his lid for the delectation of the curious; the 'time-traveller' is armed with a collection of circuit diagrams and, because able to classify the black box as of a certain type, can describe – beyond a peradventure – the contents of the box. The 'necromancer', in contrast, offers a pair of spectacles, viewed through which the black box appears to be a glass box.

This third concept of empathetic reconstruction is less ambitious than alternative interpretations. Definitions of situation, intentions and means–ends reasoning, are adduced[8] in order to make sense of the facts as known. Such mental furniture is not directly apprehended by empathetic experience nor logically deduced from knowledge of the past and of human nature. No ontological claims may be made on behalf of empathetic 'necromancy', therefore, and it may be more reasonable to speak of empathetic 'construction' than of empathetic 're-enactment' or 'reconstruction'. Necromantic explanation is also epistemologically limited. Action is not accounted in the sense of a necessary connection obtaining between evidentially known actions and empathetically re-enacted intentions, nor of a constant or statistically probable conjunction holding between actions and inferred intentions. Past action is only explained in the weak sense that if we but suppose certain things to be true, we cease to be puzzled and find the actions as familiar and intelligible as the more comprehensible behaviours of contemporaries.

If we accept the concept of 'period' as encompassing, among other things, the notion of distinctive cultures, world-views, systems of belief and ways of thinking, characteristic of different ages, it follows that 'transhistorical generalizations' about human nature can only take us so far and that 'literal' re-enactments of thought and feeling, even if possible, would be less than perfectly intelligible. It is the historian's task to render what is alien about past mentalities sufficiently recognizable to the contemporary reader for him to accept them as his 'own', but to do so without reducing their distinctive and diacritical features. Thus the historian will explain ideas, values and mores that Caesar would have taken as self-evident, and will do so in terms that Caesar may not have understood. More important still, the historian will presume to unpack taken-for-granted assumptions that Caesar may not have been aware of making. The number and nature of these assumptions is one measure of the conceptual distance between Caesar's world and our own. It is this conceptual distance, this dislocation in the world-views of past and present, that the empathizing historian seeks to remedy. When successful, he does 'bring the past back to life', but not by re-creating thought as it was – although his work creates this illusion – nor even by building a bridge of words across time. He achieves his aim by using the conceptual apparatus of the present to construct a model of mind different from that of the present into which known facts can be slotted and made good sense of.

These 'models of mind', whether relating to periods, societies, groups or individuals, amount to factually exemplified 'transformation rules' by means of which the unfamiliar is transmuted into the recognizable. Put another way, the historian writes footnotes to present-day ideas, values and norms, which enable us to apply knowledge and understanding of contemporaries to predecessors. Everyday experience thus substitutes for a science of human nature, and common-sense stands in for a deontic calculus.

Empathetic construction thus offers no more scientific or epistemologically sound account of human behaviour than we are inclined to accept in everyday life. What it does offer is a prophylactic against tempero-centrism. Whether dealing with individuals or collectivities, the historian is reluctant to see past behaviours as aberrant or irrational. That Joan of Arc may or may not have been a paranoid schizophrenic is of less interest than the reasoning employed by the Church to determine the provenance of her 'voices'. Similarly, the historian will only with reluctance adjudge the blind King John of Bohemia a deluded fool for his fatal charge against the English ranks at Crecy. The historian's attitude to the past should be one of humility.

> Whenever he [the historian] finds certain historical matters unintelligible, he has discovered a limitation of his own mind; he has discovered that there are certain ways in which he is not, or no longer, or not yet, able to think. Certain historians . . . find in certain periods of history nothing intelligible, and call them dark ages; but such phrases tell us nothing about those ages themselves.[9]

As exegesis of Collingwood, the view of the historian as 'necromancer' is exceedingly dubious. For example, although the empathizing historian may be said to explain action 'from the inside', as it were, he does so from the inside of *our known-*

in-common world not from that of our predecessors, and this is unlikely to be what Collingwood had in mind. This in itself would not occasion undue concern were it not uncertain whether such empathetic constructions can be regarded as worthwhile *explanations* of past action.

Empathy and historical explanation

Does the overt conjuring of spirits and covert making of models count as explanation or is it, in Sartre's phrase, 'mere poetry'? We have said that history rests upon common-sense, everyday empathy. We have also said that empathic construction of action and meaning amounts to the reduction of a puzzle, to a rendering of the strange and unintelligible down to the recognizable and comprehensible, if not invariably to the homely and the comfortable.[10] If history begins and ends with lay common-sense can it pretend to offer academically respectable explanations of the past? Can it even claim the status of a discipline? It can in as much as it is grounded in an evidence-based methodology and offers causal as well as empathetic explanations. But to consider empathetic reconstruction of past meanings as a legitimate part of the discipline, it is necessary to prove them something more than everyday glosses upon the past.

But what other sorts of explanation are offered in history and can these apply to action? At the level of historical biography it is permissible to explain individual action in terms of empirically observed regularities or patterns of behaviour. Thus, the fact that in the 1930s the young Viscount Knebworth flirted with fascism may be dismissed as fairly typical of many young men of his class and generation.[11] But this does not work for history on a larger scale. If we note that, unlike the SA, the SS recruited disproportionately from the class of propertyless intellectuals, we have a question of some consequence. Observation of regularities and patterns gives rise to questions not answers. And explanation of the regularity may not supply the reason for any individual German joining the SS!

What of the possibility of applying covering laws to history? In the case of human action, covering laws would supply an action schema wherein the observed behaviour is shown to be conditional upon certain possible configurations of intention, means–ends reasoning and definitions of situation, i.e.:

$$((S_1 . I_1 . R_1) \wedge (S_2 . I_2 . R_2) \ldots \wedge (S_n . I_n . R_n)) \supset A_x{}^{12}$$
IF ((Perceived Situation$_1$ AND Intentions$_1$ AND Means–Ends Reasoning$_1$) OR (Perceived Situation$_2$ AND Intentions$_2$ AND Means–Ends Reasoning$_2$) . . . OR . . .),
THEN Action of type *x*.

It is quite clear that we have no choice but to accept covering laws; they are implicit in all our statements. We could predicate nothing to other minds without the knowledge (empirical or axiomatic) of what predicates are possible, how these tend to cluster for individual personalities, which clusters are unexceptionable and which problematic, and so on. (Furthermore, unique events cannot be accounted solely in terms of other unique events or singular conjunctions of the same.) What is not so obvious is that historical explanation is *about* covering laws. The physicist assumes 'laws of nature' constant throughout the space–time continuum, explanation of natural phenomena holding good wherever and whenever a given conjunction of events obtains. The historian makes a contrary assumption such that, while possibilities for intelligible meaning are constrained within the boundaries of our common humanity, the cultures, 'forms of life', *Weltanschauung*, in which this humanity finds expression vary by time and place. Thus, although the full repertoire of thought and feeling may, in all probability, be found in any age, relative incidences appear to vary and the universal elements of human experience configure into very different mental milieu. It is for this reason that the *universals* of action and experience presupposed by unstated covering laws are of limited interest to the historian. In studying the past the historian's task is not to explain in terms of the universals (= science of human nature) but to do so by reference to models of distinct, if genetically related, 'forms of life'. Rather than elucidate psychological ground-rules for the species, he must use available evidence to articulate logically, or rather humanly, possible worlds.

But is this simply to relocate 'covering-law' theories inside the temporal boxes historians call 'periods'? Why can we not say, 'If a man of Caesar's position, character and abilities, *living in late Republican Rome*, confronts a situation of type x_n, he will tend to perceive his situation as S_n, employ the following means–end reasoning r_n and intend i_n, which perceptions, reasoning and intentions, dictate crossing the Rubicon'? Perhaps we can no longer speak of 'laws' but we would still employ law-like propositions amounting, in any individual case, to a theory of a period or, if unexplicated, to a 'sense of period'. Unfortunately, neither a model nor a sense of period may be employed to yield law-like explanations. Universal covering laws may, in principle, be so used because they are formulated on the basis of our contemporary knowledge of human behaviour; that is, the laws established on the basis of one set of data may then be applied to another. But a model of a period generalized from in-period data cannot supply a conditional explanation of these selfsame data.

Excepting the marginal case wherein individual action is dismissed as typical of a class, place and time, we must reject the possibility of *conditional*, and hence of causal, explanation of action. Nor may actions be explained ideographically by reference to the personal meanings and intentions of actors, if only because it is impossible to distinguish between valid re-enactment and mere solipsism. What may be construed, argued and analysed, are the *social meanings* attributable to an action given its authorship and temporal location. Armed with a model of mind (= a set of transformation rules) appertaining to a class, place and time, the historian is entitled to construct the meaning of Caesar's actions, not for Caesar, but for 'the collective consciousness' of Rome. In essence, the historian is saying to his readers, 'Had we been born into late Republican Rome and privy to the information presented, this is, in general, how we would have made sense of Caesar's actions.'

It may be objected that few, if any, historians seem to work in this way, that they write as though concerned to *tell it like it was in the past*, rather than, as here argued, to *discuss what may be most legitimately said about the past*. In general, they probably do, but this in no way affects the epistemological status of their conclusions. More serious is the charge that the idea of 'period' is not as prominent as here stated. Just as when dealing with events historians concentrate upon the froth and flux of 'happenings' rather than upon underlying trends and regularities (what Braudel calls the 'conjuncture' as opposed to the 'structure' of events),[13] so they pay more attention to individual and institutional *action* than to *Zeitgeist* and *Lebensform*. None the less, whether discussing Cromwell's behaviour at Drogheda or the role of 'the crowd' in the French Revolution, historians take care to remark the differences in collective consciousness between 'then' and 'now', and in so doing present what amounts to a model of mind applicable to a social group and a period of time. One strand within Annales history[14] has brought the reconstruction of 'collective mentalities' to the forefront of historical enterprise; but, in the main, it has remained in the background, obliquely hinted in such dicta as 'read till you hear them speak'.

One reason why historians write as though the empathetic reconstruction of past meanings yields conditional explanations of past actions may be because they are committed to a narrative that oscillates between two different modes of explanation, the empathetic that aims for recognition and understanding of behaviour, and the conditional/causal concerned to arbitrate significances and elucidate connections. It is thus useful to view historical narrative as a rope braided from two types of thread – *action* and *event*, what people do and what happens to the world.[15] Problems arise when historians casually or wilfully tangle these threads, analysing MacDonald's premiership, for instance, as though splitting the Labour Party was an *action* of his rather than an *event* consequential upon, among other things, his actions.

Accepting the convenience of the distinction between empathetic construction and conditional/causal explanation, the claim that empathetic constructions of social meanings and elaboration of 'models of mind' count as historical explanations may be assessed by first considering theoretical assumptions and, second, rules of procedure. The brand of empathy here advanced rests upon four assumptions:

(a) The *perspectives of the past are likely to differ from those of the present*. We cannot expect to penetrate the actions and meanings of predecessors by reference to the set of values and mores, logics and ideas, that we apply to contemporaries.

(b) We share a *common humanity* with people in the past. No hypothesized 'form of life' within which we cannot empathetically operate may be applied to the past. To be admissible as an empathetic construction applicable to the Assassins of Alamut, for example, historians must be able to say, 'Yes, I could live inside that culture and, given those ground rules, the Assassins' behaviour appears quite natural.'

(c) Past 'forms of life' are *genetically connected* to the historian's own. The anthropologist can 'penetrate' an alien 'form of life' by the simple expedient of becoming part of it. Lacking this advantage, the historian is disciplined and guided by the fact that within any cultural tradition past 'forms of life' are developmentally related to those of the present. However narrowly the historian may specialize in the France of Louis XI or the England of Edward IV, he must construct a 'form of life' that not only fits the apparent facts of the case but that also slots neatly into the unfolding history of the European mind.

(d) People in the past behaved *rationally*. For both individuals and collectivities, the historian strives to posit modes of rational action and transitive meaning. This is not to say that he expects to discover economical and efficient means to ends, or to be confronted by logically valid philosophies and theologies; but he does presume that systems of meaning were reasonably coherent and cohesive, and that our predecessors strove to avoid what, given their beliefs, would be *recognized* as logical intransitivity.

Peter Lee notes that historians

> are not content to give up when confronted with an action which resists the construction of any rationale. It is a kind of standing presupposition of history that (unless there is evidence to the contrary) people act for reasons which, from their own point of view at the moment of setting themselves to perform the action, are good reasons.[16]

Empathetic constructions may also claim acceptance as historical explanations because, quite clearly, not any construction will do. Many may be advanced to make sense of some particular action but some can be shown to be better than others. Thus, while no procedures can guarantee the sufficiency of any one empathetic explanation, it is possible to advance criteria wherewith to arbitrate the merits of rival accounts. These are the criteria of coherence, consonance, efficiency and parsimony.

Coherence refers to the 'sense of conviction' inspired by empathetic construction, or, more formally, to measures of internal consistency. As aforesaid, the assumption of rationality does not require the historian to impose a totally harmonious, sanitized and logically transitive, world-view upon a period, nor to present individual behaviour as the careful and conscious unfolding of some master-plan; but he is obliged to argue and evidence such changes of direction, dislocation of meaning and structural contradiction, as obtain. Although it can be expressed in formal language, the coherence criterion is, at bottom, nothing more than an invitation to empathize within the world or situation constructed by the historian and say what it feels like. There is a story that after a flight in the latest American supersonic bomber, General le Mays, head of SAC, reduced the order for the plane because, as he put it, 'it doesn't fit my ass'. When historians disagree, the reader is entitled to prefer the empathetic construction that 'best fits his ass'.

Equally obvious is the requirement for *consonance* with other accounts. If, for instance, a history of King John attributes intentions and meanings that jar against the generally accepted construction, or 'sense', of the medieval mind, this attribution must be scrupulously weighed and argued. The historian must also consider how well an empathetic account slots into its historical context. A study of the concept of monarchy in seventeenth-century England, for example, must always keep one eye on the sixteenth and eighteenth centuries.

The *efficiency* of an empathetic construction of individual intention or collective consciousness is gauged against the evidence falling within its range of convenience, that is, does it satisfactorily account for all the data that it ought? There is considerable room for manoeuvre in any appraisal of efficiency, partly because the interpretation of evidence is, in part, an empathetic activity (since no proposition can, of itself, tell us how to make sense of it), and partly because the documentary record evidences intention less clearly than action. We are more sure that Elizabeth I authorized Mary Stuart's execution than that she intended her death. Similarly, we have a more secure view of the discussion minuted by Hossbach than of Hitler's actual war plans – if, indeed, he had any!

Finally, empathetic construction should be *parsimonious* inasmuch as there should be no simpler or less exotic alternative construction of comparable coherence, consonance and efficiency.

In sum, what may be said on behalf of our 'beautiful woman'? She cannot satisfy the strict philosopher by arguing her right to be. She cannot prove the necessary existence of her nose, her toes, nor of any other part of her. But she is entitled to retort, 'Show me that the whole is not pleasing, that my toes are out of sorts with my nose, or demonstrate any discord between my parts and the historical objects with which you have filled my world, and I'll be content to withdraw. Yet I'll not depart because unable to explain how nose and toes come to be, nor why they are as they are; and history would be the poorer for my compliance.' And because we like happy endings, the philosopher is seduced.[17]

But what of the teacher? Because empathy is crucial to history it does not follow that secondary schoolchildren can usefully address its subtleties or that appropriate ways of teaching and assessing it can be devised. These questions are addressed in the following two sections.

II. HOW ADOLESCENTS MAKE SENSE OF 'EMPATHY'

What does a history student understand by the exhortation, 'Imagine you are Savanarola having a bad day'? Does he perceive an opportunity for 'creative English'? Does he produce the usual descriptive essay in the first instead of the third person? Or does he engage in an altogether more complicated and peculiarly historical enterprise? Precisely how pupils construe the instruction to empathize depends upon the nature of the task posed, the ways in which they have been taught, and the assumptions they hold about predecessors and the place of intention and action in historical narrative and explanation. These assumptions, in so far as they are accessible, yield evidence of what can and needs to be taught.

Adolescent construction of people in the past[18]
On the basis of phenomenologically orientated interviews conducted with 156

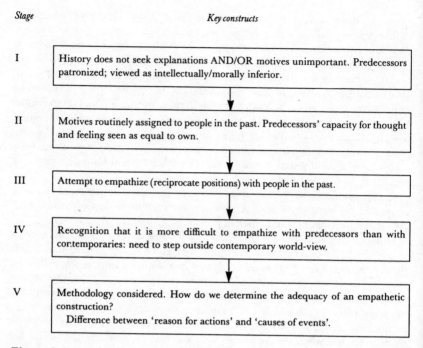

| Stage | Key constructs |

Figure 3.1

15-year-old examination stream adolescents as part of the evaluation of Schools Council Project *History 13–16*,[19] the developmental model shown in Figure 3.1 may be tentatively advanced.

Stage I: dry bones and a sense of superiority[20]
The presumption of a shared humanity with people in the past is so deeply embedded in the historian's consciousness that few teachers stop to question whether or not their pupils think in this way. And many do not, mistakenly confusing cultural and technological supremacy with biological superiority. Less able pupils, in particular, are disposed to

regard their predecessors as *similar* to themselves in precisely those respects in which they differ (the way they thought and felt), and *different* or inferior to themselves in respect of the humanity common to all (their capacity for thought and feeling). Thus, somewhat paradoxically, people in the past are seen as little more than modern men in fancy dress while, at the same time, all oddities in beliefs and practices are attributed to moral and intellectual inferiority. The Elizabethans chose to flog and hang beggars in preference to putting them on social security because their rich men were more wicked and miserly than ours! The Ancient Egyptians persisted with bizarre and inefficacious remedies because, as one boy put it, 'they were closer to the monkeys in them days, weren't they sir?'[21]

Biological historicism is rarely to the forefront of pupils' minds. When asked, for instance, why the cavalry charged at Peterloo, they may advance reasons as though the past were the playground writ large, peopled by the same personalities and coalitions having more or less similar attitudes and aspirations – the men questing for power and prestige, the women sitting in the back row doing things to fingernails. The latent presumption of moral and intellectual inferiority emerges, however, when pupils are faced with what appears especially cruel or crass behaviour, or when required to contrast past and present. In this latter case, people in the past are thought 'more primitive' than ourselves, and their technology and institutions to be inferior because their *brains* were 'less advanced'.

The second, and independent facet of stage I thinking is the routine failure to consider motives. As suggested above, almost any 15-year-old can respond to the question, 'Why did Lord Liverpool do...? What were his reasons? What was in his mind at the time?' But the question may be answered without the pupil having any idea of why it matters. Perhaps it is supposed to be of 'great note and interest' like Napoleon's piles or Pitt's predilection for port. And unless explicitly requested so to do, adolescents at stage I simply fail to consider motives. For some, this is doubtless because history is a descriptive not an explanation-seeking discipline: 'You can't explain it – it just happens.... You say they [events] happened and leave it at that' (Schools Council Project pupil). Other adolescents see history as a clear-cut, hard-edged record within which speculation about motives has no place:

SUB: History is about what actually happened not what a certain person wanted to happen [Written statement.][22]

INT: [Referring to the above]: When an historian wishes to explain 'what actually happened', would it help him to know what people 'wanted to happen'?

SUB: No. Action can be seen.... You can't judge why people did things.

INT: Why not?

SUB: You can't look into their minds.

INT: But would it help the historian if one could?

SUB: No.... It doesn't matter why people do things.

INT: Why not?

SUB: It's no good having a good reason for something if you don't do it. (Non-Schools Council Project pupil)

It is important to note that while the average IQ (AH4) score of stage I construers is lower than for subsequent stages, such ideas are a product of teaching as well as of general intellectual ability.

Stage II: assumption of shared humanity and routine stress on motives
The pupil at stage II begins to be surprised at and even puzzled by the beliefs and behaviours of his predecessors. This signifies a tacit acceptance of the fact that the people engaged in what may appear unreasonable and sometimes unpleasant activities are quite as human as his contemporaries. Historical questions about people in the past only become meaningful when pupils learn to

clearly distinguish the History of the culture from the Natural History of the species. Once the premise [of shared humanity] is accepted, moreover, the child can begin to sympathise with his predecessors, and may even see something of the viewpoint of such stereotypical demon kings as the work-house master and factory owner.[23]

Experience with Schools Council Project *History 13–16* suggests that more or less all examination-stream candidates can be taught to approach history in ways consistent with the 'shared humanity' premise. All can also be taught to routinely ascribe and question motives. Some may even articulate the concern with motivation as a principle of historical inquiry:

INT: How do you decide why something happened?

SUB: You must examine the motives to find why it happened. (Schools Council History Project pupil)

This response sounds glib and somewhat mechanical, subsequent inter-rogation revealing the girl to think of 'motives' as somehow given by the past rather than posited by the historian. She is typical of stage II thinking in that her questions about and ascription of motives is in no way empathetic.

Even when discussing 'intentions', pupils at stage II tend to explain 'from the outside'. The Mormons obeyed the dictates of Brigham Young *because of their religion*. Doctors opposed Pasteur and Lister *because they were conservative*. Such explanations are valid as far as they go, but actions are viewed as occurrences accountable by means of generalized stereotypes, rather than in terms of the meanings they held for people at the time. Equally, when explaining the behaviour of named individuals the stage II construer frequently refers to character in lieu of motive. Thus, Custer disobeyed orders and precipitated the Little Bighorn debâcle because 'he was a bighead'. And when genuine motives appear to be advanced, they tend to be mechanical inferences deduced from consideration of what was done. Why did Essex rebel? 'Because he wanted to be king and boss people around!' Use of ahistorical stereotypes of human behaviour allow some sort of reason to be given, and given without thought, for any and every action.

Nor does the provision of source materials necessarily assist the pupil towards a more empathetic response. Contemporary opinion concerning Essex's 'ambition' and 'wounded vanity' might justify a student in concluding that Essex felt 'ill-used', but this may still be to view the behaviour of Essex 'from the outside'. If evidence about Essex's mental processes is *used* in the same way as evidence of Essex's dress, physiognomy and behaviour, no empathy is involved.

In sum, while pupils at stage II frequently use the language of motivation, they tend to explain action in terms of the actor 'being this or that sort of person' or 'experiencing one of a number of stereotypical emotions'. They also tend to blur the distinctions between what someone *did* and what they *wanted to do* (Nelson ordered his ships to close with the French because he wanted to close with them), and between a description of action and a judgement upon the consequences of action (Lloyd George split the Liberal Party much as a teacher might split a class into two groups).

Stage III: everyday empathy applied to history

An adolescent may empathize with his teacher by mentally projecting himself into the teacher's shoes and trying to view the situation from the teacher's point of view. This does not entail sympathy for or identification with the teacher; indeed, a pupil better able to empathize with his teacher is better able to deceive and disrupt should he be so disposed.[24] Nor has empathy anything to do with the ability to reverse sensory perspectives, to imagine the physical aspect of the classroom presenting itself to the teacher's eyes. In like manner, empathy in history does not involve the mere imaginative projection of sensory faculties into a different physical world. An imaginary stroll through Viking York, recounting the sights thereof, may be 'imaginative reconstruction' but it does not count as 'empathy'.

Despite being set such unpromising tasks as require them to 'sympathize with predecessors' and 're-create scenes from daily life', many adolescents clearly attempt to [re]construct the attitudes and ideas, values and mores, of people in the past. It is the mark of 'empathy' that such [re]construction typically involves an imaginative projection of the self into the situation of the other. One boy, for instance, explains why we may fairly presume resentment against the Versailles treaties to be a genuine reason for the acceptance of Hitler by the German people and not a rationalization after the event:

> I mean, if one knows, I mean one can tell that the Versailles Treaty would've influenced people if you yourself feel a sort of pang of . . . if you yourself had any great patriotism towards Germany you'd feel a pang of . . . whatever, and you yourself would be influenced. (Schools Council History Project pupil)

This boy goes on to discuss the empathetic reciprocation of positions in a more abstract vein:

> we can feel what other people'd feel in their situation. By knowing the character of human beings we can judge what their motives'd be and what they'll tend to do.

Although we can hear the teacher talking out of his mouth, this pupil has clearly demonstrated the ability to practise what others preach.

More impressive, and far less common, is a *third-person empathizing* that approaches the detached empathetic modelling of the professional historian. In the following example, a rather gifted boy tries to explain why large numbers of presumably decent Germans acceded to Nazism:

> if there's no way, with Hitler controlling things, the state, of knowing if they're the majority's plans, they can be made to seem like it . . . . There's more, much more chance than given one or two people to work on – it's like being a gang member on his own and then in the gang . . . . It's the psychological force of numbers on your free will – it makes you willing to surrender it and want what you think others want. More people buy things they don't want in a supermarket than they do in a corner shop, and it was the same in Germany. (Schools Council History Project pupil)

This boy is not imagining how a Nuremberg rally 'would have' or 'could have' affected him, but he is arguing empathetically none the less. Having made the general statement that people genuinely wish to think as others think, and are hence vulnerable to the false or manufactured consensus, he unifies past and present experience by means of the 'gang' and 'supermarket' analogies. More felicitous examples could doubtless have been chosen, and a more specifically historical analysis of the concepts of 'volk' and 'racial will' would have gone a long way towards explaining the almost ecstatic surrender of individual mind and conscience to the superego of the crowd; but this empathetic analysis is exceptional none the less. Yet it is exceptional 'empathy' rather than exceptional 'history', potentially as applicable to crowd hysteria and political extremism in contemporary Britain as in Weimar Germany. This limitation is transcended at stage IV.

Stage IV: historical empathy

Adolescents at stage III attempt to think themselves into alien *situations* but not into alien *minds*. They may assess the impact of the Versailles treaties, the Great Inflation, the occupation of the Ruhr, the activities of the Freikorps and so on, upon the way people thought, but they will not work from the premise that the heirs of Bismarck, Siemens and Fichte are likely to have viewed these phenomena somewhat differently than would a contemporary Briton (or German). The assumption that past values and mores, beliefs and attitudes, even what passes for common-sense, may be different – and perhaps very different – from those of today, is the advance made at stage IV.

Reconstruction in 'the round' of 'the Renaissance mind', for example, is clearly beyond adolescents as a practical accomplishment. Yet it is not beyond most O level candidates (and talented CSE pupils) as a principle that they can recognize and operate. They may rarely hit the mark, but they frequently show evidence of aiming in the right direction. And this is sufficient – they understand something of history even if they are not, and may never become, mature and competent historians.

A few pupils can even explain why it is more difficult to understand predecessors than contemporaries; for example:

[You can't just put yourself in someone else's shoes because] as a child's influenced by his background . . . at home . . . so we're influenced by the world around us and the situation in which we live in . . . . So all these influences – you have to allow for all these influences when you're doing it [i.e. empathizing] . . . . There's always an influence behind an influence and there's no root – the influence further back . . . [Even if] the roots don't change then somewhere along the line they'll change [people's ideas?] and in the changing they'll change everything in front of them. (Schools Council History Project pupil)

The argument here is less than clear, but the pupil appears to be saying that even if situations ('influences') remain the same, the ways in which they are viewed will change and, because history is continuous, this will of itself change the situational constraints moulding future perspectives.

Stage V: empathetic methodology

At stage V pupils begin to question what empathetic construction means and how it may be accomplished. Pure scepticism, however, about the possibility of 'knowing other minds' signifies nothing more than misunderstanding of what the historian is about. An adolescent who retorts, 'How should I know why Essex rebelled? He's dead and gone, and – were he still alive – I couldn't look inside his head', has missed the point. In construing the exhortation to empathize as a request for *facts* that cannot be supplied, such a pupil mistakes the nature of the empathetic enterprise just as surely as if he had supposed the 'causes of the First World War' to be somewhere listed in documents of the period.

Methodological questions posed at stage V include the comprehensibility of sources produced within a world of meanings and priorities different from our own;[25] the extent to which contemporary culture affords a firm basis for hypothesis about those cultures from which it developed; and the problem of what is to count as 'rational' when rationality itself may be supposed to change; for example:

> I know you can try and see something from someone else's point of view, but rationalism changes – that's one of the great lessons of history and we've learned that if nothing else . . . . We might be able to solve that in part because I should think rationalism would change rationally. (Schools Council History Project pupil)

Few adolescents trouble their minds with such questions in the main because only a minority of 15-year-olds are able and disposed so to do, but partly because few teachers find it profitable to address these issues with even good O level sets. Most teachers, however, would wish to teach examination groups to stage IV, to the level of genuine historical empathy, and experience suggests realization of this objective to be fairly unlikely with a minority of O level and perhaps the majority of CSE candidates. For such pupils, the teacher must accept the pre-empathetic stage II and the empathetic, but non-historical, stage III as worthwhile goals.

This is only half the story, however. Having discussed what adolescents think they have to do when enjoined to empathize, the question of *why* they think the elucidation of motive and meaning important, of what connections they see obtaining between *history as action* and *history as event*, remains to be investigated. And here the evidence of the Schools Council History Project Evaluation is more extensive.

Adolescent construction of intentional action

Following from the theoretical analysis conducted in section I, we would expect adolescent ideas about empathetic explanation, about what may and may not be explained by reference to meanings and intentions, to be closely linked to ideas about causal explanation. This expectation is confirmed, but not as we might anticipate. Depending upon the way questions are phrased, average and able 15-year-olds readily employ two distinct languages – the personal language of meaning and intention and the more analytical language of cause and effect – without seeming to be aware that these languages attach to separate, if related, modes of explanation. This particular conceptual jigsaw contains four pieces: 'what people did', 'what happened', 'why people did what they did' and 'why what happened did happen'. Adolescent attempts to assemble these pieces into narrative and explanation are described and analysed in Figure 3.2.

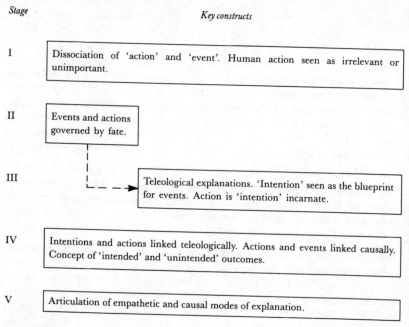

Figure 3.2

Stage I: dissociation of actions and events

Adolescents construing historical narrative at stage I make no attempt to relate 'actions' to 'events', nor to align explanations of 'why people did things' with explanations of 'why things happened'. For some, history offers description without seeking explanation, 'intentions' and 'causes' consorting on equal terms with bills and battles. Perhaps overaccustomed to dealing with first-order concepts of varying levels of abstraction and incomprehensibility – primogeniture, Privy Council, poll tax and so on – the stage I thinker never grasps that 'causes' and 'intentions' are higher order (organizing or structural) concepts wherewith to evaluate and articulate the former.

For more able pupils, a similar consequence follows from a disposition to view man as powerless to affect or command his own historical destiny:

SUB: [Opines that the historian need pay no regard to motives.]
INT: If people in the past had not have made plans, what difference would that have made to history?

SUB: It wouldn't have made any difference.

INT: Why not?

SUB: You can't stop accidents and coincidences; they'd just carry on. (Non-Schools Council History Project pupil)

What is here meant by 'accidents and coincidences' is uncertain, but the sense of human impotence in the face of impersonal historical forces is clear enough.

More sophisticated arguments against the significance of intentional action rest upon a tacit distinction between history as 'the past' and history as 'events considered noteworthy by historians':

SUB: History is just a record of past mistakes. If everything turned out as it was planned there would be no history, save that of the success of the plan. [Written statement.]

INT: [Referring to the above]: What makes you think that history is *just* a record of past mistakes?

SUB: It's just that accidents seem to be more apparent than plans . . . so that's what the historian notices most and writes about. (Non-Schools Council History Project pupil)

This pupil is highly intelligent and his construction of man as patient not agent in the historian's version of history may well mirror the teacher's classroom presentation. Again:

Things do happen when unintended and so more is made of it in history; usually if things go as planned there is nothing much to make history. (Written statement. Non-Schools Council History Project pupil)

For certain purposes it may be useful to classify stage I ideas according to whether pupils construe intentional action as (a) genuinely inconsequential, (b) of little interest to historian, or (c) merely adding to a purely descriptive, non-explanation seeking butterfly-collection. For present purposes, however, it is convenient to combine construct categories wherein what people 'do' is seen as irrelevant to 'what happens in history'.

Stage II: a superordinate fate

For adolescents admitting a substantial role to human action in history, first ideas about what may and may not be explained by reference to 'intentional action' are naturally grounded in beliefs about everyday life. The question of action in the past does not seem so very different from the problem of action in the present (which problem being to explain why events sometimes accord with intentions but more usually do not). Stage II construers resolve this problem by subordinating both intentional action and unplanned events to a single, overarching fate:

SUB: It's Fate.

INT: What's that?

SUB: It's something that can't be stopped . . . . It just happens and you can't stop it.

INT: But what is Fate?

SUB: It's Destiny.
INT: Is Fate only involved when accidents happen?
SUB: It's involved all the time. (Non-Schools Council History Project pupil)

The grounding of this theory in everyday life rather than in history as such is clearly evident in the following excerpt:

SUB: No one can change or affect in any way what has happened or what will happen in the future therefore all we can do is accept it. [Written statement.]
INT: [Referring to the above]: How do we explain why things happened in history?
SUB: I don't know . . . Luck and Fate.
INT: What are Luck and Fate?
SUB: I'm not sure, but it might be God.
INT: How much control do we have over our history?
SUB: Very little.
INT: What can we control?
SUB: Ourselves – No, we can't control the future for ourselves.
INT: Why not?
SUB: I want to be a WREN and I might have worked very hard to be one but have something wrong I can't control like flat feet.
INT: Is all history like that?
SUB: It's Luck or Fate.
INT: How do you know?
SUB: It can't be anything else.
INT: Why not?
SUB: I've no idea. (Non-Schools Council History Project pupil)

Adolescent ideas about fate are anything but clear. It may attach to God, to individuals (who may be 'lucky' as they may be tall or beautiful) or to the shadow order of events themselves (a logic manifest in its outcomes but not in its operations). What is certain is that it denotes the arbitrary and the uncontrollable aspect of life, not the random and statistically predictable. As Piaget notes, 'subjects not yet in possession of the operations susceptible of disclosing a true causal order are not capable either of recognizing the existence of fortuity'.[26] The stage II construction of fate is generalization from, or perversion of, the concept of *intention* fulfilling the role played by the *causation* concept in the historian's scheme of things. (It is significant that such pupils obliged to construe *cause in history* do so as though it refers to some *property* of the causative event which, in turn, 'makes' or 'creates' an effect.)

Relatively few adolescents think in this way and, of those so doing, many also construe in terms more characteristic of stage III.

Stage III: teleological explanations

At stage III pupils allow a significant historical role to *intentional action*, conceding that because 'people make history' the historian must look to motives and meanings ('plans') in order to explain what happened. The problem of failed plans, of occurrences contrary to human desire, is solved by positing a species of Manichaean universe containing various quasi-intentional factors coterminous with, but independent of, human intentionality; for example:

> SUB: . . . it all depends on what actually happened.
> INT: What does?
> SUB: History.
> INT: In what way?
> SUB: Well, *what* happens is most important, then *why* . . . so if they didn't plan it, it must have been an accident and that's why.
> INT: So when the historian tries to explain why things happened, will he want to know about the plans of the people involved even if these plans went wrong?
> SUB: No, he'll want to know about the accidents. (Non-Schools Council History Project pupil)

As at stage II, the adolescent is concerned to explain why events sometimes turn out other than as intended, but the preferred explanation is altogether more homely and commonsensical. Plans go wrong:

> SUB: Because something unexpected butts into it like . . . . Say you plan a picnic and the car breaks down, that's like an accident.
> INT: Did people's plans in history go wrong for any reason other than mechanical failures and natural disasters?
> SUB: They could've become ill . . . like all of a sudden.
> INT: That's a sort of natural disaster.
> SUB: Oh hell, yes it is, isn't it . . . . No, I can't think of any.
> INT: If natural disasters hadn't occurred, would history have come about exactly as people intended?
> SUB: Yes. (Non-Schools Council History Project pupil)

More usually, 'human error' serves as the complement to intentional action:

> SUB: Sometimes people did things wrong but they didn't really know they're wrong in the first place when they did them but they realized after when it's gone wrong.
> INT: You mean they made mistakes?
> SUB: Yes – mistakes.
> INT: If people hadn't made mistakes, would all their plans have come true or would accidents still have happened?
> SUB: . . . no, I don't think they would really, because everyone's human and everybody makes mistakes at some time and . . . from a mistake some of the best things've been found out. (Schools Council History Project pupil)

'Mistakes' are variously defined as 'not thinking things through to the end', 'sneezing at the wrong time', 'dropping the nitroglycerine', and so on. These are the sort of 'mistakes' Robinson Crusoe could have made in his solitude.

Why do adolescents tend to think in this way? Piagetians might argue that pupils fail to *decentre* and approach the general problem of *action* in history from the egocentric perspective of a monadic universe; that is, a stage III thinker approaches the problem as though he were the only person with goals and aspirations. In a 'universe of one' the rules would be much as here described in Figure 3.3.

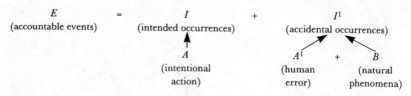

Figure 3.3

Sub-class A^1 is clearly a quasi-intentional factor comparable to the fate of stage II. But what of sub-class B? Does this category of factor betoken the co-ordination of causal and intentional modes of explanation? Probably not, because the logic articulating the concepts 'action', 'accident' and 'outcome', seems to remain that of intention not causation, of purpose not contingency. Explanation of unexpected events I^1 in terms of 'human error' and 'natural calamity' amounts to a rejection, not assertion, of contingency and fortuity because both types of actor operate upon and distort the action schema A serving to blueprint reality I. Imagine a computer program designed to play chess. Imagine the program to have a good record against grand masters. Suspend disbelief and also imagine the computer losing a game to a 7-year-old. Something has obviously gone wrong, yet while we may speak of program limitations we would not necessarily postulate programming error, a computer fault or interruption in the electricity supply.[27] But this is how stage III thinkers seem to approach action and outcome in history. For the logic of cause and effect they substitute that of intentional design (cf. the Aristotelian concepts of *efficient* and *final* causes). The relation of *action* to *outcome* is given by that of *intention* to *action*.

This extension of intentional logic to the whole of history (an extension consummated by the construction of 'cause' as a species of agency or property of antecedent, causative events)[28] entails, ironically enough, a degradation of the status of *intentional action* in history. When pupils either infer *intention* from *outcome*, or evaluate previously determined intentions against recorded outcomes, the entire business of human motive and meaning becomes at once simple and disastrously vulnerable to cock-up. The conclusion becomes inescapable that people in the past were not too smart and, for the most part, seem not to have known their own damn business. More sophisticated stage III thinkers appear to transcend such banalities in asserting, for instance, that 'people can't control everything' and 'there are always things outside our control' but, when asked to explain further, they invariably regress to the truistic 'because people are not perfect' and 'because we always make mistakes', thereby locating the problem in the frail, flawed nature of the actor and not within the inherent uncertainty of the universe acted upon.

That stage III thinkers do not 'decentre' is evident; that they cannot do so is less certain. Piagetian psychologists may be tempted to suggest that stage III thinkers cannot think formally or, at the least, fail to apply formal operations to history. But it is also possible to locate the problem in the adolescent's historical premises not his everyday logic, in his ideas not his reasoning. If so, it should be readily corrigible once teaching is directed to this end.

It is surprising that adolescents well able to take into account the motives and meanings of others in the conduct of everyday life tend to construe intentional action in history as though their predecessors operated within closed-set universes wherein, explosions and bad weather apart, public actions were as insulated from the intervention of others as were private intentions. Why should this be so? Piagetians note that any given stage or sub-stage of operational thinking is not simultaneously manifested in all areas of experience (horizontal *décalage*) such that thinking in history may lag far behind thinking in mathematics or everyday life. But again why? One possibility is that unlike everyday social intercourse, the goal of historical explanation is unknown and the starting place unclear. Considering occurrences as *intentional actions*, whether individual or collective, the historian is concerned to reconstruct intelligible meanings for behaviours in order to assemble narratives that appear to describe conceptually coherent episodes within a logically transitive universe. He also wishes to render events causally explicable, by establishing the necessary conditions and particular circumstances surrounding that occurrence. The historian thinks in this way almost as an ideational reflex; it is second nature. But stage III adolescents employ 'action' as a single unitary concept and fail to distinguish its *stimulus* and *configural* aspects. That is, they fail to consider action as, on the one hand, the incarnation of *intention*, and on the other hand, as an event within the world that may be a necessary condition for other events. Failure to make this distinction leads adolescents to view the connection between intention and outcome teleologically; that is, either intention, made manifest in action, blueprints an outcome (because action is the stimulus for an outcome it also shapes or configures that outcome); or intention fails to explain or contribute to the explanation of an outcome (action does not configure an outcome, hence does not serve as a stimulus either, and can thus be ignored by historians). This latter conclusion is readily detected:

INT: Is knowledge of these plans important to the historian even when the plans went wrong?

SUB: No, 'cos they didn't cause anything then if they went wrong. (Non-Schools Council History Project pupil)

Another boy argued that an historian studying the Battle of Talavera would wish to know about Wellington's plans, but not those of the loser, Soult (*sic*), because these were plans (= blueprints) for something that never happened, namely a French victory. Such arguments are almost the *sine qua non* of stage III thinking.

In some ways stage III ideas are first-base for adolescent thinking about *intentional action* in history. Stage I is essentially negative and stage II looks to be an aberrant dead-end. Having said this, an entire stage of construal seems to be missing. It is attractive to postulate a developmental stage at which adolescents see history as an epic saga of heroic exploits, dirty deeds and clever wheezes, without fretting overmuch about fate, accident and such like quasi-intentional agencies and categories. It seems reasonable to expect that they should do so but even pupils wedded to the notion of the Great Man who makes history in his own image, concede a role to Accident in deference to mortal clay and the unsympathetic aspect of the natural world. As one boy remarked, 'you can always catch something and die before you've finished'.

Stage IV: the genesis of causal explanation

At stage IV adolescents use the language of *causation* as well as of *intention* and do so even when 'accidents of history' are mentioned:

SUB: [Asserts the importance of both intentional acts and accidents.]
INT: Why are accidents important?
SUB: Because they shape the events for years to come.
INT: How do they shape events for years to come?
SUB: It depends on the event.... The Treaty of Versailles caused many things like the last war, but that wasn't its purpose.

Understanding of motive and meaning is now thought important whether or not outcomes turned out as desired and expected, for example:

SUB: ... plans could go wrong but they could still affect things.
INT: Good.... Is a plan which goes wrong of any interest to the historian? Could it help the historian to explain the event even though the event was not exactly as planned?
SUB: It can, yes, because... a plan was meant in a certain way and that'd affect how it'd go wrong. (Schools Council History Project pupil)

Characteristic of stage IV thinking is the idea that people act within a world of actors, that the other characters on stage are more important than backdrop, props and trap-doors. Of course, adolescents conduct their own affairs in the full knowledge that this is so, but only at stage IV do they construe this commonplace 'from the outside', as it were, and apply it to history. Whereas at stage III 'intentional action' is considered in a 'freeze-frame' situation, just as though people operate *out of time* in a universe unchanging but for the impact of their wishes, their mistakes and the intercession of the odd earthquake, they now envisage a plurality of agents functioning in overlapping action-spaces:

SUB: ... the world's very complicated and we're bound to cross over each other. (Schools Council History Project pupil)

More elaborate is the following exposition:

SUB: History's made up ... [on?] thousands of people, countries and things, and they all influence each other.... You can plan for yourself or [in?] large numbers of people so long as they've similar ideas to your own – this doesn't mean your plan'll definitely go right but you've a reasonable chance ...

[Plans going awry follow from] two things coming together usually unintentionally. The two incidents aren't accidental – it's just the fact [that?] they crossed. (Schools Council History Project pupil)

Pupils able and disposed to construe the world as a field for uncoordinated actions inspired by contrary and often incompatible intentions, may be expected to grasp much of the true nature of historical narrative and explanation. It would seem that stage IV thinkers should quickly learn to construe chance in terms of combinatorial probability not *deus ex machina*; to apprehend why discussion of cause carries no savour of the necessary or the inevitable; and to appreciate why both modes of explanation, the causal and the empathetic (= the intentional), are essential to history. On occasions this expectation is fulfilled; for example:

SUB: Well . . . we're all making history all the time – whatever we do's history – but that's not the same as controlling it.
INT: How is it possible to *make* history without *controlling* it?
SUB: If you . . . you can intend what you do . . . but what you and others make together's unintended by anyone really. (Schools Council History Project pupil)

Despite overstating his case, this boy understands 'free will' in history as referring to the 'freedom to act', the freedom to choose between genuine alternatives, not as the 'freedom', or rather the 'power to bend a compliant universe to one's will'.

Unfortunately, this degree of sophistication is rare. The stage IV thinker is able to conjoin causal and empathetic explanation, but the two modes remain imperfectly articulated. Adolescents able to distinguish intended and unintended outcomes and who accept that 'plans can cause other things to happen' (non-Schools Council History Project pupil) rarely grasp that both sorts of outcome are causally explicable and that intended outcomes are not *entirely* explained simply by noting that they were intended by someone or other. Equally, typical stage IV thinkers regard unintended outcomes as messes to be accounted for by showing how the mess arose, by explaining how 'everything gets in everything's way . . . it's like too many cooks spoiling the broth . . . they're all making different things but using the same saucepan – or kitchen might be better' (non-Schools Council History Project pupil). Two modes of explanation are employed, selection of one or the other depending upon whether outcomes were intended or unintended, that is:

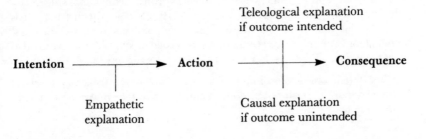

Teleological explanation
if outcome intended

Intention ⟶ Action ⟶ Consequence

Empathetic
explanation

Causal explanation
if outcome unintended

The atavistic reversion to teleological modes of explanation also accounts for a somewhat surprising feature of stage IV thinking, the disposition to consider intended and unintended outcomes as mutually exclusive possibilities. Either things go as planned or there is an unholy mess. Adolescents thus operate a closed alternation model of possible outcomes rather than the open disjunction model assumed by historians, that is:

Intended consequence(s) | *OR* | **Unintended consequence(s)**

instead of

Intended consequence(s) | *AND/OR* | **Unintended consequence(s)**

This is all the more noteworthy since stage IV thinkers generally admit the possibility of multiple outcomes – but seem to restrict them to what is *either* intended or unintended. A few adolescents, it must be admitted, can transcend this; for example:

> SUB: . . . people make history but only a small piece of history and are only indirectly responsible for long-term consequences. The consequences are long-term effects whereas desires of people are only short-term. (Written statement. Schools Council History Project pupil)

But it is the exception not the rule.

At the root of the problem is the failure of stage IV thinkers to properly distinguish the stimulus and configural aspects of intentional action (cf. stage III). Pupils need to learn that intentions are relevant to the elucidation of all action, both successful and unsuccessful, and that all outcomes may be explained causally, whether intended or not.

Stage V: articulation of empathetic and causal explanation
Although there is no evidence of 15-year-old adolescents properly articulating empathetic and causal modes of explanation, there is every reason to suppose that some may be taught to do so. Most adolescents act on the assumption that they themselves are elements in the calculation of others, and many are able to transfer this common-sense insight to history. Building upon these foundations, it should be possible to teach pupils why it is necessary to question both the 'causes of events' and the 'reasons for actions'.

The impact of teaching upon adolescent thinking[29] is evident in Table 3.1.

These results are significant at < p.01. They should, however, be treated with caution. The high incidence of stage IV constructions looks distinctly odd, particularly in comparison with the dearth of stage V constructs. It is possible that interview procedures biased respondents towards stage IV thinking and that this stage is either over-recorded or stage V under-recorded in consequence. Taken as they stand, these results suggest that

> while few if any adolescents will attain completely satisfactory levels of understanding, much can be done to enhance how they make sense of what they are taught;

Table 3.1 Matched pair comparisons: constructions of intentional action in history (pairs are matched for sex, IQ and sociocultural background)

Groups	Stage I	Stage II	Stage III	Stage IV	Stage V	N
Schools Council History Project pupils	4	3	14	57	—	78
Control pupils (following conventional history courses)	17	10	34	17	—	78
N	21	13	48	74	—	156

teaching methods and approaches should be geared not only to the general ability of pupils but also the ideational stage attained;

methods should directly address and exploit the ideas pupils already have, however misconceived these may be;

empathetic work should be aproached from two directions: reconstruction of the meanings, individual and collective, of people in the past, and analysis of the individual's role in history (i.e. the role of 'intentional action');

projective approaches to empathetic reconstruction are overused and should be augmented by techniques more likely to direct attention towards the differences between past and present world-views, and to provoke the examination of alternative possibilities rather than the generation of unitary reconstructions verified by existential fiat, that is, 'I've imagined I was there and this is what happened . . .';

pupils need to be taught to distinguish 'explanation of action' from 'explanation of the consequences of action' more thoroughly than is done at present.

What do these recommendations mean in practice? How may the teacher reliably assess the empathetic thinking of his students and, having done so, what teaching approaches are suggested? No adequate answers may be offered to these questions. We are still at the bottom of the learning curve, but a start has been made by teachers of Schools Council History Project pupils and a summary of this experience may prove of interest.

III. TOWARDS A PRACTICAL PEDAGOGY

Whether or not beauty can withstand the onslaughts of a sceptical philosophy, experience suggests adolescent 'beginners in philosophy' to be perfect suckers for a 'beautiful woman'. Equally evident is the frequency with which they bungle the liaison. For instance, in one secondary school in south-east England pupils devote term 3 of Year 4 to a study of country houses. As a concluding exercise, girls write an 'empathetic reconstruction' of life below-stairs at the turn of the century. The vitality and power of their work testifies to an interest and involvement in the exercise. Indeed, some opera, recounting torrid affairs with 'the young master' in soft-pornographic detail, may even be publishable! But is imagination and emotional involvement, in isolation from all historical virtues save a few cribbed particulars and the avoidance of gross anachronism, sufficient to distinguish history from historical fiction? Is erotic and rhapsodic prose as valuable as cold analysis, however immature? And what learning of value is thought to accrue from the imaginative displacement of adolescent Saturday nights from 1983 to below-stairs broom cupboards in 1900? These questions are thrown into greater relief by considering a second empathetic exercise, set in the aforementioned school, that required pupils to imagine themselves 'saucepans in the kitchen of a great house'. This is just not on since, while the ideas and sensibilities of servant girls may be thought to vary by place and period, those of saucepans are – on the best guess – reliably constant throughout space and time. Unlike the human condition, the 'hardware condition' is not a fit subject for the empathizing historian.

Some approaches to teaching and assessing empathy

What, then, can be said about the teaching of 'empathy' in history? Methods may be classified according to the nature of the empathy demanded (descriptive or explanatory), the nature of the activity required (enactive or reactive) and the logical structure of the task (synthesizing particulars, projecting personal responses, forging connections, disconfirming expectations, adducing alternatives or resolving incongruities (see Table 3.2).

Table 3.2

Nature of empathetic response	Logic of task	Nature of activity	
		Enactive	Reactive
	Synthesis of particulars		Biography
Descriptive	Personal projection	Drama	Projective exercises ('Imagine you are . . .')
		On-site re-enactment	Imaginative reconstruction ('What was it like?')
	Adduction of alternatives	Games and simulations	Decision-making exercises*
Explanatory	Forging connections	Games and simulations	Link culture and economy*
	Disconfirming expectations	Experimental re-enactment	Disconfirmation exercises*
	Resolving incongruities		Empathetic dilemmas* Structured contrasts* between past and present

*These approaches may be instantiated in written work, class discussion and computer-assisted learning packages.

1. *Biographies*[30]

Biographical exercises are normally presented as written assignments, for example, 'Write a biographical sketch of Fergus O'Connor as a Chartist leader', and demand synthesis of data derived from primary and/or secondary sources such that the finished product amounts to an interpretation of its constituent parts. Empathy both follows from and contributes to a gestalt effect: a sense of character and purpose holds together and, at the same time, emanates from what is – for adolescents – a series of discrete episodes set against a shifting background of national events. Experience of SCHP coursework suggests the traditional biography to be too demanding for all but the most able adolescents. For the generality of candidates, the necessity to relate the particular to the general, the minutiae of an individual career to the wider historical context, while simultaneously organizing and interpreting relatively large numbers of data, remains unfulfilled.

More successful are exercises restricting attention to single events but that none the less require pupils to consider an individual's character and motives over a longer period of time, that is, the 'spot' biography, for example, 'Who was most responsible for the execution of Mary, Queen of Scots in 1596: (i) Elizabeth? (ii) Walsingham? or (iii) Mary herself?' The average adolescent is better able to cope with this more factually limited and highly structured exercise, while the capable pupil is encouraged to consider the position of each participant within 'a context of actors' each of whom had his own goals and viewed events from a unique perspective.

2. *Drama*

Among what Americans call 'gee whizz' history methods, drama is one most readily justified as an aid to empathy. If a pupil acts the part of – and, in a sense, 'becomes' – Alonso the Horrible, he may better sympathize with and understand the character. Unfortunately, it is uncertain how far sympathetic resonances with Alonso predispose pupils to deeper understanding of or 'elective affinity' with Torquemada, Himmler and so on. It is, in any case, possible to argue that too close an identification with predecessors inserts a subjective impediment between historical characters and an understanding that should, as far as possible, be dispassionate. It may be fortunate that drama must of necessity remain a very occasional, albeit spectacular, weapon in the teacher's armoury.

3. *Projective exercises*

The *reactive* complement to dramatic enaction is the projective exercise. As a rule, this takes one of three forms: the direct invocation to project one's psyche into the past ('Imagine you are a rat on the North-West Passage . . .', and so on); the personal diary ('You are a Toltec warrior about to be sacrificed to Huitzilopochtli; complete your diary for the day'); and the letter home, most usually from one illiterate to another.[31] The following 'letter' was submitted as coursework by a Grade 5 CSE candidate in north-west England:

Dear

Dad its Great here at Vindolanda the fort is quite cosy. The view is fantastic we are always insulting our commander.

The Stonegate is quite a Smooth Road but it is very long actually it stretches from Carlisle to Corbridge.

It was built by Agricola one of your best mates. It has quite a number of forts on it.

The latrines are really modern with new sponges. The commander has his own private latrine and he has two sponges. We put some fish Glue on his Sponge the other day for a laugh but the commander was not ammused we are know on three weeks hard labour.

Any way weve got to go that's John and I by the way.

Yours faithfully
Placeni

PS Looking forward to seeing you.

Apart from the avoidance of some obvious anachronisms (e.g. 'fish glue' not super-glue) and the realization that Roman latrines were 'modern' once upon a time, there is little evidence of genuine empathy. Indeed, some teachers damn this letter on the grounds that 'modernity' is a modern concept of improbable currency in Roman Britain. But there seems little point in noting sophisticated vices in work bereft of simple virtues. Nor is this letter atypical of empathetic (re)constructions submitted for CSE coursework. Except for a small minority of adolescents with genuine literary talent, such projective exercises do not afford pupils fair opportunity of displaying what, if any, empathetic understanding they have gained from history courses. It is also difficult to see what adolescents learn from 'imagining themselves to be Roman legionaries'. To reconstruct an historical context is difficult; to project oneself back into this context with conviction is improbable; to project oneself back as one would have been given the experiences of a Roman soldier and minus those that shaped the projecting personality is, for an adolescent coming to terms with the historian's craft, near impossible. In sum, while the projective exercise may remain a useful experiment in empathetic appraisal, it cannot carry the burden of empathetic instruction or assessment.

4. *On-site re-enactment*

This technique substitutes an historical site for a dramatic script as an aid to the imaginative projection of the psyche into the past. For example, the history staff of one Yorkshire school, dismayed by the gung-ho Pict slaying that characterized empathetic (re)construction of life on the Roman Wall, took pupils to Vindolanda and re-enacted, as far as was possible, twenty-four hours of garrison life. Sanitary and sexual arrangements, of course, remained those of the twentieth century. The exercise was successful up to a point, written work reflecting the loneliness, physical discomfort and remorseless tedium, of the soldiers' lot; but pupils failed to convey the sense that here was 'world's end', a frontier dividing the known and the ordered from a realm of mist and madness. For adolescents, though strangely accoutred, the centre of the universe remained Leeds a few miles down the A1, not Rome many leagues distant. By dint of considerable preparation on the part of history department staff, pupils succeeded in empathetically (re)constructing the *situation* of people in the past, but not their *perspective*.

5. *Imaginative (re)construction*

Imaginative (re)construction differs from the projective exercises previously discussed in that the pupil is required to project himself into another situation as observer not participant. Questions like, 'Take an imaginary walk through the streets of Salford in 1870; describe the sights', are less demanding than invocations to adopt the perspectives of predecessors, but the answers are usually disappointing and as difficult to mark. The *reactive* complement to *enactive* on-site re-enactments, imaginative (re)construction exercises, appear to have little to recommend them.

6. *Games and simulations*

Techniques demanding an *explanatory* mode of response differ from those previously discussed in several respects: first, the pupil is required to empathize in order to solve some problem, to explain a puzzle or to make sense of some apparent nonsense; empathetic construction is used for some purpose other than the production of an empathetic description. Second, the pupil has to recognize what game is being played; for instance that, re the case in question, an historian would offer an explanation from 'the inside' not 'the outside'; simple cues of the form 'Imagine you are . . .' are rarely present. Third, tasks are usually more finite and closed-ended than are traditional invocations to empathetic rhapsody. Fourth, the logical structure of tasks is more varied and, at times, elusive.

One family of approaches requires pupils to adduce alternative practices or beliefs on the basis of a supplied normative framework and experience of adduced alternatives in action. For example, one simulation currently being designed is entitled 'The Strangers: Nacirema Sailors among the Esenapaj'. The class is split into two, each half learning an interlocking series of mores and laws dealing with the exchange of goods, relations between the sexes and physical contact. Each 'tribe' practises and perfects its 'culture' in isolation from the other. A group of Nacirema sailors is then shipwrecked on Esenapaj shores. The challenge is to learn sufficient about the Esenapaj 'culture' to avoid death, by starvation or by execution. The problem can only be solved by adducing a complex of practices substantively different from but structurally similar to those of the Nacirema.

Other games and simulations teach pupils to forge connections between discrete particulars, constructing thereby a coherent 'form of life' from a chaos of detail; or to 'hunt the rule' in a game for which only the object and regulatory procedures are known. A good example of the latter is the 'Barter' game[32] wherein pupils are led to discover and apply rules of exchange appropriate to a medieval village economy.

7. *Decision-making approaches*

Many decision-making games and micro-computer programs have been written, but the approach may be usefully applied to routine classwork, particularly when the objective is to force an evaluation of behaviour in the context of possible alternatives for action, for example, 'Why did Custer do *x* when he could have done *w*, *y* or *z*?' This approach may involve a cycle of exposition, written work and discussion, revolving around a series of decision points located within a story.[33] Analysis of events leading up to the Little Bighorn debâcle might conform to the following cycle:

Exposition:	Teacher gives background to the Indian War and recounts the story of Custer's campaign up to the *first* decision point (e.g. Custer's departure from the route ordered by General Terry).
Assignment:	'(i) What could Custer have done at this point? What were the alternatives?
	(ii) What would have been the most sensible thing to do? Explain your answer.
	(iii) What did Custer actually do?
	(iv) Why did he do this rather than any of the other alternative courses of action you worked out (see your answer to (i))? What were his reasons? Use evidence to explain your answer.'
Discussion:	Pupils will come up with different answers to (i), (ii) and (iv). They should discuss why they have done so and whether or not some answers (and arguments) are better than others.
Exposition:	Teacher continues story up to the *second* decision point (e.g. Custer's decision to divide his forces).
Assignment:	(As above but related to the second decision point.)

Although ideally suited to pupils of average and below-average ability not normally disposed to consider what someone 'could have done' when seeking to explain what they 'did do', this approach may also prove of value with more able adolescents. For example, in debating the question 'What do we need to know before we can say why Custer behaved as he did?', a teacher may aim to extract and exemplify categories of knowledge at several levels of sophistication:

knowledge of character (low-ability pupils are well able to link Custer's disobedience to his 'bigheadedness');

knowledge of intentions (reference may be made to Custer's political ambitions);

knowledge of definition of situation (O level and good CSE candidates should refer to the fact that past experience led Custer to anticipate flight by the Sioux and to employ tactics that proved successful hitherto);

knowledge of contemporary standards and expectations (able pupils may make reference to contemporary norms and mores, for example, that Indian tactics were despised as cowardly).

A teacher might also wish to focus the attention of able pupils upon the difference between the information accessible to Custer and that available to the historian with benefit of hindsight.[34] Pupils could make lists under three headings: what we know to have been the case; what Custer knew for certain; what Custer expected to be the case; and reconsider their verdict in the light of data contained therein. Equally, with bright pupils, connections between 'freely willed action' and 'force of circumstance' may be explored by asking why alternatives for action were limited. A species of counterfactual game may be played by supposing circumstances to have been other than they were and asking how this could have affected possibilities for action. Developments such as this perhaps lend themselves to 'computer-assisted' rather than to 'black-board-based' pedagogy but, viewed as a family of methods embodying a common logical gene (the adduction of alternatives), decision-making approaches constitute a major class of weaponry in the empathetic armoury.

8. *Exercises linking culture and economy*

A second family of approaches, already mentioned in the discussion of games and simulations, requires pupils to forge logical connections between ostensibly independent areas of experience and, thereby, to (re)construct some facet of a past 'form of life'. This technique is particularly effective when the connection to be made is between some aspect of *culture* (ideas, beliefs, practices) and what may be loosely termed *economy* (means of production and distribution; the material bases of communal life). For pupils of average and below-average ability such exercises, whether used for teaching or assessment purposes, should be highly structured; for example:

' "You are foolish to make them so strong. They will still be here when their owners are dead." (Comment of an Indian Chief on first seeing British houses during a visit to London.)

Which of the following features of Indian life best explain the attitude of the Indian Chief to British houses?

Belief in Spirits   Love of Nature
Nomadic Way of Life   Warrior Society

Explain your choice.'[35]

Despite the less than felicitous phraseology, this question is successful for several reasons: first, it presents pupils with an empathetic problem: why should it seem foolish to build houses with a design lifetime in excess of fifty years? Given the assumption of a shared humanity, this problem may only be resolved by positing a system of values and beliefs very different from our own but within which the attitude expressed makes good sense. Second, the extended objective format[36] shows pupils what an adequate answer looks like and sets a precise challenge, namely to forge a connection between the question posed and one or more of the four answers supplied. Finally, by offering two *cultural* and two *economic* options, the question caters for pupils able to do no more than link attitude to housing to some other belief or beliefs, as well as for fairly able adolescents who can first locate the problematic attitude within a complex of beliefs and then proceed to relate this to the material, or economic, bases of Indian life.

Questions designed for more homogeneous ability groups can be shorter and less complicated; for example:

'It is likely that had the Plains Indian been a farmer growing crops and not a buffalo hunter, he would have been more willing to look on his land as something that could be bought and sold.
    Explain why this is so.'

This question is appropriate to a good O level group.

9. *Experimental re-enactment*

Experimental re-enactment is superficially similar to on-site re-enactment previously discussed excepting the absence of Thespian paraphernalia and authentic historical sites. More profound is the fact that experimental re-enactment poses a problem to be solved not a scene to be relived. The problem need not be very elaborate, as in the case of a teacher who took a class of 13-year-olds on to the school playing fields, supplied similar tools to those available to the megalith builders and asked them to construct a perfect circle of equally spaced stones. After witnessing sixty minutes of growing frustration, the teacher demonstrated how it was done and pupils previously dismissive of crude stone circles were mightily impressed. They also learned some mathematics. This exercise led on to class discussion of the relation, or lack of relation, obtaining between technological level and intellectual ability as pupils conceded that Stone Age people must have been pretty smart to achieve what they did with the tools and resources to hand. This and other exercises, albeit not all of this type, were designed to persuade adolescents of one of the fundamental premises of historical empathy, namely that we share a common humanity, an equal *capacity* for thought and feeling, with people in the past. It may be expected that this understanding would transfer to different cultures in today's world but remains an as yet untested hypothesis.

10. *Disconfirmation exercises*

Experimental re-enactments such as that described above rely for their impact and effectiveness upon the shock effect of things being other than was confidently expected or predicted. Pupils are puzzled by their own inability to create a simple stone circle – it looks so easy and, anyway, mere primitives could do it so why cannot they? Surprising facts, facts at odds with avowed expectation, cannot be easily assimilated within existing ideational schema and thus afford the teacher an opportunity to force an accommodation of such schema to new realities.

This strategy can also be used within the classroom. For example, the author witnessed one lesson in which students of Elizabethan England were presented with a woodcut showing sentence being passed upon the Puritan pamphleteer John Stubbs (see Appendix I). Already familiar with the political and religious background to the incident and having discussed Stubbs's motivation and the reasons for so harsh a punishment, an O level class was asked 'What would be the first thing that Stubbs would say on losing his hand?' As soon as things had quietened down, this was amended to, 'What would be Stubbs's attitude to Elizabeth and her ministers? How might he react?'

Various predictions were advanced, ranging from making common cause with the Catholic opposition to the attempted assassination of Elizabeth, all of which reflected the themes of hatred and vengeance. The teacher went through the motions of advancing a contrary case and was argued down. Pupils then committed their ideas to paper. A primary source (see Appendix II) was next distributed which, to the consternation of the class, stated that Stubbs, on losing his right hand, doffed his bonnet with his left and shouted 'God Save the Queen'. After some heated discussion, first, concerning the reliability and provenance of the evidence, and second, about the likelihood of Stubbs dissembling his true feelings and intentions, the class were persuaded to accept the report at face value. Discussion now centred on this question: 'How could Stubbs have been sincere in this protestation of devotion?' and 'Why did pupils fail to predict his reaction? What information about Elizabethan England had they ignored?' At the end of the lesson, one boy summed up the debate by saying, 'I got it wrong because I thought how I'd react if the Queen did that to me. I forgot that I'm not a Puritan and don't live in the sixteenth century', or words to this effect. As a technique for transmitting an historically sound perspective upon Elizabethan religion and politics, this approach and any others that attempt to force pupils to reflect upon their own ideas is dangerous and likely to mislead. But the evidence of public examinations suggests that, unlike raw facts, an historically sound 'sense of period' cannot in any case be transmitted to this age group, especially when – as above – time and ingenuity are necessary simply to make adolescents aware of the illegitimacy of empathizing with predecessors as though they were contemporaries.

11. *The empathetic dilemma*

Disconfirming pupils' expectations or predictions and, thereby, making them aware of logical intransitivities within their ideas, is a teaching technique applicable to concepts other than empathy and subjects other than history. Approaches based upon the identification and reduction of apparently incongruous data are, in contrast, more suited to teaching empathy than anything else. Such approaches are also useful for assessment purposes. The basic technique involves presenting pupils with information about what people did or believed that simply does not make sense from a contemporary perspective. The challenge is to use background knowledge of the period in order to make sense of it. The example in Figure 3.4 is taken from a 16 + Trials Paper for Schools Council Project History 13–16.[37]

A selection of responses to the question in Figure 3.4 (grammar and spelling corrected to render comparison of 'empathetic' contents easier) illustrates both the virtues of this type of exercise and the difficulties of assessing empathetic understanding:

Source G

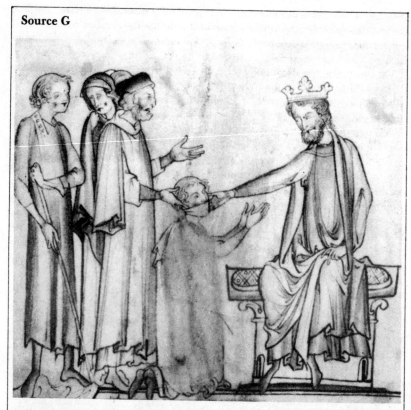

A thirteenth-century manuscript showing King Edward the Confessor treating scrofula, a skin disease, by touching it with his hand.

'When people like those shown in Source G were not cured they often followed the King around, being touched over and over again. Why did people living in the Middle Ages still believe in "cures" like these *even if they did not work*?'

Figure 3.4

(a) They wouldn't think the 'cure' hadn't worked only that it hadn't happened yet. Being touched by the King wasn't a scientific cure it was something that God did, so it isn't like something not staying in orbit proving the theory of gravity wrong, it's more like me saying I'm going to take you to a football match this season and you ask every match and I say no but may say yes next time. Only it's more complicated because of the need to have faith. If you start worrying about miracles and wondering if they happen after all, they won't work. So they've got you both ways. Either you believe even when it doesn't work or you stop it working. And if you take this bit away you might find everything else

you believe in falls down as well. You can't believe in the King and God
without believing in miracles and that kings are put there generally to
rule over you. It was called the divine right of kings by Louis XIV a few
hundred years later.

(b) Some people who touched the King would get better if they waited long
enough and courtiers and priests would then say 'It's a miracle' to flatter
the King and get rewards. Faith sometimes works as well, especially for
hypochondriacs who only think they're sick. Doctors give you anti-
biotics for colds even though they don't work. It keeps the patients
happy and believing in doctors.

(c) They believed in these things because they were superstitious and
religious. Religion is a main factor in medical development through
time. It started with the Egyptians and then potions and ended with the
Salvarsan trial when religious people opposed cures for syphilis. It's
always been the same, religion has only helped medicine a little bit and
held it back a lot.

(d) They carried on being touched because they thought the King was
supernatural. The Middle Ages were primitive and backward and
people weren't as good at thinking things out.

How should these responses be assessed? For many teachers, the absence of
any affective element, the paucity of emotional commitment and imaginative
flair, is commensurate with a lack of empathy. Evaluated by reference to 'a
warm glow around the heart' or 'cold chill in the bowels', these four answers
are uniformly deficient. But they are clearly different and, equally clearly,
reflect different conceptions of what should count as an historical answer to the
question posed. May they be assessed according to the historical accuracy, or
felicity, of the (re)construction offered – that is, for the degree of *authentic*
empathy that each may be thought to contain? But this is to demand the
impossible and could only encourage rote instruction of the least desirable
kind. Imagine an art teacher attempting to teach the principles of composition
and colour theory to average 15-year-olds. If successful, he may be able to
detect an understanding and appraise the application of these principles, but
he cannot expect the resultant paintings to qualify as more than worthless
daubs. Nor can he expect understanding of the principles taught to be co-
extensive with artistic talent or skill with a brush. The 'best' paintings will not
necessarily be produced by pupils who demonstrate effective learning of what
was taught. The history teacher is in the same position – he must be able to
evaluate teaching in terms of its manifest impact upon pupil performance, but
he cannot expect pupils to produce work of historical value. Of course, this
does not follow if 'motive' and 'sense of period' are taught as though they were
dates or lists of bills and battles; but such teaching is comparable to learning art
by tracing Dürer drawings.

   An alternative approach to the appraisal of these responses is to regard them
not as pieces of historical writing but as *evidence* of pupils' historical thinking, of
the assumptions they bring to the subject, of the way they make sense of what
they are taught. A criteria-related mark scheme incorporating four levels of

empathetic and pre-empathetic understanding and conforming to the developmental models described in section II may be advanced:

Level 1:   No valid application of historical knowledge or empathetic understanding. At best, truistic common-sense and historicism.
   – 'They believed these things because they were thick/stupid/a bunch of dimmos.'
   – '. . . not advanced like us.'
   – '. . . backward and superstitious; lived in primitive times.'
   Explanations either *tautological*
                  biological
                  historicist

Level 2:   Valid historical analysis but 'from the outside'. No evidence of empathetic understanding.
   – 'Believed in supernatural cures because lived in a religious age; pre-Renaissance.'
   Conditional explanation substituted for empathetic.

Level 3:   Explanation 'from the inside', but only *everyday empathy*. Genuine attempt to show how the Royal Touch could have seemed reasonable to people at the time, but reconstruction remains locked in twentieth-century world-view – no attempt to recreate an alien form of life and way of thinking.
   – 'Faith cures occasionally effective (placebos; spontaneous remissions)'
   – 'Effective religious and royal propaganda – people would always hear about miraculous cures; nothing to counteract this.'
   – 'People desperate and had nothing to lose because no alternative recourse.'

Level 4:   Genuine *historical empathy*. Attempt to show how belief in the Royal Touch was reasonable to the *medieval* mind.
   Genuine attempt to shed twentieth-century preconceptions and to recreate alien world-view. Reward any answer that clearly attempts this even when less than completely successful.
   – 'Disease wages of sin; cure signals forgiveness; forgiveness must be merited; following the King around may be construed as a penance.'
   – 'King merely the instrument of God's purpose; this instrument must be "clean" and in a state of grace.'

12. *Structured contrasts between past and present*

Along with the empathetic dilemma, this type of exercise may be recommended as a standard, routine approach to the teaching and assessing of historical empathy. Adolescents experience difficulty in making the leap from everyday to historical empathy, being generally disposed to impose contemporary values and ideas upon the past. The necessity to think, or to try to think, in period must be learned and repeatedly reinforced, and exercises embodying a contrast between past and present are useful inasmuch as they signal to pupils that past behaviour and attitudes are incongruous when viewed from the perspective of the present. The following example is taken from a CSE examination paper:[38]

' "What can be more ridiculous than the idea of trains travelling twice as fast as stage coaches! We should as soon expect people to let themselves be fired off upon one of Congreve's ricochet rockets as to trust themselves to the mercy of such a machine going at such a speed." (*Quarterly Review*, March 1825.)

We treat as normal the fact that Concorde flies at more than twice the speed of existing airliners. Why, then, did people find it "ridiculous" for railway trains to travel "twice as fast as stage coaches"?'

Although more appropriate to O level candidates, this question worked reasonably well at CSE. An annotated version of the mark-scheme is given below:

Level 1: Recreation of a particular set of circumstances

Candidates argue to the effect that the circumstances in which railways were introduced were in no way comparable to those obtaining during the launch of Concorde: the suggested parallel is false because circumstances were different.

Many arguments rather elliptical with no mention of Concorde at all; for example:

> Lots of silly stories were told to frihten pepl of railways by the canal and turnpike men. Great Duks and mps did not want to sell their land and of a dirty noisy train spoil hunting and told lies about it killing all the cows and pasengers could not breath when they went fast ... [explanation of support for railways omitted] The public were not very sophiastikold they only read cheep broodsheets and ballards even tho there was no page 3 in them days. they believed lots of the lies they wrote in the ballards ...

The implication here is that, unlike Concorde, railways suffered a barrage of hostile and mendacious propaganda. This is true as far as it goes, but the candidate construes all fears and theories, for instance about the physiological effects of high-speed travel, as lies and propaganda. There is no attempt to explain how it was possible for people at the time to believe these ideas.

Level 2: Empathetic reconstruction of situation

Candidates attempt to reconstruct what it was like to ride as a passenger in an early train. Again most contrasts with Concorde are implicit; for example:

> they tried to jump on and off trains to fetch their hats because they were used to doing this on stagecoaches. It was dangerous to go twice as fast as a stagecoach if you kept the same habits and forgot where you were .... A famous actress had a ride in 1830 and got burnt by the red hot cinders. They set their clothes on fire and had to be put out all the time. She enjoyed it but other people were scared of burning to death. The cinders got worse the faster the train sped along.

Other responses mentioned problems with tunnels, the high accident rate, the decapitation of people riding on top of carriages stage-coach style, etc.

Level 3: Empathetic analysis of perspective

Candidates recreate and *explain* the point of view of people in the past. There is an attempt to see things through the eyes of the average man in 1825, given his society and, interestingly enough, given his *history*; for example:

> Concorde goes twice as fast as a jumbo jet, but this goes twice as fast as propeller-driven airplanes. Airplanes go twice as fast as cars and some cars go faster than locomotives. Today people get used to going faster and faster but they had not in 1825. For thousands of years NOTHING went faster than a horse could ride or wind could blow a ship. Then railways were invented and went a lot faster and people worried about what would happen. If a spaceship was pulled faster than light by a Black Hole the astronot would worry a bit.

This response is short on fact but long on sense of history. In the unsuccessful 'astronaut' reference, the candidate is attempting to find a contemporary parallel for the steam locomotive.

Level 4: Empathetic reconstruction of period

One or two candidates attempted to locate railways on the wider canvas of early nineteenth-century life and thought. As might be expected, no more than a few hints of anything approaching a 'sense of period' were recorded; for example:

> looked at great iron monster clanking their pistons, hissing steam and smoke and fire. 'How different from our sleek pony's', they thought. 'What iron and fire can do Nature cannot', they wondered . . . . They all know Nature and what nature could do, so they wondered if a horse was as fast as Nature was meant to go. Perhaps Nature could not stand going faster and should not try.

Despite the literary extravagance and lack of factual precision, this response does capture something of the impact of steam upon the nineteenth-century imagination. Whether or not there is sufficient evidence of a sense of period, of the intrusion of iron and fire and steam into a world of muscle and sinew and elemental forces, for this to qualify as a Level 4 response remains open to debate, however.

The twelve approaches to teaching and assessing empathy listed above are far from exhaustive, and discussion of contents, uses and implications has been sketchy in the extreme. Taken as a whole, however, they exemplify a view of current and possible practice consistent with the position outlined and arguments advanced in sections I and II. This view is summarized below.

Desiderata for teaching and assessing empathy

(a) *Adolescents cannot be taught to empathize 'authentically'*. Within certain limits, facts can be marked 'correct' and 'incorrect', but the products of adolescent empathetic construction are more or less justifiable in terms of the facts a pupil knows or believes to be the case, the assumptions he makes about his predecessors and his conception of what counts as empathetic or intentional explanation in history. Thus to condemn a candidate's work because he is empathizing from a limited and error-ridden data base is to miss the point. Equally, to dismiss empathetic constructions as incompatible with what *we* know about Essex's motivation or the role of religion in sixteenth-century society is to vitiate the whole enterprise, in so far as we cannot reasonably expect 15-year-olds to reproduce the considered conclusions of professional historians unless these conclusions are taught as facts to be memorized and reproduced. It also follows that history teachers should not avoid questions, especially empathetic dilemmas, to which they know no certain answer (= sombody else's theory); indeed, such questions might prove to be most suitable material for teaching since the teacher may be more disposed to arbitrate the merits of rival empathetic constructions.[39]

(b) *Empathetic construction should be taught and assessed as a cognitive not an affective activity* more akin to the elaboration and justification of hypotheses than to creative writing. This is not to argue against an 'affective' component of historical empathy – though this may signify no more than that 'construction' gives the impression of being 'reconstruction' – but is rather to contend that affective empathy cannot be taught without degenerating into indoctrination. For our beautiful woman to be more than a tawdry drab, she must be approached with more philosophy than poetry, more head than heart, and the free rein of imagination must bow to the buckle and harness of decorum and responsibility.

(c) *An understanding of history cannot be taught to adolescents in the round.* When using sources to construct a sense of period pupils should not simultaneously consider problems of evidence. Equally, until a certain level of understanding is reached, pupils should not be expected to deal with cause and effect while analysing problems of intentional action.

(d) *Teaching and assessment should seek to mesh aims excogitated from analysis of the nature of the subject with the ideas adolescents hold at given stages of conceptual (i.e. ideational not operational) development.* The aim of teaching empathetic construction thus entails the precise formulation of objectives defining a set of logically constituent propositions (the assumption of rational action; differences in perspective between past and present; etc.) and a set of developmentally primitive concepts signposting the route by means of which, on the best evidence available, adolescents acquire understanding of historical empathy. The general model outlined in Figure 3.5 may also be used to validate criteria – related mark schemes, even though it is unlikely that more than a few schemes will exactly conform to the whole or any fraction of this model.

Teaching should address the ideas pupils have at any given time and seek to force progressive accommodations to new data and unforeseen implications. The adolescent should be confronted with the limitations and absurdities in his own ideas, bearing in mind that what he is able and disposed to recognize as absurdities and limitations is dictated by these selfsame ideas.

(e) *Teaching methods requiring empathetic explanation are, in general, more effective than those demanding description* and, in particular, exercises constructed around

Figure 3.5 Hierarchically ordered objectives for teaching and assessing empathetic construction

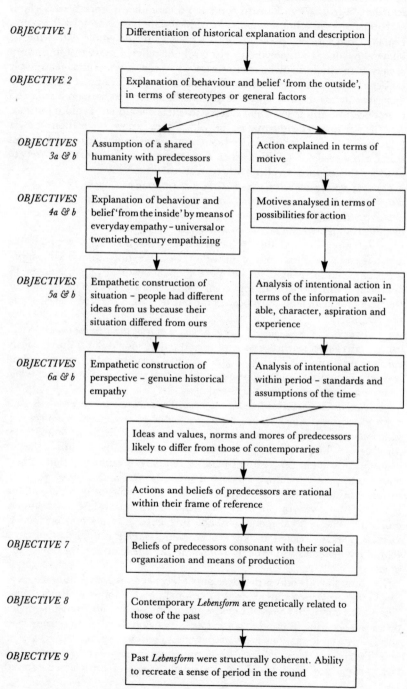

OBJECTIVE 1 — Differentiation of historical explanation and description

OBJECTIVE 2 — Explanation of behaviour and belief 'from the outside', in terms of stereotypes or general factors

OBJECTIVES 3a & b — Assumption of a shared humanity with predecessors | Action explained in terms of motive

OBJECTIVES 4a & b — Explanation of behaviour and belief 'from the inside' by means of everyday empathy – universal or twentieth-century empathizing | Motives analysed in terms of possibilities for action

OBJECTIVES 5a & b — Empathetic construction of situation – people had different ideas from us because their situation differed from ours | Analysis of intentional action in terms of the information available, character, aspiration and experience

OBJECTIVES 6a & b — Empathetic construction of perspective – genuine historical empathy | Analysis of intentional action within period – standards and assumptions of the time

Ideas and values, norms and mores of predecessors likely to differ from those of contemporaries

Actions and beliefs of predecessors are rational within their frame of reference

OBJECTIVE 7 — Beliefs of predecessors consonant with their social organization and means of production

OBJECTIVE 8 — Contemporary *Lebensform* are genetically related to those of the past

OBJECTIVE 9 — Past *Lebensform* were structurally coherent. Ability to recreate a sense of period in the round empathetic dilemmas and contrasts between past and present practices and beliefs should form the routine, everyday staple of teaching for empathy.

What may be said in conclusion? Various ways of dealing with our beautiful woman have been devised, the more effective of which involve stripping her finery, marring her features and serenading her with historical logarithms. Whether or not consummation is devoutly to be wished under these conditions, no 'beginner in philosophy' is qualified to determine.

APPENDIX I

John Stubbs having his hand cut off.

APPENDIX II

Elizabeth takes action against the Puritans in 1583

From this time forward she [Elizabeth] began to be a little more incensed against the Puritans . . . . And indeed within a few days after, John Stubbs of Lincolns-Inn, a fervent hot-headed Professor of religion, . . . the author of this book, William Page who dispersed the copies, and Singleton, the printer, were apprehended. Against whom sentence was given, that their right hands should be cut off . . . . Hereupon Stubbs and Page had their right hands cut off with a cleaver, driven through the wrist by the force of a mallet, upon a scaffold in the market place at Westminster. The printer was pardoned. I remember [being there present] that when Stubbs, after his right hand was cut off, put off his hat with his left, and said with a loud voice, 'God Save the Queen'.

NOTES

1. Collingwood, R. G., *The Idea of History*, Clarendon Press, 1946.
2. Gardiner, P., *The Nature of Historical Explanation*, Oxford University Press, 1952.
3. Martin, Rex, *Historical Explanation*, Cornell University Press, 1977.
4. Walsh argues for a set of propositions about human behaviour applicable to all men at all times (Walsh, W. H., *Introduction to Philosophy of History*, Hutchinson, 1951). While a set of universally applicable predicates would effectively define human nature, it is less than clear that this would greatly assist the historian. The dangers of equivocation would also be considerable.
5. The most highly developed of these theories is that of the 'practical inference schema' advanced by von Wright, G. H., *Explanation and Understanding*, Routledge & Kegan Paul, 1971. Peter Lee, in a penetrating critique of these models, asks 'How can an *action* be the conclusion of an inference?' ('Explanation and understanding in history', in Dickinson, A. K., and Lee, P. J. (eds), *History Teaching and Historical Understanding*, Heinemann Educational Books, 1978).
6. Martin, op. cit.
7. Collingwood, op. cit. It is obvious that many generalizations are transhistorical but, as will be argued later, these are of marginal interest to the historian.
8. The distinction between *deduction* and *adduction* in history owes much to Martin Booth, although the author is far from confident that Dr Booth would approve the use made of it in this chapter. (Booth, M., 'Inductive thinking in history: the 14–16 age group', in Jones, G., and Ward, L., *New History Old Problems*, University College of Swansea, 1978.)
9. Collingwood, op. cit.
10. On occasions, the historian may be obliged first to create the puzzle, the sense of strangeness about the past, by showing good reasons why late twentieth-century perspectives do not quite fit. For example, to people with fixed prejudices about 'radical politicians on the make', the motivation of so picaresque a figure as John Wilkes may appear readily comprehensible. But the historian should enjoin caution and invite consideration of alternative interpretations.
11. Barnard dismisses this mode of explanation as trivial. 'It is one thing . . . to grasp the point of an action in terms of roles and rules or common understandings, but quite another to blandly assume that this is all there is to it, that meaning *must* be found in customary practices.' (Barnard, F. M., 'Accounting for actions: causality and teleology', *History and Theory*, 1981.)
12. Von Wright, Dray and others would argue a distinction between such 'practical inference schemas' and covering laws. The position taken here, however, is that while 'practical inference schemas' may perhaps be used to illuminate the ethical or prudential quality of some action, the lack of *logical* connection between intended outcome and action taken to bring about an outcome necessitates importation of covering laws to explain why a person of particular character and abilities in a given situation at a given time would consider one set of means more efficient than any other. Schemas of practical inference may only dispense with covering laws if the process be deemed enthymematic, that is, a syllogism wherein one premise – dealing with intentions and perceptions of means–ends efficiency – is suppressed.
13. Braudel, F., *The Mediterranean and the Mediterranean World in the Age of Philip II*, Fontana, 1972.
14. See particularly, Mandron, R., 'L'histoire des mentalités', *Encyclopaedia Universalis*, 1968; and Foucault, M., *The Archaeology of Knowledge*, Tavistock, 1976.
15. *Actions* are regarded as *events* when the historian wishes to offer a *conditional* instead of or as well as a *hermeneutic* explanation. But since historians rarely consider it worthwhile to state the sort of explanation on offer, they also find it irrelevant – not to say silly – to mark 'action' and 'event' in this way. The distinction assumes significance, however, because it is by no

means clear that all *events* may properly be treated as *actions*. Methodological individualists would argue that explanation of the Oklahoma dust bowl or of the German inflation could be reduced to explanation of the behaviour of participating individuals, 'collective consciousness' to the sum of individual consciousness. This theory has been savagely attacked by Stephen Lukes and others, and seems an unnecessary and extravagant piece of theology in any case. It may also be possible to reduce individual action to a complex of electrical discharges across synaptic bridges (see the 'scientific realism' of J. J. Smart), but little is gained thereby.

16. Lee, op. cit.
17. A classical philosopher like Carneades would certainly be seduced if an empathetic account could be shown not only to be 'reasonable', but 'evidently true' in the sense of it being more acceptable (coherent, efficient, parsimonious, etc.) than all alternative accounts. The validity of an account follows not from the operation of a trustworthy methodology upon verified data, but from a process of open competition given a set of agreed criteria. We cannot claim an absolute right to advance any empathetic explanation on the basis of what we know and are skilled in doing, but we can argue that if an explanation is requested, a particular one is preferable to all others. Arguments over which and what is 'preferable' will, of course, always be with us.
18. This analysis rests upon the view of empathetic (re)construction outlined in section I. The reader will demur to at least the extent of his disagreement with the philosophical position previously sketched.
19. Interviews were but one technique employed in this evaluation, and adolescent ideas about empathetic reconstruction were only assayed in passing. See Shemilt, D. J., *History 13–16: Evaluation Study*, Holmes McDougall, 1981. Methodology matters are more thoroughly considered in a forthcoming paper, 'A babble of voices: adolescent ideas about evidence'.
20. 'Stage' is not used in any Piagetian sense in that

    (a) the model deals with ideation not ratiocination, that is, with the premises pupils bring to history rather than the *logic* wherewith they operate upon it;

    (b) the content and sequence of stages are neither stable nor invariant, inasmuch as they reflect the outcomes of particular teaching regimes (traditional world, European, British and social–economic syllabuses as well as Schools Council Project *History 13–16* in its trials phase) as much, and perhaps more than, the logical and psychological structures of history method and the adolescent mind.

21. Shemilt, op. cit.
22. Written statements were derived from an Elicited Construct Test and used as the basis for interviews. Interviewees were thus talking about their own ideas, the ways in which they make sense of history, not about history as such.
23. Shemilt, op. cit.
24. An adolescent may empathize with Adolf Hitler, and ponder his distaste for Himmler's lampshades and habit of drawing the blinds whenever his train passed through bombed cities, without a shred of sympathy or fellow-feeling for the Führer.
25. No proposition, and hence no source, can be self-indexing, that is, tell the reader how to make sense of it. Propositions only make sense within, and are intended to be indexed by, the 'form of life' within which they were produced. Source interpretation therefore demands empathetic construction of this past *Lebensform*.
26. Piaget, J., and Inhelder, B., *The Growth of Logical Thinking*, Basic Books, 1958.
27. Adolescents here view *intention* as akin to a DNA blueprint for biological *outcomes*. Short of defects in the DNA helix (= mistakes) and environmental catastrophe (= volcanoes), the mature organism is encoded in the genetic blueprint.
28. See Shemilt, op. cit.

29. A shift from knowledge-based to concept/skill-based objectives is the most likely explanation for the attainment differences recorded in Table 3.1. Teachers are only now beginning to devise teaching approaches directly geared to the new objectives.

30. A more extensive discussion of the uses of biographical exercises is to be found in *Explorations in Teaching Schools Council History 13–16 Project*, TASC/SREB, 1981.

31. The historical absurdity of many projective exercises is of minor consequence; they could be even less historically credible without undue harm arising if they could be shown to work. Unfortunately, they appear to have scant utility for either teaching or assessment.

32. Birt, D., and Nichol, J., *Games and Simulations in History*, Longman, 1975, is the best introduction to this approach.

33. See *Explorations*, op. cit., for a fuller discussion of the decision-making approach.

34. This suggestion owes much to Dickinson, A. K., and Lee, P. J., 'Understanding and research', in Dickinson and Lee, op. cit.

35. This question is adapted from a Schools Council History CSE paper issued by the East Anglian Examinations Board in 1979.

36. Extended objective questions employ a format akin to that of multiple-choice questions but reserve all marks for the justification offered in support of candidate choice. There is, in fact, no right answer to the question.

37. The paper was trialled in 1982 by the Associated Examining Board and the Southern Regional Examinations Board as part of the work towards the provision of a 16 + History 13–16 syllabus.

38. This question is adapted from a Schools Council History CSE paper issued by the East Anglian Examinations Board in 1979.

39. The futility of attempting to assess *authentic* empathy is illustrated by the results of an experiment wherein examiners gave less credit to an *authentic* 'letter from the trenches' than to student reconstructions of the same. See Elliot, D. M., *Testing Skills in History*, SCEEB, 1980.

4. Historical Imagination

P. J. LEE

I. INTRODUCTION

Consider the following two (imaginary) history teachers' comments in the margin of two different pieces of children's work:

'A nice story, but in the end it's sheer imagination.'
'A sound piece of work, but it lacks imagination.'

What weight should one attach to these two critical remarks? Which is the more serious criticism? Suppose they occurred in the reviews of the work of two professional historians – would one weigh them in the same way?

Historians and teachers of history have ambivalent attitudes to imagination. A good historian, it seems, must have imagination, and a mediocre one lacks it. ('No imagination!') Too much of it, however, and the result is not just a mediocre historian, but a downright bad one. ('Sheer imagination!') One might be forgiven for thinking that exercising one's imagination in history is playing with fire – better to be safe and let scholarship slide a little in the direction of pedantry. Such a view would make imagination marginal to history, like icing on a cake. But side by side with this 'marginal' account there is a different version, which makes imagination more central. Without imagination, historians can only go through the motions; no amount of evidence, however 'hard', can be a substitute.

Men's actions can be the subject of detailed research, and enumerated . . . .
But what went on in their minds . . . can only be known by inference, and to understand it, if it is to be understood at all, intuition and imagination are necessary.[1]

Statistics and imagination are for the historian what oil and petrol are to the internal combustion engine: an excess of one will not compensate for lack of the other.[2]

The trouble is that 'imagination' covers a wide range of activities and achievements in history, and carries with it connotations deriving from the arts which in some cases appear to conflict with the fundamental tenets of history. Bearing in mind such difficulties, what basic distinctions can be made in the concept of imagination? Following Furlong's classic general analysis, we may distinguish between (i) '*in* imagination', (ii) 'supposal', and (iii) '*with* imagination'.[3]

In a history lesson a child imagines he is engaged in fighting William at Hastings: maybe he has just decapitated William with a swing of his axe. He is doing this *in* his imagination. The teacher has other concerns. 'Suppose you were Harold', he says, 'Where would you put the housecarls in the line of battle?' (He might have said 'Imagine you are Harold . . .'.) A pupil replies. Perhaps he argues for splitting up the experienced housecarls among the untrained local fyrd, to steady them. He has *supposed* he was in Harold's position, and that, like Harold, he had certain specific problems. If the pupil does his supposing with real insight, and makes perceptive selections from the wealth of possibilities open to him (given the evidence he has), we might also say that his supposal is done *with* imagination.

Note that the child taking part in the Battle of Hastings *in* imagination may depart from what evidence suggests occurred during the battle. What is imagined may in that sense be purely *imaginary*. Whether or not this is the case, there are likely to be images involved here – of Saxon and Norman combatants – but they will not necessarily be present in all such cases. *Sympathies* may be engaged, and *identification* with some agent may take place. What the child does in imagination may be the result of supposal, and more or less controlled, but it may be much freer than this. It may develop a life of its own, or it may constantly be referred back to basic suppositions. Similarly, where the pupil is *supposing*, he may do it with the help of goings-on *in* imagination, a kind of directed and controlled daydream. But he might equally do no such thing, and still come up with the same suggestion.

Whatever may be said of (i) and (ii), it might seem that the notion of doing history with imagination is more problematic. For an activity to be done with imagination there must be a certain amount of freedom available. How much is there in history, where the point is surely to get it right?[4] The goal of history as a discipline is the production of knowledge: historical knowledge acquired by employing evidence according to certain principles. If this is true, then whatever picks out historical imagination from imagination in general must recognize the constitutive role of evidence in history. In central cases of historical imagination the latter must be tied to evidence in some way, and so in history imagination cannot be creative in the same way as in literature, painting or music. It is tempting to say that the merely imaginary (fictitious) can play no part in history. This would be putting the point much too simply, and I will return to the issue later, but there is some truth in the assertion.[5] At the same time, history has no mechanical rules for the discovery or use of evidence, and so there is a prima facie case for claiming some freedom for the historian, and hence the possibility of doing history with imagination.

II.   EVIDENCE, INTERPRETATION AND IMAGINATION

In section I, I made the easy assertion that historical imagination must be tied to evidence. In some respects this is a misleading claim, and Collingwood puts the matter more carefully: '.the historian's picture stands in a peculiar relation to something called evidence'.[6] It is misleading to say simply that imagination is tied to evidence, because the implication seems to arise that the evidence is fixed and logically prior to any exercise of imagination. For Collingwood the historian's picture of the past is a construction of his imagination in interaction with his evidence. The historian decides what to make of his evidence; the evidence does not dictate to him. Imagination in this constitutive sense Collingwood calls the 'a priori imagination', and claims that 'It is ... the historian's picture of the past, the product of his own a priori imagination, that has to justify the sources used in its construction'.[7] Collingwood does not make it entirely clear whether the 'picture of the past' in question is a very general formal concept, or a detailed and substantive one. He refers on the one hand to detailed examples derived from a knowledge of physical laws and on the other to an innate and general idea of the past: any attempt to decide here exactly how far he meant to go in allowing the historian's picture of the past to determine his reading of the evidence would require more space and skill than are available to me.[8] Perhaps one could more modestly say (with Collingwood) that evidence does not oblige us to believe anything by itself, but only in conjunction with a conception of the world and how it works. But this conception includes (at least) a concept of a past without which there could be no evidence, and perhaps also more substantive conceptions of what any part of the past could be like. These conceptions provide (at least) prima facie limits on what we can imagine. Hence one might say: 'It is impossible to suppose ...'. Elton calls this 'the last test', and applies it to the claim that changes in the composition and powers of the Privy Council in the sixteenth century took place gradually: 'Is it possible to envisage a situation in which one part of a group of men is gradually turned from privy councillors into councillors at large, a title hitherto unknown?'[9] But such conceptions cannot set firm limits on their own; the world is often more complex than we can imagine, and evidence can turn up that may force us to accept what once we could not imagine.

For my purposes in this chapter, there are two things to emphasize. First, evidence is created by questions, and what questions ought to be asked is a matter of judgement. There are no determinate rules for asking questions, and so no possibility of simply working mechanically through prescribed steps in using evidence. Because there is some freedom here, there is the possibility of using evidence with imagination. Second, where supposing is concerned, the premises are supplied by evidence. I will return to this later.

If the notion of evidence appears at first sight to close down the opportunities for imagination, that of interpretation seems to open them up again: there is a good deal of freedom whatever the sense of historical interpretation being employed. So once again we have the possibility of doing something in history with imagination. The degree of freedom, however, will depend on the kind of interpretation, and in no case will any old interpretation do. For example, in interpreting what was meant by certain words, there will in the end be a very limited range of possibilities if we are to be correct. The writer of a document in which the historian is interested may often be presumed to have had a very limited number of meanings in mind. Misinterpretation and misunderstanding is possible only where there is also the possibility of correct interpretations. Kitson Clark gives the example of Chartists and even Liberals using language apparently appealing to violence and revolution, and threatening that crowned heads might roll, prior to the disturbances in Lancashire and parts of Yorkshire in the late summer of 1842.

> After studying the matter as far as I could, I decided that the explanation was relatively simple. This inflated language was natural to large sections of the community at that date, they inhaled it from the plays they saw, the novels and poems they read, and the speeches and sermons they listened to with avidity.[10]

His original interpretation had been wrong. This sort of case depends closely on evidence, and freedom to take words as meaning this or that is limited to ambiguities, intentional or unconscious, in what the speaker or writer meant.

Where the interpretation at issue is of a whole corpus of evidence – for example how Gildas or Nennius are to be taken (in arguments about the existence of King Arthur), or how Bede's *Ecclesiastical History* is to be interpreted – there is likely to be more freedom, because it is harder to be sure that a corpus of this kind was unequivocally meant in just one or even several limited ways. Thus David Dumville argues that Gildas cannot be understood in the straightforward way in which John Morris interpreted him: almost as if he were writing a kind of chronicle. On the contrary what he was offering was an allegorical and religious exhortation.[11] The argument here turns partly on what was meant by Gildas (which still allows a degree of openness of interpretation) and partly on what the significance of the material is as evidence in answering certain kinds of historical question. Plainly what was meant will affect the significance of the evidence, but the latter is also a matter of judgement and ingenuity in seeing that any given material can be put to work in different ways and to answer different questions. There is at this level a good deal of room for interpretation *with* imagination. Thus Stephens argues that Bede's *History* is not so much a history of the Church as the first English history.[12]

Further up the scale interpretation may be understood as seeing historical events as events of a certain kind (for example a revolution, or a renaissance, or a decline). Walsh has characterized an important element of this – the linking together of events under appropriate conceptions – as *colligation*.[13] It is almost axiomatic among historians that there is considerable freedom of interpretation at this level, and much historical argument concerns the merits of rival interpretations. Whether the late Middle Ages are to be seen as a period of decline, or as the first steps towards the new world of the Renaissance; whether it is true or simply the 'myth of the French Revolution' that it was a bourgeois revolution otherthrowing feudalism; or whether pre-capitalist economic changes are to be envisaged as Malthusian or Marxist, are not matters to be settled by algorithms or mechanical decision procedures. Indeed it is sometimes possible at this level to employ different interpretations simultaneously without contradiction, allowing ample room for operating *with* imagination. But even here the concepts employed for a colligation must not strain the evidence or unduly distort the material, and an interpretation must not be thought of as exhaustive when it is not. Nor must interpretations that enshrine contemporary meanings be confused with those imposed in hindsight by historians. Imagination cannot be allowed free rein for, as Elton pointed out in a review of certain developments in history teaching, if all we are after is conceptual agility and internal coherence, we need not trouble ourselves with history at all: Tolkien's Middle Earth will do.[14] Tolkien's world exemplifies the creative imagination as opposed to its historical counterpart, for Middle Earth is a coherent, complex world with its own past, created by Tolkien, and (merely) imaginary.

III. UNDERSTANDING, EMPATHY AND IMAGINATION

Empathy, understanding and imagination are related in complex ways in history. The argument of this section will be that empathy is part of (and a necessary condition of) historical understanding, and that imagination as supposal is *criterial* for that same understanding.[15] I have given a sketch of one important aspect of historical understanding elsewhere, and there is a detailed account of empathy in the preceding chapter of this book.[16] The discussion that follows, therefore, raises questions about empathy and understanding only so far as is necessary to elucidate their connections with historical imagination.

Like imagination, empathy has associations that are problematic for history. If imagination has associations with the merely fictitious, empathy is associated with fellow-feeling, shared emotions, and even identification with some other person. Rather than try to enforce some standard meaning by appeal to etymology or by simple legislation, I will try to make one or two crude distinctions, and see what aspects of empathy can be harnessed to history.

Empathy is sometimes conceived of as a *power*, as something we use to discern other people's thoughts and feelings, perhaps directly or non-inferentially. This is not an indication that mysterious powers are at work, but that we share a common form of life at a very basic level with all other humans, and at the cultural level with those in our own society. We pick up signs as to what people mean and want without conscious ratiocination, and although we can make mistakes, or be fooled, we often get it right. But in history we are not in direct contact with the people we study, and do not enjoy mutual relationships with them; in consequence empathy as a power has no role in history.[17] In fact empathy in history is much more like an *achievement*: it is knowing what someone (or some group) believed, valued, felt and sought to attain. It is being in a position to entertain (not necessarily to share) these beliefs, and being in a position to consider the impact of these emotions (not necessarily to feel them). In this way empathy is closely related to understanding. Empathy (as achievement) involves grasping the internal connections between an agent's beliefs and goals, or between the values and beliefs of a social group, and this is a necessary (but not sufficient) condition for historical understanding.

Empathy may also be regarded as a *process*. Here it is easy to drift into thinking that empathizing is a special means of finding out, which leads back into a position very similar to the one in which empathy is viewed as a power. But in history we find out what someone believed or wanted by looking at the evidence, and we justify our assertions by referring to that evidence. (This does not rule out intuition – we may still have 'hunches' – but unless we can produce some public evidence, we cannot expect anyone to take much notice of them.) In the end 'empathizing' in history is intelligible only as the task for which empathy in the previous sense is the achievement. Such a bald statement needs qualification, however, for it is possible (finally) to treat empathy as a *disposition* or *propensity*. In history this amounts to the disposition to take into account other points of view. Acquiring this disposition is an essential part of learning to think historically. Empathy is often characterized as 'affective', whereas if the foregoing remarks are correct it makes at least as much sense to regard it as 'cognitive': nevertheless, here there *is* a link with the 'affective domain'. The disposition to take account of other points of view is like the 'rational passions' that must be acquired in learning any academic discipline. We would not accept that someone had properly grasped mathematics if that person had no concern for accuracy or cogency, or that a student who showed no interest in truth had really understood what history is about. Perhaps it is in this sense that someone with no disposition to empathize cannot be said genuinely to have learnt history. Historians must want to achieve empathy with their subjects. But this does not mark off empathy from other aspects of history: historians must also want to make true statements, respect evidence and so on.

Empathy as achievement is closely related to important aspects of historical understanding. Understanding actions in history presupposes empathy as achievement, because it involves seeing an action as appropriate in terms of the agent's goals and intentions, and his view of the situation. Of course the agent may be mistaken about the situation, and actions do not always turn out as intended: what an agent thinks he is doing may be very different from what a historian wants to say he actually did. Moreover a historian may wish to characterize an action in terms unavailable to the agent, either because the concepts did not exist at the time, or because the agent could not know at the moment he performed the action that the concepts in question could apply to what he did. For (at least) these reasons, there is much more to historical understanding than the achievement of empathy. But without empathy there could be no historical understanding of action, which is why acquiring the disposition to empathize is an essential part of learning history.

Understanding in the sense at issue may, roughly speaking, be broken down into knowing an agent's goals and intentions, knowing the situation in which he acted, and seeing how these provided reasons for the action that is to be understood. Goals and intentions may be complex, ramified, and qualified in an immense range of ways. The situation in which the agent acted needs to be seen both from his own point of view, and from that of the historian, and may be conceived in static or dynamic terms. The 'dynamic' view is analysable in terms of conditionals: if so and so is done (happens) then such and such will be the case. Where it is beliefs rather than actions that are to be understood, there are important differences, but once again the central feature of understanding is seeing things as reasons for beliefs. And, with further qualifications, a case could be made out for a similar account of understanding social practices.

The problems for children is understanding why someone acted or failed to act in history are immense. There are no rules of relevance for what is to count as part of the agent's concerns. The distinction between the agent's and the historian's knowledge and point of view is a difficult one, and it is harder still to oscillate between these points of view in the way often required if understanding is to be achieved. Dynamic characterization of an agent's situation and its interaction with his goals demands conditionals, often counterfactual in the light of historians' knowledge; and the alternative courses of action and their consequences that figure in these conditionals must be assessed against one or more specifications of the agent's goals. Some courses must be ruled out.

Two examples will serve to illustrate what is involved, and provide concrete material in the context of which to make connections with imagination. The two passages are the work of very intelligent fourth-year boys, who had just completed half a dozen lessons on the origins and course of the French Revolution up to Thermidor. They are not chosen as representative examples of typical children's work, but as giving a particularly clear picture of some elements of imagination and understanding in history. The question to which the passages are a response was 'What would I do if I had found myself in the same circumstances as Louis XVI in 1789, and why?'[18] This exercise represents a reaction on my part to the view taken by many in the class that Louis XVI's behaviour was in a curious sense the work of a mental defective, and to that extent unintelligible: anyone can see what he should have done.

1. With his country in economic ruin due to an inefficient tax system and several wars the king, Louis XVI, was in a difficult position. The chancellor, Necker, had been giving inaccurate budgets to make people believe that the country had a surplus when in fact there was a vast deficit. He could continue to govern until all monies ran out, or start afresh. He chose the latter expecting the nobles to rush to his aid at the chance of power. However, they blackmailed him into calling a States General. This should have meant an outright victory for the nobles, but, public opinion forced the king to revise the States General more in favour of the middle classes.

When the S.G. finally met, there was a walkover victory for the peasants. At this point Louis could have:

(a) dissolved Parliament, but this was not practical since he needed money from the nobles. He could have used the army to force nobles to 'pay or be damned' but since many of the army's officers were also nobles this was not practical;

(b) abdicated. Never. Since although Louis was a weak monarch, he ruled by absolute right and would not give up his powers easily;

(c) joined the bourgeoisie and taxed the nobles – dangerous. There were enough nobles around to overthrow him.

(d) carried on his non-committal attitude and tried to keep both sides as happy as possible.

This of course is what he did but it was no permanent solution. A more permanent solution however was found in 1794: – he was executed.

2. Louis XVI had great problems as a monarch but I think he could have done a better job at the governing of his country.

I would have been stronger and more forceful. He didn't seem to know what was going on, or he did and didn't act. When the other monarchs threatened to invade, I would have got the people's support in Paris, the non-agricultural workers and made them see reason. The country we were so proud of was going to be invaded. He should have tried to stir up the people's patriotism and sent all the rebels and the army into war. He may have been able to stop the crises. He could have fled the country in 1793 and saved his life.

When the Girodins gained power the king could have made a pact with them. The Girodins had all the people behind them and therefore gained all the people's support.

When the war went badly the king should have said: 'There is not enough effort being made, more guns and ammunition must be made, more people should get into the army and fight.'

The people might have rallied together and won the war and therefore the king would have been popular.

Example 1 sets out very clearly some of Louis's problems, and works systematically through some possible courses of action. The form in which the answer is given is entirely the pupil's own, but it is a form that illustrates something of what underlies an understanding of Louis's actual behaviour. First, the circumstances in which Louis found himself are outlined, and second, a range of alternative steps that might be thought open to Louis – the situation in dynamic terms – are assessed. In addition to wider constraints, the constraints upon Louis's action imposed by his own view of the world are referred to in (b). It is noticeable that nowhere are Louis's goals explicitly set out. Instead we are presented with an overall sketch of some relevant concerns in which goals and estimates of the situation interact. It is assumed in general that Louis wished to remain king, and preferably king in reality, not just in name; in (b) it is pointed out that Louis 'would not give up his powers easily', but in (d) it is hinted that something less than those powers might be acceptable in the short run. Understanding the action here involves coming to see that apparent alternatives are ruled out by Louis's goals and his view of his situation. The structure of the answer is provided by a systematic elimination of the alternatives, and Louis's actions are understood as (from his point of view) 'the thing to do in the circumstances'. The remark at the end moves beyond the frame of reference laid down by Louis's point of view, and at the same time comments wryly on his predicament.

Contrast all this with Example 2. Here the circumstances in which Louis found himself scarcely enter into the picture, except as manipulable occasions for decisive action on the part of Louis. In consequence there are no constraints on action, which is seen simply as a matter of *force, will, effort* and *decision*. 'I would have been stronger and more forceful'. When exhortation is called for, the schoolteacher model seems only too evident: 'There is not enough effort being made'. In Example 2 the picture we are offered of Louis is that of someone utterly feeble-minded and idiotic. There are obvious steps open to him that weakness of will or lack of grasp prevented him from taking. ('He didn't seem to know what was going on, or he did and he didn't act.') Louis's actions (or lack of action) don't make any sense and cannot be understood. We may want to say that this picture is not totally unfounded: no doubt Louis's grasp of what was happening and his readiness to take decisive action were both sadly wanting.[19] The point is not that understanding requires approval, but that it must be based on an awareness of the agent's position. The lack of this in Example 2 makes Louis's behaviour unintelligible.

Where does imagination come in here? One way of answering this question might be to ask how far the difference between Examples 1 and 2 could be adequately described by claiming that 2 'lacks imagination'. Both pupils know in some sense what happened to Louis, what events were going on around him, and that such events posed problems. But where one is (with qualifications) able to see what these events would mean to Louis (given evidence as to Louis's point of view) the other cannot. He has the 'same' set of events to consider, but he is unable to see them in the way Louis would have been likely to see them. He cannot (or does not) entertain the complex of considerations required. Another way of putting it might be to say that he is unable to follow up the consequences of a certain set of beliefs and goals, to use his knowledge to make sense of events from a point of view not his own (and thus to make sense of Louis's actions). The second pupil is unable to 'cash' what in one sense he already knows. Is it a lack of imagination? In so far as the pupil fails to maintain a set of suppositions, it is natural to say that imagination (as supposal) is what is missing. But there is another way in which imagination comes in.

The events of the French Revolution are not just a series of fixed elements, like still pictures caught once and for all 'as they really were' by a camera. They can be correctly described by a vast range of overlapping descriptions, and because there is no mechanical decision procedure for determining which description to employ, there is the possibility of being more or less 'imaginative' in seeing events as one thing or another. That is to say there is room here for doing things 'with imagination', or without.

The pupil in Example 2 carries out his task without imagination, in failing to see (for example) that the war was not just a war, but meant particular things to particular groups of people, and was itself an opportunity for or constraint upon further action. And here the connection with imagination as supposal is clear: lack of imagination in this sense is a failure to 'cash' what in some sense is already known.

The exhortation 'Use your imagination!' is an exhortation to cash knowledge we already have. Consider this passage from Powicke discussing the disinheritance of the 'rebels' of 1265:

Who was to say whether a man had been a rebel or not? The only definition given by the crown was that he was an accomplice of Earl Simon. The knights appointed in each shire were the 'seizers [seisitores] of the lands and tenements of the accomplices [fautores] of the late earl of Leicester'. More writs than can be counted begin with these words. The confusion to which they gave rise, the jobbery which embittered the lives of their victims, can easily be imagined.[20]

Here Powicke is in effect saying '*Use* what you know, what I've already told you. Put yourself in their position, look at things from their point of view – it's not hard given what I've told you of the situation.' And the implication is 'Then you'll understand'. Understanding in the sense discussed here involves empathy as achievement, which in turn means being in a position to entertain beliefs and goals that one need not share. It is the idea of entertaining points of view other than one's own that provides the link with imagination as supposal. Where there is conclusive evidence for the views of some historical agent, and the connection between those views and the agent's action is clear, imagination may barely enter into things. True, knowledge of the agent's beliefs and goals must not remain inert: the historian must see them as bearing on the relevant action. Where he cannot share the views of whoever he is studying, he must entertain them consistently enough to follow the reasons that give the action its intelligibility, setting aside his own beliefs. But while the schema here may be 'Suppose one believed this and wanted that, what follows?', the role of imagination is minimal, because what the agent believed is already known under a description that ties it to the action in question. In the light of the evidence as to the beliefs of trade union leaders about the Taff Vale decision, even a historian whose own views about the role and value of unions differ radically from those of his subjects will need little imagination to follow their actions in attempting to overturn the consequences of the decision. But where the same historian is trying to understand how people could see trade unions as desirable at all, it is a different story. Even in the case of particular events there is often no conclusive evidence, for although it may be clear how someone (or some group) saw things in general terms, there may be no specific evidence about his (their) reaction to the particular event or situation with which the historian is concerned. Supposal, and hence imagination, comes in here in a much more substantial way. Suppose one had lived through such and such events, believed this, and wanted that, how would one see the event in question? Imagination carries some implication of going beyond the evidence, at least in so far as what is conclusively given can hardly require imagination.

This is not to say that it is a special faculty that works without evidence. The precise relationship between a historian 'using his imagination' and the evidence in connection with which it is used will vary with what evidence is available, and the relationship will in any case be a complex one. Sometimes it is a matter of working out what events will amount to from some agent's point of view. Sometimes an action that is known to have been performed under one description – say, signing a treaty – is, on the basis of evidence as to the agent's goals, policies and beliefs, redescribed as something else – say, buying time.

Steps like this where the historian goes (perhaps tentatively) to a greater or lesser extent beyond the evidence, but on the basis of evidence, should ideally be supported by further, independent evidence. But the notion of further and independent evidence here is not so clear-cut as it is in natural science, where predictions are deduced from theories and tested against future events.[21] Sometimes extra evidence in the form of physical objects like charters or minutes or diaries will turn up: extra in the sense of not being available when the tentative suggestion at issue was made. But more often it is a question of looking again more closely at what evidence there is. If something is seen in a new light as a consequence of closer inspection, or of evaluation on the basis of different assumptions, it will not appear to the outsider as independent supporting evidence so much as part of a particular interpretation of what evidence there has always been.[22] It is tempting to say that imagination must always be backed by evidence, but it would be nearer the truth to say that when it is supposal, imagination starts from evidence and then returns to (often the 'same') evidence with the ability to see it in a new light. Evidence does not come in as a kind of last resort, as if an artist's imaginative construction is suddenly discovered to match a photograph. Imagination as supposal leads us to 'read' the evidence in one way rather than another.

Imagination as supposal, in which we 'cash' what in some sense we already know (provided we think about history 'with imagination'), can be illustrated both from what historians have written about their activities and from their substantive work.

> Men's actions can be the subject of detailed research and enumerated, so with much less certainty, can the influences which possibly affected their actions and so can their words. But what went on in their minds escapes exact scrutiny and classification. It can only be known by inference, and to understand it, if it is to be understood at all, intuition and imagination are necessary; it can never be discovered by means of the mere accumulation of detail, however massive that accumulation may be.[23]

Here Kitson Clark is contrasting imagination with quantitative techniques in history, and in this context the reference to intuition is a natural one. Evidence is often inconclusive: there are no fixed rules or mechanical procedures that, if followed step by step, guarantee correct conclusions. It has already been argued that intuition has its place in history, provided it is never allowed to become the court of appeal, and Kitson Clark sets similar limits.[24] Except for the possible implication that mind is essentially (rather than partly) private, the conception of imagination suggested here is close to the one I am trying to set out.[25]

Exemplification for this kind of view is provided by Christopher Hill.

> It has become fashionable . . . to argue that the miseries of the workers during the Industrial Revolution are the *ex post facto* invention of sentimental historians, especially of . . . J. L. and Barbara Hammond. It can be shown statistically that both the national income and average wage rates went up after 1780. Therefore, it is argued, factory workers must have been better

off . . . But the Hammonds were more gifted with historical imagination than their critics . . . .

It is, for instance, not enough to demonstrate simply that in the same number of hours a man could earn more in a factory than as a domestic worker. At home, however long his hours, he was his own master. If he chose to take an hour or a day off, and be that much poorer, he was free to do so: and this freedom could not be measured in cash. In the factory his nominal earnings might be higher. But this was offset by a strict discipline, of a sort to which he was entirely unaccustomed, enforced by severe fines for trivial misdemeanours, so that even the net financial outcome might be less: in working long hours not of his own choosing his sense of personal freedom and dignity was impaired. We may suppose, looking back after two centuries, that the imposition of labour discipline was easily accepted because its necessity is obvious to us: men have to start at a given time in the morning, work regular hours, continuously, at such speeds and in such temperatures as are required for the industrial process. But all these must have seemed enormous hardships, and intrusions on his liberty, to the former domestic worker, with no clock in his house, living perhaps some miles from the factory, and with no means of transport other than his legs. Above all, he abandoned the right to choose when he worked, for how long and at what intensity: and what is freedom, as Milton asked, but choice?[26]

This passage could almost have been written to illustrate Kitson Clark's comments; like his remarks, it sets imagination against the formal rules involved in statistics, and concerns itself with understanding of a kind not opened up by the 'mere accumulation of detail'. In the first place we have here a picture of history done with and without imagination. The implication is that there is no mechanical way of treating evidence, because we have no mechanical procedures that can determine how evidence is to be seen, what questions are to be asked of it, or how it is to be understood. Hence the Hammonds, working 'with imagination', saw that for a historian to set hours worked against pay received is 'not enough'. It is not enough because (in the second place) imagination involves seeing what we (in a sense) already know – more money for the same hours – in a different light. What we know cannot be treated as atomistic snippets of information, but must be related to other things (seen, as Kitson Clark said, as a whole). And what relates it, and to which other things, is decided by – among other considerations – the points of view of the agents involved. The mere description ('accumulation of detail') of pay or factory working conditions is not enough. The historian must entertain sets of beliefs and goals not necessarily his own, and with them a conception of what is normal or reasonable (perhaps enshrined in habits), and bring all this to bear on his description. And in so doing he *re*-describes it. This is imagination as supposal. Of course, the fact that there is no mechanical way to do this does not make it a matter of free flights of imagination, of mere subjectivity. Hill says at one point 'We may suppose, looking back after two centuries, that the imposition of labour discipline was easily accepted because its necessity is obvious to us.' But if we did suppose this Hill argues, we would be wrong. The mistake would have been to make twentieth-century suppositions, which is in reality not to make any suppositions (engage our historical imagination) at all, but to go on thinking in the ways to which we have become accustomed. This is a mistake because the evidence does not allow us to say that such ways of thinking were normal in the eighteenth century. This amounts to an example of the failure of historical imagination – a lack of imagination. But it also shows that imagination is tied in history to evidence, and is not free floating and viciously subjective.

The task of imagination as supposal is to change our point of view: then everything looks different, and we can begin to understand.

> We look back with twentieth-century preconceptions. After two hundred years of trade union struggle, wage-labour has won a respected and self-respecting position in the community. But if we approach wage-labour from the seventeenth century, as men in fact did, we recall that the Levellers thought wage-labourers had forfeited their birthright as freeborn Englishmen, and should not be allowed to vote.
>
> ... We should not allow hindsight to prevent us from entering imaginatively into such feelings. If we grasp the aura of unfreedom which still clung around wage-labour in the eighteenth century we shall not be so impressed by statistics which suggest that wage-labourers might be better off than craftsmen or squatters on commons; and we shall understand why the freer craftsmen formed the vanguard of early trade unionism.[27]

Nothing in what Hill says here demands that we must share the feelings of those we seek to understand; nor are any mysterious processes involved in getting straight about them. Once again it is a matter of cashing what in a sense we already know – of looking at things from a different point of view. Grasping 'the aura of unfreedom which still clung around wage-labour' is knowing that people believed and felt certain things, and being able to see the implications of this knowledge. Imagination requires sensitivity in appreciating the way in which beliefs and feelings bear on other beliefs, feelings and actions. Lack of imagination means that the requisite knowledge remains inert. To say that hindsight must not be allowed 'to prevent us from entering imaginatively into such feelings' is to warn us of the dangers of just this kind of 'cognitive inertia'. 'If we approach wage-labour from the seventeenth century, as men in fact did' reminds us to shift our position, not to change our beliefs, and to appreciate what such a shift would mean in terms of feelings, not to share those feelings.[28]

It is often argued that good history is impossible without *sympathy* for the period or individual concerned. But in history sympathy is more a matter of recognizing the appropriateness of feelings or beliefs than of sharing them. Even in everyday life, where having sympathy for someone may sometimes mean sharing that person's feelings or emotions, it is often more a matter of recognizing that the feelings are appropriate, given the way the person concerned sees the circumstances. Hence we can say 'I sympathize with your feelings, but...', or even 'I sympathize with your position, but...'. Historical sympathy may imply agreement with the most basic assumptions and presuppositions of a period (as far as it makes sense to talk like this); it may even imply agreement with the moral tenets and style of life of some social group at some particular time. Such agreement is not necessary, however, for good history, and if it is more than loose and general, may turn into mere partiality: agreement with one set of contemporary assumptions implies disagreement with others.[29] Sympathy for the eighteenth-century Englishmen in Hill's passage does not mean concurring with their beliefs and goals, or sharing their feelings. To praise a historian for his sympathy for what he is studying is in part to indicate what he does *not* do – namely jump out of his account to show his audience how misguided, stupid or wicked some way of doing things was. More positively, such praise implies that because he recognizes the appropriateness of his subjects' emotions, given their assumptions, the historian is more likely to be able to entertain their views in a consistent manner, to have insight into their consequences, and to pass all this on to his audience. The practical difficulties in this are of course particularly acute where the historian's views are antipathetic to those of his subjects. Carr spoke of the historian's 'need of imaginative understanding', and adds

> I say imaginative understanding, not 'sympathy', lest sympathy should be supposed to imply agreement. The nineteenth century was weak in medieval history, because it was too much repelled by the superstitious beliefs of the Middle Ages . . . to have any understanding of medieval people.[30]

A notion connected with sympathy, and sometimes treated almost as a synonym where children's thinking in history is concerned, is *identification*. In mature history identification is almost always historically destructive, and usually a sign of a failure of imagination. Unlike supposal it is a surrender of control, and in precluding free movement between points of view it precludes understanding: once a historian has identified with his subject, there is no possibility of distinguishing between the subject's view of what was happening, and what historians now know about it. Separated from notions of supposing, entertaining and evidence, identification and even sympathy are signs of partiality, lack of detachment, or just plain bias.

It might be argued that agreement in beliefs is one thing, and shared feelings another; it is the latter that is demanded by historical imagination. But the price of tying imagination too closely to feelings is to make it a mere marginal romantic epiphenomenon of history. To see why this is so, one must understand the relation between feelings and beliefs. It would be absurd to suggest that to follow the connections set out by Hill, it is necessary to share the feelings that correspond with the belief that wage labour is demeaning or unfree. Moreover, in some passages of history such a necessity would render the historian's task in principle impossible (rather than merely difficult). Emotions and feelings have a cognitive basis – it is beliefs that distinguish fear from hope, jealousy from anger, and so on. I cannot share the triumph and hope of a politician immediately after an election if I know that his assessment of the significance of his victory for the future was wildly wrong. And what would be the position of a historian unable to accept the beliefs concerning providence discussed in this excerpt?

One cannot begin to understand Cromwell's part in the Revolution until one grasps his vision of man's life in the universe. The intricate pattern of events was made by the continuous intervention of God, who was weaving on the loom of destiny not merely the grand design which we call history, but countless webs of detail which make the experience of each individual soul. In the main pattern He would bring about war . . . by causing King Charles to harden his heart, and then ensuring, against all the rules of probability, the victory of His Saints. . . . But if one also scrutinised a corner of the colossal tapestry, the Isle of Wight and Carisbrook Castle, for example, whither Robin Hammond had just gone in search of a quiet life clear of political problems, there also one could discern 'a chain of providences'. It was to the Isle of Wight and nowhere else that God sent 'that person' (the King). In all this there must be 'some glorious and high meaning'. One catches a glimpse of the King with Berkeley and Ashburnham moved like pawns round Hammond, who was one of the elect, for the trial and perfection of his spiritual life. At the same time, moved by the same invisible hand of God, each of them is playing his part in the drama that ended on a scaffold in Whitehall.[31]

There is no reason to suppose that Brailsford believed in the workings of providence, yet he would have to share this belief if he were to be able to share the feelings that in certain circumstances such beliefs might entail. Lacking these beliefs, for example, he cannot share Cromwell's emotions during the 1649 campaign in Ireland. The upshot of this is that if historical imagination is not to be a marginal luxury in history, but has some central role, the account we give of it cannot make its occurrence in vast passages of history impossible. And this would be the consequence of tying it too closely to feelings.

There is another aspect of historical imagination in which cashing what we already know plays an important part. A historian is not operating as an isolated consciousness, but as someone taking part in a public activity. His reconstructions must take a form that allows others to work through them. Part of his job is to enable his audience to follow what is happening, and to cash what is offered. Gilbert Ryle contrasts two biographers of Napoleon (both of whom he regards as historians).

From the quite efficient but unimaginative biographer we learn what, of course, we do need to learn: how long the battle of say, Waterloo lasted, how much ammunition was expended, and how big the casualties were. From the quite efficient but also imaginative biographer we learn these things too, but, so to speak, we also smell the gunpowder and we also hear the horses' hooves squelching in the mud of the sunken Belgian road. The former biographer duly classifies the weather in meteorologically correct terms, as a heavy and steady downpour; the other personally acquaints us with the weather, by describing the riflemen's [sic] water-filled boots, and their rain-soaked rations.[32]

The connection between the historian's imagination and his audience's is a close one. However much the historian spells out the implications, the audience must draw some of them itself. A steady downpour means waterfilled boots, but waterfilled boots mean something for the morale of the troops. And this in turn means...?[33] If the historian is unimaginative, he is less likely to provoke the imagination of his audience; hence Ryle can run together the differences the downpour made to the participants and the question whether or not the audience is made aware of these differences: '[The unimaginative biographer] neither makes his readers think, nor does he think himself what actual midmorning differences a heavy rain might have made or did actually make to the concrete actions and passions of the participants in the battle.'[34] The metaphor Ryle uses to elucidate the contrast between the imaginative and the unimaginative biographer is instructive: 'instead of treating the concepts of "heavy rain" and "ammunition shortage" as cheques to be banked, [the imaginative biographer] treats them as coins and notes that are means to be exchanged here and now for consumable commodities.'[35] Whereas the unimaginative biographer sticks to 'good beaten track concepts along which his intellectual feet are content to take their wonted and quite indispensable paces', his imaginative counterpart goes beyond this:

> He employs these very same concepts, [but] they serve also as springboards. *Because* he has found in the records that the rain was heavy or that ammunition was running short, he wonders about the hungry rifleman's rations, and he wonders about the belatedness of the mules and pack-horses – and wondering he looks for evidence in the soldiers' letters, say, for comments on the state of their mid-day rations or of the depth of the mud in the Belgian road.[36]

Here Ryle is emphasizing that history is the sort of open, unmechanical activity that can be performed *with or without imagination*, and – in the example he offers – is giving a description of the way in which *imagination as supposal* enables both historian and audience to cash what they already know by following out its implications, and taking another point of view. At the same time he (correctly) stresses the crucial relationships between historical imagination and evidence. Ryle's imaginative biographer employs concepts as 'springboards', just as the first pupil in the French Revolution example (p. 91) went beyond the concept of 'war' to ask what the war in question meant to different groups of people – whereas the second pupil did not.

The connection between imagination and understanding underlying the account given here is of fundamental importance. Understanding is not a state, or special kind of experience, or a mental process, but something akin to an ability (but not an ability to do just one sort of thing for any one thing that is understood). There are public criteria for understanding, and a claim to understand is tested against such criteria. (I can think that I understand, but others may deny this claim on the basis of what I can and cannot do, and whatever 'Aha-experience' I may have had, I can later come to agree that I had not understood.) Criteria for understanding are as varied as the circumstances and activities in which understanding may be claimed, and even if the range is narrowed to include only (say) understanding people, or (rather differently) understanding their actions, it would be a task beyond the scope of this

chapter even to begin to map out such criteria. Nevertheless, in so far as understanding involves being able to do things, it makes sense to speak of understanding some past agent in the same way. Elton condemned the injunction
that historians should read in a period until they can hear their subjects speak
as mere 'amateurishness': 'The truth is that one must read them, study their
creations and think about them until one knows what they are going to say
next.'[37] One criterion for understanding someone in the present is that we are
able to say how that person will react to some hypothetical event, because we
know something of his past experiences, his beliefs, preferences, present goals
and policies, and so on: and because we can see what, from this point of view,
the event in question will look like. (Of course we may get it wrong: the
relevant beliefs are not always obvious, and real events may change someone's
beliefs and goals; but if we get it right one criterion of understanding has been
met.) To put it another way, in the case of understanding a person, one
criterion is that we are able to 'use our imagination' – to cash our knowledge,
to entertain beliefs and attitudes other than our own, and to see their implications. It was said earlier that imagination as supposal is a necessary condition
of understanding. This is perhaps a slightly misleading formulation (which
might, for example, be taken to imply a causal connection): more precisely,
imagination is *criterial* for certain kinds of understanding.[38] And if it is past
people who are to be understood, it is not altogether unnatural to put things as
Elton does: if we really understand them, if we know them well enough and can
cash that knowledge, we know 'what they are going to say next'. Hence
historical imagination as supposal is not a special faculty, or a mysterious
process. It is not even just a particular manner of thinking, although in some
respects it is that. In other ways it is more like an achievement. The imaginative historian will have done certain things that the unimaginative historian
will not have done. Whatever mental goings-on there have been 'in his head',
judgement as to whether a historian has been imaginative or unimaginative
will depend on public criteria. It is his work that displays his historical imagination or the lack of it, not the tales he tells of his experiences in researching or
writing it.

IV. IMAGINATION AND THE 'IMAGINARY' IN HISTORY

There is a tendency among historians (and teachers of history) to deny any
interest in what *might* have happened. The historian's task, it is assumed, is to
discover what *did* happen: the merely *imaginary* has no place in history. How
else, it may be asked, could history be distinguished from fiction? History is
based upon evidence, and how could there possibly be evidence for what (*ex
hypothesi*) never happened?

   No doubt this view represents a salutory warning against empty romanti-
cizing, against historians or pupils 'letting their imagination run riot on all the
more agreeable things that might have happened'.[39] But as a self-denying
ordinance it is unenforceable. If the concept of cause comes into history at all,

and if it is sometimes to be analysed in terms of necessary conditions, then what would have happened if some antecedent condition had not occurred must enter implicitly into historians' assessments. To say that *A* is a necessary condition of *B* is to say that if *A* had not happened, *B* would not. Since *A* did occur, and with it *B*, the historian is committing himself to speculation. The non-occurrence of *A* and *B* and the consequences that might have ensued instead are imaginary. Similarly, events are sometimes construed as moving in a certain direction: 'left to themselves' things would have gone in such and such a way. But then someone or some group (or some 'accident') 'intervened', and things took a different turn. Without this person or that event, the course of events would have been very different from what it actually turned out to be.[40] The following passage, taken from a debate between Brian Simon and Marjorie Cruikshank on the 1902 Education Act, illustrates this.

> Now for various reasons there was built into the School Board system factors which were *bound to lead* to an accelerating concern with education. The Boards themselves were directly elected, . . . so that parents were involved in the developing systems. The system of finance, while imposing strong restraints, did allow some advances to take place. For these and other reasons . . . the most progressive of them were *bound to thrust upwards*, and they did so extremely rapidly.[41] [my emphasis]

For Simon, Morant and Balfour checked a movement in which events were taking a certain direction. It is worth stressing that he is writing from a Marxist standpoint, and that the assumption that the intervention of a person or group of people may set events on a different path is not simply a liberal one.

Nor is this just a case of Marxist speculation. Consider this passage from Elton: 'The question which matters is whether the Lutheran Reformation was really necessary; or whether the Church could have been renewed and restored by the widespread movement of Christian humanism which looked to Erasmus.'[42] Here we are invited to imagine a possible world in which Luther and his 'more revolutionary position' had not existed, and asked to wonder whether in such a world, Christian humanism could have 'renewed and restored' the Church. The point of this exercise is to see that without the popular support won by Luther's more radical positive stance, Christian humanism would have had a purely marginal effect. This is 'what would have happened if . . .' with a vengeance, but there is nothing illegitimate about it.

Very occasionally, this kind of move is made openly and explicitly. A particularly interesting example is Geoffrey Parker's 'If the Armada had landed'.[43] Parker's strategy is to marshal the evidence available now to assess the strengths and weaknesses of the English and Spanish on land, their morale under certain conditions, and the chances of Spanish success given what we know of Parma's orders and his likely plans. 'If Medina Sidonia had succeeded, against all the odds, in landing the army of invasion on England's shores, what could have been achieved? Were the means provided by the Prudent King equal to the ends he had in mind?'[44] What is involved is a detailed examination of the problems, the effectiveness and equipment of the Spanish, and of their opponents, much as would have had to be conducted by a contemporary, or by Philip himself attempting to answer the same question, but with benefit of hindsight and knowledge unavailable to the participants. The scenarios developed in the discussion are imaginary: they never came about. But if in this sense the whole thing is 'sheer imagination', in another sense it is not. At every point in the calculation the argument turns on evidence. Parker admits that 'any – or none – of the scenarios . . . might have happened. . . . . We do not know, and no amount of speculation or calculation can enlighten us.'[45]

Why then 'play a parlour-game with the might-have-beens of history', especially if (as Carr goes on to say) 'they have nothing to do with history'?[46] One reason is given by Parker himself: 'a counterfactual approach . . . is essential when the historian wishes to assess the feasibility of a course of action or a policy'.[47] Why should we want to assess the feasibility of a course of action that failed? Because it sometimes helps us to understand why such a course was embarked upon, and because our decision about this determines the use we can make of the failure of the Armada as itself evidence for our assessment of Philip II and his scheme. But Parker could have given another, perhaps more important, reason for such imaginings. The failure of the Armada has (at least in English history) generally been considered an event of some importance. Much of its importance flowed from its consequences. Now to say it is a consequence of the failure to get troops ashore that 'the Counter-Reformation was not to triumph throughout Europe', is to say that this failure was a necessary condition of the lack of success of the Counter Reformation.[48] Indeed, Garrett Mattingly, trying to weigh the different claims for the importance of the Armada, and to give support to his own assessment (that it was decisive in its effects on European opinion as to God's purposes), explicitly offers his own might-have-beens: 'Without the English victory at Gravelines and its ratification by the news from Ireland, Henry III might never have summoned the courage to throw off the League's yoke, and the subsequent history of Europe might have been incalculably different.'[49] Mattingly takes only the first step along this 'imaginary' path, and characterizes the multiplicity of alternatives that these open up as 'incalculable'. But were anyone to challenge his assessment, it is hard to see how more might-have-beens could be avoided, and the challenge itself must assume that certain things would have happened anyway, even without the defeat of the Armada.

It is wrong, then, to say that the purely imaginary has no part in history. But even the imaginary, when it appears in history, must be tied to the evidence. The kind of counter-factual imagination discussed here is a form of negative supposal: if so and so had not happened, what, on the basis of the evidence, would have followed? Something of this kind is involved, at least implicitly, whenever causes as necessary conditions are invoked; and frequently such imaginings lie behind attributions of importance in terms of consequences. What is supposed did not happen, and is thus (*ex hypothesi*) merely imaginary, but it is not mere fancy, or imagination without control or constraint.

If the imaginary has a role in history, how is it possible to draw a line between history and historical fiction? What is usually called historical fiction accepts what historians have established as a set of factual premises within which a story may be told. The merely imaginary in these circumstances is generally confined to the level of events that historians, in saying a battle or a revolution or a price-rise occurred, are implicitly taking to have happened, but are unable to characterize. Often there is simply insufficient evidence to say much at that level at all; at other times there is enough for exemplification, but not enough to tell a coherent story. The writer of historical fiction bases the imaginary on evidence, but none the less invents what the historian is unable to reconstruct. Suppose there had been an individual with this particular set of experiences, who believed so and so, lived in such and such circumstances, and became involved in this (historical) series of events: what might have happened to him? The people in the story resemble ideal types; they embody a particular configuration of beliefs, goals and economic and social roles which are at least historically possible, and which, given what historians have established on the basis of evidence, amount to a highly probable combination. Ideal types are employed in history, anyway – Maynard's Russian Peasant, Brenan's Andalusian Anarchists, Soboul's Sans Culottes – but in historical fiction they perform deeds, have conversations and personal relationships, and suffer day-to-day events for which there could be no evidence, because these things never happened. Ideal types in history illuminate and exemplify wider matters, but in historical fiction they are given all the trappings of (imaginary) life.

Imagination in historical fiction must recognize the constraints imposed by evidence and established historical fact, but at the same time it must meet the ordinary literary criteria of coherence, human possibility and so on. From this standpoint, it is also normally part of the point of historical fiction to evoke a response, and the author may actively seek to produce emotional reactions in his reader. The story is usually told very much from one point of view, and in this sense at least there is rarely any attempt to maintain a historian's detachment. In the case of children's fiction (and perhaps of adults' too?) the reader is encouraged to identify with the hero, which demands living *in* imagination. And to the extent that the work forces the reader to accommodate to the hero's world, and not merely assimilate it to his own, it demands imagination as supposal too. Writing historical fiction is not doing historical research, and reading it is not (in some respects) like reading history. But it can lead to empathy as achievement, and an appreciation of a period, if from a narrow point of view, by making it easier to cash historical knowledge. Too easy, it might be said: historical understanding demands movement between a range of points of view, some of them never held by (or even comprehensible to) the people under investigation. This, of course, is one of the things that makes history difficult for children, and historical fiction, in narrowing the range of viewpoints but exploring one or two in detail, may have a much more important place in learning history than it has generally been given.

V.   IMAGINATION, IMAGES AND THE 'REALITY OF THE PAST'

Historical fiction, in company with true historical stories, has another role. A story in which one can 'immerse' oneself may, by dimming current reality, strengthen awareness of the reality of the past. There is a paradox here: how may a piece of fiction strengthen a sense of the reality of the past? I will come back to this; but a prior question obviously arises: just what is involved in talk of the awareness of the 'reality of the past'?

It is a curious phrase, but one that teachers often employ in trying to describe what children (and many adults) lack, and I do not think it is entirely a piece of mystification. Plainly the past is not present, and no one is claiming that. The point is that people and societies did exist in just the way we now exist. It is easy for both children and adults to see history as a catalogue of formal, almost empty statements, and to treat established historical facts as a kind of abstract pattern or calculus in which terms are manipulated for mysterious academic purposes, or for examinations. For such people, there is no possibility of (or point in) cashing such historical knowledge as they have – if they can be said to have historical knowledge at all. It is formal and empty because while its statements have esoteric relationships with each other, they have no contact with or application to the 'real' world. Hence abstractions are not translatable into concrete terms, and there is no exercise of imagination as supposal (implications of beliefs, goals and so on are not seen): this means that there is a failure to see that the same sort of connections applied in the past as apply now. It does not occur to someone who lacks a sense of the reality of the past to make the connections he would make if he were confronted with some present person or action. With all this goes a certain arbitrariness in handling historical knowledge, and a failure to understand that past and present are overlapping, not discontinuous, categories. In contrast, it is obvious that for many people (including a great many children) the 'real' world is not a more or less instantaneous present, and in consequence historical knowledge, far from being inert and formal, is rich in implications.

What brings about these different approaches to the past? Clearly a historian in writing imaginatively (as with Ryle's biographer) may make it easier for his audience to cash what is offered, grasping what it amounted to in concrete terms. Consider, for example, this description of the execution of Mary, Queen of Scots:

> So she held the crucifix high, visible all down the long hall, as she flung defiance at her judges, and her voice rose with a kind of triumph above the voice of the Dean of Peterborough, always higher and clearer than his rising tones, arching over the vehement English prayers the mysterious dominating invocations of the ancient faith. The Queen's voice held on for a minute after the clergyman had finished. Her words were in English now; she was praying for the people of England and for the soul of her royal cousin Elizabeth; she was forgiving all her enemies. Then for a moment her ladies were busy about her. The black velvet gown fell below her knees revealing underbodice and petticoat of crimson silk, and she stepped forward suddenly, shockingly, in the colour of martyrdom, blood red from top to toe, against the sombre background. Quietly she knelt and bowed herself low over the little chopping-block. 'In manus tuas, domine . . .' and they heard twice the dull chunk of the axe.

There was one more ceremony to accomplish. The executioner must exhibit the head and speak the customary words. The masked black figure stooped and rose, crying in a loud voice: 'Long live the Queen!' But all he held in his hand that had belonged to the rival queen of hearts was a kerchief, and pinned to it an elaborate auburn wig. Rolled nearer the edge of the platform, shrunken and withered and grey, with a sparse silver stubble on the small shiny skull was the head of the martyr. Mary Stuart had always known how to embarrass her enemies [50]

Here the historian's description is as concrete as it is possible to make it within the range of what the evidence allows, and what imagination as supposal and a general knowledge of the time suggests. Phrases are selected carefully. 'Then for a moment her ladies were busy about her': the evidence does not tell us exactly what movements they made, but the choice of description gives us as clear and rich as possible an idea of the range within which they fell, and the succeeding sentence informs us as to the results. We are told what we would have seen and heard if we had been there, and if our attention had been turned to the main business of the day. And we are told what it all meant – how Mary, for example, intended her actions to be taken, and how (given what is known of those present) they were likely to react. (Mary stepped forward not just suddenly, but shockingly.) To this extent it is possible to say 'It is as if we were there'.

Part of our reason for putting things in this way might be that there were certain goings-on *in* our imagination. We might have images of Mary in scarlet, of the executioner in black, of the expectant assembled onlookers, and so on. It is tempting to say that a passage like Mattingly's makes us think of events as real (in the general sense already discussed) precisely because it conjures up images. Certainly the concrete and detailed description is central here, and such a description allows images to come easily to mind. In following a story (narrative history or historical fiction), concrete details make it easier for us to turn our attention away from current reality, and to pay attention to what is happening as described or narrated. This dimming of current reality makes it easier to treat whatever we are attending to as itself real; and in the end, provided our attention is not disturbed, the past may seem 'more real' than the present. (This resolves the paradox about historical fiction mentioned at the beginning of this section.) To say the past seems 'real' in this sense is just to say that it demands our attention more pressingly than the present.[51] Once again there is a temptation to equate this with having images, and to say that the more vivid they are, the more they will take over from ordinary perception, as if reading a compelling history book were a kind of (guided) hallucination. No doubt for some people in some circumstances there is truth in such an account. But while following a narrative may involve the dimming of current reality, images are not necessarily involved. What is central is attention to what is happening in the narrative, whatever sort of thing it may be. Some things that happen cannot be imaged, and it is not always concrete details of a perceptual kind that are relevant to our ability to cash what a historian is telling us. A political argument or development will be vivid or real to the extent that it compels attention, and it will only do this if it enables us, or better encourages us, to follow it in such a way as to see its consequences and implications – in short, if it is not allowed to remain inert.[52]

An awareness of the 'reality of the past', then, is closely connected in different ways with imagination as supposal, with (sometimes) goings-on *in* imagination, and with the historian's ability to write *with* imagination. Images are often valuable here, and what produces a sense of the reality of the past may also help to produce images (where they are relevant). But this sense of reality is not a matter of having images, and neither is historical imagination in general.[53]

VI. IMAGINATION AND LEARNING HISTORY

This chapter has touched only on some salient aspects of imagination in mature history: qualifications may have to be made if it is to be applied to *learning* history. It is possible, for example, that imagination as supposal might be developed through immature and partial (as opposed to impartial) sympathy; it *may* be necessary for children to share the point of view of the people they are studying if they are to see its implications for action or for other views. It may even be necessary at some stage for them to identify with historical agents. But these are empirical questions, and as yet no clear evidence exists to support or refute such hypotheses – at least in history. Nor is it clear how far children must have had similar experiences to those past people they are learning about – even the prior question (which is not empirical) of what is to count as a 'similar' experience remains virtually unexplored. Similarly, we do not know whether exposure to examples of historical imagination (in the form of historical fiction, for instance) is a prerequisite for the development of children's own imagination.

What we do have is general psychological evidence on the wider issue of understanding other persons, much of which is largely perceptual, with children asked to say what can be seen of some array of models or objects from a different point of view.[54] Such work is important, but it must be recognized that in history points of view encompass much more than the visibility of physical objects. Characteristically it is more a matter of what beliefs, purposes and values were held, what considerations borne in mind, and what weight attached to them. Nevertheless, in so far as much of the work is inspired by dissatisfaction with Piaget's general account of egocentrism in young children, derived in particular from his 'three mountains' experiment, it shares a major concern with history.[55] It is probably fair to say that early work tended to support Piaget's conclusions: namely that young children fail to realize that other people have different points of view from which they will see different things, and indeed that very young children regard their viewpoint as the only one possible. The implications of this egocentrism for historical imagination in school are gloomy, but it is not clear that we have to accept them. There is not space here to give a comprehensive account of the arguments involved, but it is worth raising one or two central questions.

First, Flavell has suggested that children are often capable of making inferences that allow them to put themselves in someone else's position, but do not necessarily see the need to make such inferences.[56] The distinction between the capacity and recognition of the need to exercise it is suggestive for history. If Flavell were right, the capacity would set limits to empathy (as achievement) and understanding, but recognition of the need to exercise it would be decisive for imagination. Under what circumstances are children likely to recognize this 'need'? How is willingness to make the required suppositions, to cash the knowledge they often already have, acquired? Is it, as Flavell suggests, a process of training people to make certain responses automatically in certain classes of cases?[57] Or is it more a matter of helping people to see the relevance of such exercises of imagination? It is almost as if one needs imagination to see that exercise of imagination is necessary in a particular case. For unless I can see that someone else's position, being different from mine, makes a difference – unless I *do* cash my knowledge of his position in at least a minimal way – I can have no reason to try to see what those differences are. This is not really paradoxical: once the general point has been grasped that different points of view make a difference (have consequences) it will be clear that imagination is required in specific cases. In everyday life a failure to recognize the necessity of seeing another point of view is likely to be met with fairly rapid feedback, sometimes unpleasant. In history the penalty is only incomprehension, and schoolchildren in large classes have to live with that on at least a temporary basis as a normal part of school life. ('Deferred understanding' might be a useful sub-category of 'deferred gratification'.)

Flavell's research also connects with some of the remarks made earlier in this chapter about sympathy and imagination. His work suggests that it is difficult not only to work out the substance of another person's point of view, but more especially to maintain it consistently in active competition with one's own perspective. Flavell's evidence derives from tests employing visual arrays, where his subjects found it hard to keep in mind that what they could see was not visible to the person with whom they were supposed to be co-operating.[58] There seems a prima facie case for thinking that the task in history will be harder, but this cannot simply be assumed without research evidence. It is even possible that absence of a strong conflicting visual stimulus may make it easier to bear in mind alternative points of view in a consistent way. But it is clear that in history everything is more complicated: beliefs, values, and their appropriate emotional loadings have to be suspended, and others entertained in their place.

Secondly, experimenters are increasingly aware of the need to see how things look from the child's point of view. Margaret Donaldson has stressed that for all thinking the task must make 'human sense', and has distinguished between 'embedded' and 'disembedded' thinking.[59] Thinking removed from its grounding in the familiar contexts that make sense of what is going on is 'disembedded'. Many of the tasks set for young children in experimental work make no sense to them, and this, Donaldson argues, invalidates many of the conclusions drawn from such tests.[60] When, for example, a perceptual test of ability to see another's point of view is set up so that it makes sense to children in terms of their own experience of intentions and meaningful situations, '4-year-olds could . . . succeed at the 90 per cent level' with complex arrays and multiple points of view. (The arrays consisted of walls behind which boy dolls had to be hidden from model policemen.) Donaldson comments:

> the *motives* and *intentions* of the characters are entirely comprehensible, even to a child of three. The task requires the child to act in ways which are in line with certain very basic human purposes and interactions (escape and pursuit) – it makes *human sense*.[61]

Donaldson's suggestions are perceptive and important, but do not clearly distinguish between the sense a task might be given by children (as opposed to experimenters), and the sense implicit internally in the context of the task. She rightly points out that what experimenters make of a conservation test, and what children assume is going on, may be quite different. But in the test described above, the point about the task making human sense has a double importance, because in a test designed to get at children's grasp of other people's points of view, what the 'people' actually built into the test (the boy and policeman dolls) are doing must also make sense. Displaced volumes or rows of objects do not themselves do things that make sense, although they figure in activities that do. Boys and policemen may figure in experimentally imposed tasks that make sense, but may also themselves *do* things that make (or fail to make) sense. In tests of children's thinking in history this is of paramount importance: being asked to see things from another's point of view must be embodied in a meaningful task, but it also involves understanding what sense can be made of what others do, and their purposes, intentions and perspectives within the task.[62]

The concept of 'human sense' is intuitively attractive, but it is not easy to see what is to count as making human sense in history. It is tempting to say that on the task side, being asked to put ourselves in someone else's shoes, and cashing what one knows, should be familiar enough from everyday life. Even allowing for Flavell's warning about failure to appreciate when such a task is called for, a general and consistent inability to recognize appropriate situations would lead to dire consequences for the child. The task, it seems, certainly ought to make human sense. Of course this still leaves history teachers with the problem of getting children to see that *history* demands an exercise of imagination in this way. Very often in everyday life the imagination called for is supposal within narrow shared limits; it is like the task Helen Borke's 3-year-olds accomplished of recognizing the emotions appropriate to easily categorized everyday situations – easily categorized because of a shared way of life.[63] In history the point is that imagination is required to understand a different way of life. Moreover in everyday life where there are often shared assumptions, people are frequently not as much concerned to see if another view makes sense as to evaluate it as true or false, or to assess its bearing on them and their concerns. Donaldson quotes Mary Henle's experiment in which adults were asked to assess the validity of various inferences. The subjects (graduate students) frequently rejected the premises or inserted their own premises, in effect evaluating the truth of the substantive assertions, not the validity of the arguments.[64] It is not absolutely clear if Margaret Donaldson is classifying the thinking demanded by this kind of task as disembedded because it asks for a (formal) assessment of validity rather than truth, or because it asks for detachment from a context in which one's own interest is considered and the bearing of the assertion on one's own concerns comes in. What *is* clear is that in the exercise of historical imagination it is often the *validity* of other people's views that is in question, and this validity is to be assessed in independence of our current concerns. So a great deal of historical thinking must in this sense at least be 'disembedded', or ' "prised out" from the supportive context of the rest of (the thinkers') experience'.[65] How far one ought still to talk of the task making human sense is in these circumstances debatable.

It has already been argued that the notion of human sense has a double importance in history: it comes in at the content level as well as the task level. What historical agents do must also make human sense. In elucidating her concept of disembedded thinking Donaldson gives this account:

> It is when we are dealing with people and things in the context of fairly immediate goals and intentions and familiar patterns of events that we feel most at home.
>
> . . . So long as our thinking is sustained by this kind of human sense, and so long as the conclusion to which the reasoning leads is not in conflict with something which we know or believe or want to believe, we tend to have no difficulty. Thus even pre-school children can frequently reason well about the events in the stories they hear. However, when we move beyond the bounds of human sense there is a dramatic difference. Thinking which does move beyond these bounds, so that it no longer operates within the supportive context of meaningful events is . . . 'disembedded'.[66]

What provides the human sense is 'the context of fairly immediate goals and intentions and familiar patterns of events'. Now at one level this context must be present in history if there is to be any understanding at all. At some level there must be common human interests – in getting sufficient food, adequate shelter, and perhaps meeting certain emotional needs for instance – shared with anyone whose actions are to be intelligible. Presumably there must also be some common rationality (as opposed to *a*rationality).[67] But what this level is, is a matter for argument.[68] The point that matters here is that much of history is concerned with coming to understand goals, values, beliefs and actions that at some level are radically different from our own, and that imagination is central in this. Donaldson's notion of human sense is highly suggestive, but not precise enough here. What exactly is crucial? Is it familiarity with the content of a task? What counts as familiarity with content? Have children got to have met similar beliefs and goals, and similar situations? How deep must the similarities be? Will a broad grasp of kinds of motives do? Is it enough to know *that* people have, as a matter of fact, often acted out of fear or envy, or must the child have felt fear and envy? Fear of similar events, or simply some childish fear? Donaldson, commenting on the relative ease with which young children tackled the 'boy hiding from policeman' task, argues we cannot appeal to direct actual experience: few, if any, of these children had ever tried to hide from a policeman. But we *can* appeal to the generalization of experience: they know what it is to try to hide. Also they know what it is to be naughty and to want to evade the consequence.[69]

The notion of *experience* brings out the complexity here. How indirect can the experience be if the content of a historical task is not to make the required thinking disembedded? Must a child have religious beliefs or is it enough to know that some people have such beliefs? Or is at least some indirect experience of religious beliefs and their consequences necessary: that is, contact with religious people acting in a context of religious belief?[70] Familiarity with content in a modern context is often cited by teachers as a major obstacle to imagination: children may simply assume that familiar beliefs and goals were current in the period they were studying, with anachronistic results.

The notions of 'disembedded thinking' and 'human sense' leave many questions unanswered, but they are useful – although crude – tools for teachers and researchers concerned with historical imagination and understanding. They also strike a note of optimism about children's rationality, dispelling some of the neo-Piagetian gloom cast over school history by repeated rediscoveries of pupils' egocentrism. Whatever else may be said, it is clear that it is the teacher's job to *make* things make human sense so far as the task itself is concerned, and to try to make sure that within the task the thinking required is at least not unnecessarily disembedded.

What then, in the absence of decisive evidence from psychologists, can be said about historical imagination in school? It is widely agreed that there is no value in children collecting inert historical information; there is no point in pupils merely being able to recite lists of events. But equally it is no good children being able to rehearse what historical agents believed or wanted, or the 'causes' of events, if this information is also inert. Imagination is essential: knowledge of people in history must be cashable. I asked at the beginning of the chapter which of two criticisms is more serious – that a piece of history is 'sheer imagination', or that it 'lacks imagination'. For a professional historian, the answer is clear. What is 'sheer imagination' is not history at all. The first criticism is utterly damning. The second is wounding, but still allows the historian his place in the guild. For school history, the question is not so straightforward. Where a professional historian can be assumed to be able to cash his information even if on this occasion he has not bothered, or has just been pedantic, at school we are working on a different basis. If a pupil's history lacks imagination, we cannot simply assume that what he has written or said makes any sense to him. If imagination is one criterion of understanding history, then lack of imagination is likely to be symptomatic of lack of understanding. And lack of understanding renders history pointless.

NOTES

1. Kitson Clark, G., *The Critical Historian*, Heinemann Educational Books, 1967, p. 170.
2. Hill, C., *Reformation to Industrial Revolution*, Pelican Economic History of Britain: 2, 1969, pp. 260-1, © Christopher Hill, 1967, 1969. Reprinted by permission of Penguin Books Ltd.

3. Furlong, E. J., *Imagination*, Allen & Unwin, 1961, *passim*.
4. 'Getting it right' is not meant to imply that in history one final or certain story can be achieved, but to indicate that evidence can refute some stories.
5. In contrasting imagination in history with literature etc., I am *not* arguing that in the latter imagination is untrammelled, free from all constraint. But the constraints are different from those in history – in particular there is no (or at least a very different) connection with *evidence*, and no prima facie ban on the (merely) imaginary. See Scruton, R., *Art and Imagination*, Methuen, 1974. Scruton emphasizes the notion of 'appropriateness' in connection with imagination (pp. 98–9).
6. Collingwood, R. G., *The Idea of History*, Oxford University Press, 1946, p. 246.
7. ibid., p. 245.
8. ibid., pp. 241 and 247. Mink, L. O., *Mind, History and Dialectic*, Indiana University Press, 1969, pp. 183–6, discusses what Collingwood may have intended. The issue is part of a much more general one in epistemology and philosophy of science. See Quine, W. V. O., 'Two dogmas of empiricism', in *From a Logical Point of View*, 2nd edn, Harvard University Press, 1961; and Lakatos, I., 'Falsification and the methodology of scientific research programmes', in *Criticism and the Growth of Knowledge*, Cambridge University Press, 1970, for a discussion in the context of physical science. Murphy, M. G., *Our Knowledge of the Historical Past*, Bobbs Merrill, 1973, pp. 22–7, examines Quine's arguments in relation to history.
9. Elton, G. R., *The Practice of History*, Sydney University Press, 1967, pp. 86–7.
10. Kitson Clark, op. cit., p.64.
11. Dumville, D., 'Sub-Roman Britain, history and legend', *History*, vol. 62, no. 205, June 1977; Morris, J., *The Age of Arthur: A History of the British Isles from 350 to 650*, Weidenfeld & Nicolson, 1973.
12. Stephens, J. N., 'Bede's *Ecclesiastical History*', *History*, vol. 62, no. 204, February 1977.
13. This extremely useful concept is slightly weakened by Walsh's use of it to embrace both conceptions derived from people's explicit purposes and policies, and conceptions 'imposed' by historians regardless of whether contemporaries would (or could) have seen things in the relevant way.
14. Elton, G. R., 'Putting the past before us', *The Times Literary Supplement*, 8 September 1978, p. 993.
15. The sense in which imagination is a criterion for understanding emerges at the end of this section. See Wittgenstein, L., *The Blue and Brown Books*, 2nd edn, Basil Blackwell, 1969, pp. 24–5; and *Philosophical Investigations*, Basil Blackwell, 1968, paras 143–55 and 179–82.
16. Lee, P. J., 'Explanation and understanding in history', in Dickinson, A. K., and Lee, P. J. (eds), *History Teaching and Historical Understanding*, Heinemann Educational Books, 1978.
17. This claim is too simple. It might be argued that if empathy in this sense were not possible in everyday life, there would be no possibility of empathy in other senses in history. And it is certainly not possible to rule out intuition entirely in history. See pp. 90 and 94–5.
18. The ambiguity here was deliberate; part of the point of setting this was to force out into the open the differences between trying to imagine one is Louis – to the extent that one entertains *his* beliefs, goals etc. – and being transposed (as if in a time machine) into Louis's circumstances as we now see them, with one's own beliefs and goals intact.
19. But note that 'Louis XVI was far from being the simple, weak man . . . that has often been portrayed by historians of the period. Rather he was endowed with a certain intelligence and with tenacious obstinacy which he used in the service of one single aim, that of re-establishing his absolute authority, even if he did so at the heavy cost of betraying the nation.' (Soboul, A., *The French Revolution 1789–99*, New Left Books, 1974.)
20. Powicke, F. M., *King Henry III and the Lord Edward*, Oxford University Press, 1947, p. 508.
21. This may well be a naïve view of evidence in natural science, and it is not one to which I wish to commit myself. The point is that *even if* in physical science there is a clear notion of

independent evidence (in this sense) at work, in history there is not.

22. See Passmore, J., 'Objectivity', in Gardiner, P., *The Philosophy of History*, Oxford University Press, 1974.

23. Kitson Clark, op. cit., p. 170.

24. ibid., p. 171: 'the working of the imagination is subjective . . . No one else can go over the steps by which the result was reached to check it and to see where an error has possibly been introduced into the process.' 'Subjective' here seems meant to draw attention to this feature of imagination construed as 'workings' or 'processes' of the mind, with the idea of intuition juxtaposed to mechanical decision procedures. There is no great harm in speaking in this way so long as it is not taken to imply arbitrariness or to deny the possibility of intersubjectivity with respect to conclusions, but analysis of historical imagination as mental process in the end proves unsatisfactory. See pp. 96–101 of this book.

25. It is less likely that Kitson Clark is subscribing here to any philosophical theory than simply warning of the practical difficulties facing historians in this sphere – again in comparison with the way in which data has to be treated to be susceptible to statistical manipulation. The passage quoted is in any case part of a wider conception of imagination: 'The "historical imagination" . . . is the power of imagining the conditions, the men, the actions of a past period as a convincing whole distilled from the disparate evidence available' (op. cit., p. 170). It is not clear what atomistic alternative this 'whole' is being set against, but there is a clear connection between a coherent account which 'makes sense' of an event or period and historical understanding in which action is grasped in its context. For history to make sense at all, and for any kind of 'whole' to be intelligible, let alone convincing, beliefs and actions must be understood. What an action is, and what an agent had in mind in performing it, is not a matter of that agent ('internally') attaching (private) meanings to it. Men's minds are not essentially (even if they are partly) private: we can discover what people intended, believed, or felt because their actions take their meanings from their place in some public context. Hence without taking a sufficiently synoptic view to bring in an adequate context, we can have no understanding. Seeing a whole depends on understanding, and understanding depends on seeing a whole. The concept of imagination connects both.

26. Hill, op. cit., p. 261.

27. ibid., pp. 261–2.

28. The impossibility of this in many cases, where feelings depend on beliefs themselves seen as mistaken, is discussed below. But in any case there are moral questions here: should one expect the historian (or his audience) to *share* the grim satisfaction of a Nazi at the fate of the Jews? See also the following note.

29. Such feelings may be a hindrance rather than a help. If there is any truth in the claim that historians must operate with some detachment and impartiality, there are obvious difficulties. (How can he, being impartial, share the feelings of both parties in an election, a battle, or a class struggle?) Neal Ascheson's review of Irving's *Uprising* (Hodder & Stoughton, 1981) in the *Observer* (29 March 1981) indicates how a historian's feelings may vitiate a whole work:

> it isn't the Nagy group's shortcomings as revolutionary leaders that interests Irving. He is, quite simply, outraged that a gang of Marxists is remembered for its courage and patriotism. In language which rises to a scream of abuse, he tries to demolish their memory.
> The whole book is written as if David Irving were shaking with uncontrollable hatred. It is a bad book . . .

30. Carr, E. H., *What is History?*, Penguin, 1964, p. 24.

31. Brailsford, H. N., *The Levellers and the English Revolution*, Crescent Press, 1961, p. 365.

32. Ryle, G., *On Thinking*, Basil Blackwell, 1979, p. 54.
33. Of course the historian cannot spell out everything. He needs imagination to see things from the point of view of his audience. What will they be most likely to miss, or falsely assume? The importance of this issue for teaching is immense. See Lee, P. J., 'Explanation and understanding in history', and Dickinson, A. K., and Lee, P. J., 'Explanation and research', in Dickinson and Lee (eds), op. cit.
34. Ryle, op. cit., p. 59.
35. ibid.
36. ibid.
37. Elton, *The Practice of History*, op. cit., p. 17.
38. Imagination as supposal is criterial for understanding actions too. One criterion for our understanding an action is that we can exhibit the action as (under certain descriptions) the thing to do in the light of beliefs, purposes, etc., taken as reasons for performing the action, in such a way as (in principle) to elicit the (truthful) assent of the agent. With past actions it is often no longer possible to obtain the agent's assent, but in any case this is not essential even with present action. Where what happened is described in such a way that it was not intended by the agent under that description, understanding will of course involve the historian's view of the situation as well as the agent's, and the criteria for understanding become more complex.
39. Carr, op. cit., p. 97.
40. See Mackie, J. L., *The Cement of the Universe*, Oxford University Press, 1974, ch. 2, and especially pp. 33-4.
41. Simon, B., 'The 1902 Education Act – a wrong turning', *History of Education Society Bulletin*, no. 19, spring 1977.
42. Elton, G. R., *Reformation Europe 1517-1559*, Fontana, 1963, p. 282.
43. Parker, G., 'If the Armada had landed', *History*, vol. 61, no. 203, October 1976.
44. ibid., pp. 358-9.
45. ibid., p. 368.
46. Quoted by Parker, op. cit.
47. ibid.
48. Mattingly, G., *The Defeat of the Spanish Armada*, Jonathan Cape, 1959, p. 334, discussing the evaluation of Froude, Motley, Ranke and Michelet. For an analysis of consequence chains in terms of necessary conditions, see Dray, W. H., 'On importance in History', in Kiefer, H. E., and Munitz, M. K., *Mind, Science and History*, State University of New York Press, 1970. Reprinted by permission of the Executors of the Garret Mattingly Estate.
49. Mattingly, op. cit., p. 336.
50. Mattingly, op. cit., p. 26.
51. If the inhibition of current reality depends upon our attention to what is happening in the narrative, the narrative must obviously be intelligible. Part of what makes it so is that it enables us to follow events from points of view that differ from our own. Here there is a link with the notion of sympathy, as well as imagination as supposal. It is distracting to find hostile or critical judgements upon this different point of view thrust upon us at frequent intervals, because our attention to what is happening (seen from this other point of view) is disturbed, and current reality is brought in upon us. Critical judgements are of course legitimate; it is just that they can be mistimed or overdone, and when they are, partly constitute a lack of sympathy.
52. Mary Warnock attempts an account of 'successful imagining' in terms of images and feelings. (Warnock, M., *Imagination*, Faber, 1976, pp. 169-73.) Such an account fails in history because images (even in the very wide sense she employs) are not central in history in the required way, and more importantly because private feelings cannot normally be criterial for *successful* imagining. If we have imagined successfully, as already argued in

section III, we will be able to do things differently; moreover, whatever our feelings, we may just be mistaken in thinking our imagining has been successful.

53. The notion of the reality of the past takes us into grander conceptions, and back to another connection with imagination. We talk about history capturing children's (and adults') imagination, of children suddenly becoming aware of the vast scope of man's history, of the procession of ages – a sudden awareness 'that men really have been around all this time' as one boy put it. These ideas are perhaps close to Kantian 'ideas of reason', which are beyond the power of imagination to represent by images. 'Imaginatively we stretch out towards what imagination cannot comprehend.' See Warnock, op. cit., pp. 56–61.

54. Another strand of research has concentrated on the ascription of thoughts or feelings to other people, often characters in specially devised stories. There have also been experiments in which children have had to communicate certain features of a visual array to a listener unable to see what the subject could see. See in particular Borke, H., 'Piaget's view of social interaction and empathy', in Siegel, L. S., and Brainerd, C. J. (eds), *Alternatives to Piaget*, Academic Press, 1978; Donaldson, M., *Children's Minds*, Fontana, 1978; and Flavell, J. H., 'The development of inferences about others', in Mischel, T. (ed), *Understanding Other Persons*, Blackwell, 1974. For a discussion of some recent work in history, see the next chapter of this book.

55. Piaget, J., and Inhelder, B., *The Child's Conception of Space*, Routledge & Kegan Paul, 1956. In the 'three mountains' test children aged 4 to 12 years were shown a model consisting of an array of three mountains. The task was to choose from a group of pictures the one that best showed what a doll would see from a particular position in relation to the mountains, or to put the doll in the right position to see what was shown in a given picture.

56. Flavell, op. cit., pp. 75–8, But see Shemilt, D., *History 13–16 Evaluation Study*, Holmes McDougall, 1980, pp. 33 and 37.

57. Flavell, op. cit., p.78. It may be that the sometimes painful circumstances in which young children have to learn to recognize other people's points of view may give them reasons for *withholding* (rather than merely failing to achieve) such recognition. A large part of early training in this area takes place in circumstances where the child is being persuaded (compelled?) to share favourite toys, to accept that Mum cannot play a game at this moment, or to cease antisocial behaviour. (I owe this point to Mrs Rosalyn Ashby of the Bramston School, Witham.)

58. Flavell, op. cit., pp. 80–1.

59. Donaldson, op. cit., p. 76.

60. See ch. 6 of Dickinson and Lee (eds), op. cit., where the same point was made against some of Peel's work. Many teachers have known this for a *very* long time, but surprisingly have sometimes accepted experimental results that have ignored it. And it is not unfair to say that much history teaching ignores the implications of Donaldson's argument.

61. Donaldson, op. cit., p. 24.

62. Where Donaldson does distinguish between the human sense of the task and what goes on inside the task, she seems to say that a task in which the content demands a grasp of interpersonal motives is easier than one that does not. Contrasting the 'boys hiding from policemen' test with the three mountains test she says 'In respect of being humanly comprehensible, the "mountains" task is at the opposite extreme. Within this task itself, there is no play of interpersonal motives of such a kind as to make it instantly intelligible' (op. cit., p. 24). Perhaps the rider 'of such a kind as to make it instantly intelligible' saves this statement from being highly controversial: if the rider means what it (literally) says the point is tautologous. If it is not meant to be tautologous it seems at least a curious thing to say, and no evidence is given for it. At times she even appears to imply that tasks involving people *as content* is what gives them human sense. But her discussion of Hewson's experiments with linked behaviour segments (p. 54) shows that a task may make human sense (fit into a

confronting them, and this knowledge is conspicuously absent. Secondly, the establishment of levels or stages of thinking is a mixed blessing in education. Stages of this kind can provide a valuable – if schematic – map of the way in which cognitive development proceeds. But the omnipresent danger is that they may function in teaching almost in the same way as racial prejudice. Suppose for a moment that the racial superiority of group *A* over group *B* were conclusively established by a culture-neutral intelligence test. Teachers would still not know how to treat any individual pupil. Any particular child from group *B* might still be far more intelligent than his group *A* classmates, despite any statistical generalizations to the contrary.[3] In a similar way, even if there were convincing evidence for an agreed set of age-related stages in historical understanding, individual pupils would still have to be assessed as individuals. The age–stage relation is only statistical, and, more important, the stages themselves are necessarily simplified models. Even where a child's thinking may in general be allocated to a given stage, his performance on any particular task may fluctuate widely according to the nature of the task, the variety of his experience, and the surrounding circumstances. For many teaching purposes cognitive stages are therefore likely to be at best misleading and unhelpful, and at worst rigid and stultifying, leading to a kind of 'stage prejudice'.

In order to discover more about the ways in which children actually behave when confronted with the 'strangeness' of the past, we have begun to work with small groups of children, recording their discussions on video-tape. (The age range so far tested runs from 8 to 18, together with one group of parents.) A group of three children is given a passage either on Anglo-Saxon oath-helping and the ordeal, or on Spartan education. In the case of the Anglo-Saxons test children are given the first question – 'Why do you think the Anglo-Saxons used oath-helping and the ordeal to decide if someone was guilty of a crime? Give the best explanation you can' – and asked to discuss what they think would be the best answer. They are told to 'chew it over' thoroughly before they write down their answer, and that they do not have to agree with each other about what the answer should be. When the first question has been dealt with, two more follow: 'Does anything puzzle you about these ways of finding out if someone was guilty?'; and then, when the second answer is complete, 'Do you think an Anglo-Saxon would have explained it in the same way as you have? If you think there would be any differences, say what they would be. If you don't think there would be any differences, say why not.' In the Spartan test some groups are asked to set suitable questions for the rest of the class, and others are given questions to answer. ('Why do you think the Spartans treated their children the way they did?' 'Does anything about the Spartans puzzle you?' 'Why do you think the Spartans stopped going to the Olympic Games?') It is made clear before the children begin that there is a considerable amount of extra information available if they feel they need it; this is emphasized in a concrete way by spreading out the material on nearby vacant tables or desks. The discussion that ensues is recorded by a TV camera. Children generally overcome most of their reticence after a few minutes of peering through the camera at each other, and seeing pictures of themselves on the monitor. Where we think it will help, we leave the room altogether, letting the subjects get on with their discussion, asking them to come and ask us whenever they need more information or to know the next question. Frequently, however, it is possible to stay in the room, thinly disguising our curiosity by ostentatiously carrying on some other task.

The final product of a session of this kind is a transcription of the video-tape, and a set of written answers. Such 'data' is clearly not susceptible to statistical analysis. What it does offer is a chance to begin to see some of the ways in which children cope with the (apparently) strange behaviour of their ancestors. We are able to see in detail their initial reactions, the strategies they employ to make sense of a past way of life, the way they use evidence and their own experience, their reasoning, the kinds and degrees of understanding achieved, and the relationship between their first response and their final position. The questions they ask themselves and each other, and the way discussion is helped or hindered by their interaction and by our feeding in new material, are additional sources of interest.

II. TRYING TO UNDERSTAND

(a) Confusion and contempt

The quotation that opens this chapter (Excerpt 1, p. 117) is typical of children's first reaction to an alien institution, or to an action that does not on the face of it make sense. It is very close to the reactions we met – in our earlier work – to Jellicoe's turn away at Jutland, and to the sort of responses we frequently see in classrooms; moreover, it is repeated for other content and other age groups.[4] Consider, for example, the following excerpt in which a group of final-year primary schoolchildren discuss the same problems. (These children were of average IQ and from non-academic backgrounds.)[5]

Excerpt 2:
JANE: . . . Stupid . . .   (1)
RICHARD: The best way of finding whether they was guilty or not
    was going and looking in Ethelred's cowshed.
JANE: Yes.
RICHARD: Find out whether the cow was there or not.   (5)
JANE: If he was really . . . if he was really saying that it had gone, or
    just was he accusing the other man because he was jealous or some-
    thing like that?
MAY: Coo, fancy putting your hand in a pot of boiling water!
RICHARD: Phew-er!   (10)
JANE AND MAY: A pot of boiling water.
RICHARD: What puzzles me . . .
JANE: If he floated he was guilty . . . phew!
MAY: What . . .
JANE: If he floated he was guilty, that means they would kill him after-   (15)
    wards.
RICHARD: Yeah but . . . yeah but . . .

JANE: It's stupid . . .

RICHARD: You got it anyway, didn't you . . .

JANE: It you drowned . . .   (20)

RICHARD: What puzzles me . . .

MAY: I'd rather sink . . .

RICHARD: All the fuss they take, I mean why couldn't they just
  say . . .

MAY: . . . you're guilty or not . . .   (25)

RICHARD: No . . . no, you stupid idiot. . . . What puzzles me is why
  do they have to do all this throwing into the water with Ethelred?
  Why don't they just go round to Ethelred's . . .

JANE: Yes.

RICHARD: . . . farm and look in all his cowsheds, search the place?   (30)

JANE: Yes.

MAY: He could be hiding something.

JANE: Could be . . . could be lost . . . It could be lost.

RICHARD: They search the whole place, then if that's not there then
  he'd be not guilty, but . . .   (35)

MAY: Yes, but how do they know it's that man's?

RICHARD: He could've. . . . He could've . . .

MAY: Yes, but how do they know it's that man's?

RICHARD: Well, they just search his place and if it's not there then
  they would know . . .   (40)

MAY: But they could search *anybody's* place . . .

RICHARD: Ethelred's . . .

JANE: They might as well do a whole search of town then that would
  cost them something.

RICHARD: Think of all the money it would take.   (45)

JANE: Yeah, that's what I thought. . . . It's a bit stupid . . . I mean the
  cow could've gone down a ditch or something . . .

The passage that formed the basis for this discussion covered two A4 sides and
described a case in which Wulfric accused Ethelred of stealing a cow. The
children's initial reaction is that the whole system was absurd, a response
resting on assumptions about the Anglo-Saxons for which there is no warrant
in the passage.[6] In the first place it is assumed that the ordeal in particular is
patently insane. During the exchange between lines 9–20 Jane assumes that
ordeal by cold water terminated not merely in the killing of a guilty subject, but
in the drowning of the innocent. Richard concurs: 'You got it anyway, didn't
you . . .' (line 19). There are no grounds for such assumptions in the passage. It
may be that half-grasped tales of witch trials are playing a part here, but for
whatever reason the children seem happy to believe that the Anglo-Saxons
behaved in an unintelligible and senseless manner.[7] In the second place,
throughout Excerpt 2 the assumption is that the system was stupid because
there were plainly much better ways of discovering if someone were guilty or
not. The passage had indicated that evidence was not brought in court as it is
now, but equally, in making clear that a different procedure would be followed

if Ethelred had been caught red-handed, gave grounds for thinking that obvious steps to discover the truth would have been taken. (The passage specifically mentions, for example, the procedures that would have been employed if the cow had been discovered in Ethelred's cowshed.) Richard, none the less, believes that the Anglo-Saxons failed to make the simplest moves to discover what had happened, or even whether a crime had taken place (line 21ff). May and Jane at first agree (lines 29–33). Part of Richard's difficulty lies in his thinking that there was a much simpler course of action – namely searching Ethelred's farm. At least this would have had a chance of establishing Ethelred's innocence. May (line 36) exposes a flaw in this – how do you know where to look? Jane's comment, 'They might as well do a whole search of town then that would cost them something' (line 43), rams the point home, and Richard agrees. At this point the children are beginning to get close to several real constraints on Anglo-Saxon institutions and perhaps partly *because* they are envisaging a 'town' in modern terms, the effort involved in a criminal inquiry looms large. There is nothing available to them, however, that will allow them to connect the scale of Anglo-Saxon society to the problems involved. An intervention was made soon after Excerpt 2 in which the group was given information on the size of the population and the scale of village life, but this information was not successfully harnessed to the problem. The discovery that there was a smaller population in Anglo-Saxon times prompted the children to wonder whether there were so few people because of 'all these punishments'! The timing of such interventions seems to be critical. (See below for a discussion of this.) In the end, Jane's suggestion that the whole business is stupid because 'the cow could've gone down a ditch or something' (line 47) returns the discussion to a concrete sticking point, based on the assumption (originally voiced by Richard) that no one would be sensible enough to try to discover whether a crime had even taken place.

At sixth-form level the reaction is similar, if more complicated.

Excerpt 3:

CATHERINE: A bit superstitious. (1)

KATE: I think I am a bit confused about how much money and everything.

JENNY: Yeah, I thought perhaps it was all to do with God . . . and everything else, but all the money coming into it has completely . . . (5)

CATHERINE: It's . . . . The oaths were so much for each person . . . depending on how much land they own. . . . So what use was money? I mean I don't understand . . .

The confusion over money arose from an initial assumption that oaths were paid for, as opposed to *valued*, in money. An intervention – explaining that no money changed hands – cleared up that point, and allowed progress to be made; but there had been no warrant in the passage for the assumption that oaths were bought. Even at sixth-form level, where possible explanations of what is going on come much more readily, there is at first a willingness to assume the worst: that what was done may well have been absurd. As the argument develops, it is suggested that the system worked on class lines – the rich would find 'heavyweight' oaths to clear themselves, but the poor would have had to go to ordeal. This provides a basis for seeing the ordeal as intelligible at least as a means of social control, but the sixth formers are still ready to assume that the innocent died in most cases – indeed the whole hypothesis that the poor were getting rough treatment rests on this assumption.

Excerpt 4:

> JENNY: Right, if you've got the oath-helping the people who *are* (1)
> higher up have got the chance to be proved innocent whereas if
> you've got the ordeal, I mean, you're not going to get out of it
> with . . .
> KATE: [Laughing] . . . whatever . . . (5)
> JENNY: . . . festering hands and getting drowned, are you? Whoever
> you are . . .
> CATHERINE: Yeah, that's . . . that's like letting the . . . um . . . the
> more important people get out of the oath-helping and the ordinary
> people don't get out of the ordeal. (10)
> JENNY: Yeah.
> [They all laugh.]

The Anglo-Saxon poor at least are thought of as easily taken in – Kate sums it up: 'They *must* have thought at some time that, you know, "Gosh, they're all dying!"' Like the primary schoolchildren, the sixth formers are content to think that the innocent, having sunk the required distance, are left to drown.[8] It is noteworthy that Excerpt 4 follows a long discussion in which some very perceptive remarks are made, and explanations of various kinds advanced (see excerpt 10 below). Despite the fact that they are beginning to get at important issues, part of the assumption of Anglo-Saxon stupidity or gullibility remains. How could people be hoodwinked into such a patently absurd system? The group makes no inquiries into the *details* of the ordeals, but simply assumes that the poor drown or die of their burns in simple-minded droves. Nevertheless, the incredulity and cynicism of the sixth formers is much more complicated and subtle than that of the primary schoolchildren. The idea that the ordeal is a foregone conclusion and spells disaster for those who undergo it is an unjustified assumption, but it is made plausible and fitted into an explanatory framework by the thesis that the institution amounts to a form of social control. A later aside by Kate shows that even incredulous first reactions do not necessarily denote any unwillingness to see a different point of view, even if in the end the cynicism triumphs.

Excerpt 5:

> KATE: Yeah. I think it would be kind of ideal if they all . . . um . . . if (1)
> there wasn't any of the oath-helpers and it was all just oaths . . . and
> you could really take people on their word. It would be really
> marvellous.
> JENNY: The thing is you can't take people on their word. (5)
> [Both Jenny and Kate laugh.]
> KATE: When I read it through at first I thought 'Gosh, you know,

they've got the right idea here'. And they're all saying 'I swear to
God I didn't steal it or I swear to God' you know. But then
again . . . [chuckles cynically].   (10)

Reactions of incredulity in the face of strange past goings-on are not confined
to the Anglo-Saxon material. Here is the response of another group of final-
year primary children, this time to a change in Spartan behaviour.

Excerpt 6:

  [The children search in the text for suitable questions to ask their
  classmates.]

  MELISSA: Look . . . [reads from text] 'and another rule they intro-   (1)
  duced said that they must stop to . . . stop going to games and
  festivals outside Sparta . . .'

  SARAH: Now that *is* a load of rubbish, what reason was there for that?
  [Said with feeling – Melissa and George both laugh.]   (5)

  GEORGE: [Has been writing painstakingly all this time, now looks
  up]: Phew!

  MELISSA: Cos they can't go to . . .

  SARAH: No, no, they used to go up to the *Olympic* games which was
  the most important . . .   (10)

  MELISSA: Yeah, in Olympia.

  SARAH: . . . festival of games, but they can't do . . .

  MELISSA: [Simultaneously]: can't go up there . . . I know, it's stupid
  isn't it.

  SARAH: It's stupid . . . what . . . what reason could they have thought   (15)
  of that?

  MELISSA: [Reading]: 'Athletics was still a very important part of their
  life . . .'

  SARAH: [Interrupting]: But you still couldn't go out . . .

  MELISSA: [Continues to read]: 'But they stopped competing outside   (20)
  Sparta.' It's stupid, isn't it?

  SARAH: [Shaking her head]: It's stupid, they, you get, you get, you
  get so used to other people wouldn't you.

  MELISSA: [Reading]:'For a long time they . . .' – look – 'For a long
  time they had won more events at the Olympic games than any-   (25)
  body else. But they even stopped going to the most famous games
  of all. They still trained very hard. But we hear of no more Spartan
  competitors at the Olympic games.'

  SARAH: Even now!

  MELISSA: Yeah, I know, its stupid.   (30)

  SARAH: We've never heard of Spartan ones . . . we hear, can hear of
  people from Greece . . .

The incomprehensibility of the Spartan decision is emphasized by its finality –
'even now' we do not hear of Spartan competitors![9] The passage that evoked
this response made the numerical relationships between helots and Spartans
clear, together with the manner in which the Spartans treated the helots. It also

set this particular rule in the context of others, mostly concerned with education, but also with the conduct of war, and with policy towards other states.

Where does this kind of puzzlement and incomprehension come from? It has its origins both in assumptions about how things ought to be done – assumptions as to the values one ought to hold and about the efficiency or inefficiency of particular practical procedures – and assumptions as to how people behave as a matter of fact. These allow children to interpret strange goings-on as indications of absurdity on the part of people in the past, before they begin to wonder whether there is not more to it all.[10] The group of third years already quoted, having made some attempt to explain Anglo-Saxon behaviour, were asked if anything else puzzled them.

Excerpt 7:

GINA: It . . . they . . . it couldn't have been a . . . really sound method, (1) could it, of finding out who was guilty or not?

MARY: It isn't, is it?

GINA: I'm not really puzzled.

MARY: No *I'm* not puzzled, just sort of shocked. [Smiles at her (5) paper.] Nine out of ten times they'd die, wouldn't they, with these sort of methods? . . . Something more original . . . I suppose they were more original in them days.

GINA: [Mumbles to herself, then]: Bit funny way of going about it, (10) innit?
[They all laugh.]

MARY: No they wouldn't shock me after half the things . . . um . . . you know, in these sort of days. They're all like this, n't they?

LINDA: [Talks inaudibly below Mary's contribution.] (15)

GINA: No. [It is not clear who this is directed at.]

LINDA: You wouldn't think of going round doing that though, would you? I mean . . .

GINA: [Talking simultaneously with Linda and Mary]: *Those* days they would. (20)

LINDA: Not *that*. If you found . . .

MARY: [Also simultaneously]: *They* would. I suppose in ten years' time they'll be saying 'Oh, they didn't go round doing *that* did they? Letting people go when they're guilty' . . . you know, that way. I suppose in ten years' time they'll all be just going . . . you (25) know . . . 'Oh, it doesn't matter. We ain't got no witnesses so you can go.'

LINDA: [Simultaneously]: In their way of thinking . . . . In their way of thinking . . . . In their way of thinking that was a reasonable approach to it or something like that, you know. [She subsides into (30) mumbling.]

LINDA and GINA: [Both simultaneously talk briefly but inaudibly.]

MARY: They must have enjoyed looking at suffering . . . because

they're not giving them a chance, are they? They might have been
guilty or again they might be innocent. (35)
GINA: [Interrupting]: That's stupid.
[Long pause.]

Neither Gina nor Mary is prepared to admit to being puzzled, and although Mary is initially 'sort of shocked' (line 5), once she starts to think about it even this is withdrawn on the grounds that this sort of behaviour was only to be expected of people 'in these sort of days. They're all like this, n't they?' (line 14). Partly on the basis of this expectation Mary draws a clear distinction between Anglo-Saxon behaviour and our own; but equally it is her conception of current attitudes to law and order that allows the distinction. She can see that in the future *our* behaviour may look odd to our successors (or perhaps even to us). How far this represents a genuine ability to move between different temporal points of view it is hard to say: what may be happening here is that a current 'soft' attitude is being criticized in terms of another *current* – this time 'hard' – attitude towards law and order.[11] Nevertheless it is interesting that, if this is so, the criticism is given weight by an imaginary future historical perspective. Mary is prepared to accept that 'their way of thinking' might make Anglo-Saxon institutions seem reasonable; yet in the end she is convinced that the system is absurd because innocent and guilty will both be likely to die in the ordeal. Gina is even clearer as the exchange grinds to a temporary halt: the system is stupid.

(b) Understanding and explaining

The examples given so far are typical of first reactions. Children seldom stick at this point (although some do) but there are grounds for thinking that if they are not given time to explore the material and their own experience, and not given questions that force them to do this, convenient and ready-made assumptions about the inferiority and absurdity of people in the past will remain undisturbed. However, it is encouraging that in most cases once children have vented their surprise at the strange behaviour they have vicariously encountered, they settle down to make sense of it.

Excerpt 8:
GINA: It was an easier way of doing it. They didn't know any other (1)
way of doing it.
MARY: [Interrupting]: Yeah. They weren't adv' ... as advanced as
us, ... I suppose.
GINA: We're not that advanced are we, when it comes to court? (5)
LINDA: [Laughs.]
MARY: Not in court ... I don't suppose so.
GINA: You can get away with anything in court now.
[Murmur of agreement from the other two. Long pause. They look
at the papers and grin at each other.] (10)
GINA: I think they just used that because they didn't know any other
way of using ...
MARY: [Interrupting]: There is no ... there was no other way, I

don't suppose. There wasn't no evidence that he *did* steal it
anyway . . . and there wasn't that he didn't.   (15)
LINDA: [Again speaking quietly, and at first inaudibly]: Oh gosh,
silly really, isn't it?

The approach of the third years here is unsophisticated, and again exposes
condescending assumptions: oath-helping and ordeal are the best a backward
people can manage. On the other hand, a basic problem is picked up – the lack
of evidence – and the children use their picture of modern life to qualify the
initial condescension. Later on the connection is made between the strange
Anglo-Saxon behaviour and their beliefs about God, but the implications are
not drawn out before an attempt is made to go behind the Anglo-Saxon
conception in order to suggest deeper and darker goings-on. (But this point in
turn depends on seeing that the background circumstances in which people
lived have to be taken into account – in this case the incidence of disease.)

Excerpt 9:
MARY: They must have worshipped him, and all that . . . God. This   (1)
bit here, if you *did* wrong he was likely to make *you*, and . . . and
your relatives and that, suffer.
GINA: [Coming in as Mary finishes]: Where is that? Oh yeah.
MARY: [Continues]: So it's not only *you*, which I would have thought   (5)
[inaudible] . . .
LINDA: [Drowning Mary]: It's the whole family . . .
MARY: Yeah . . .
LINDA: Which is a bit . . . you know . . .
MARY: I don't believe in all that *miracles* business but . . . it is a bit of a   (10)
coincidence though, isn't it.
GINA: Yeah.
MARY: [Continuing] . . . about you and your kin suffering.
GINA: But that would be all . . . um . . . [she flaps her paper struggling
to recall the point] . . . all the diseases they had flying about the   (15)
place. [They all laugh.]
GINA: They didn't [inaudible] wash much, did they?
[Linda and Mary both laugh.]
LINDA: Yeah, the Black Death [and something inaudible].
MARY: Yeah, the plague and that.   (20)
GINA: So they're bound to get diseases and things, and die off.
MARY: Mm . . .
LINDA: [Inaudible as Mary coughs]: that . . . was the punishment
that he gave to 'em. [Inaudible]: done something wrong or some-
thing.   (25)
MARY: I suppose the priests were happy about that . . . all these
people believing in God.
GINA: [Laughs.]
MARY: [Continues]: They might . . . have . . . gone into another
village, made someone go to their own village, catch a disease . . .   (30)
[They all laugh.]

At sixth-form level there is a more differentiated response, which reveals very clearly some of the problems.

Excerpt 10:

KATE: So the question is why do you think the Anglo-Saxons used (1) oath-helping in order to find out if someone is guilty of a crime? So I suppose that would be because they attached importance to God.

JENNY: Yeah, it's superstition isn't it? I mean . . . (5)

KATE: Yeah.

JENNY: Especially a crime where you haven't got any witnesses . . . I mean, if you believe in God the only witness around *is* God, isn't it? So therefore I suppose this is a way of attaching something to God. (10)

KATE: But, um, they used an oath to . . . in all kinds of . . . um . . . trials.

JENNY: But you use an oath now, don't you.

KATE: But you don't . . . . Am I right in supposing that if you say, 'I swear to God I'm not guilty' then . . . they sort of think 'Ah, he (15) isn't'?

JENNY: [Inaudible brief comment, then]: The thing is that you can swear that you are not guilty but you've got to get so many people to swear with you that you are not guilty, that they think you are not guilty. (20)

KATE: And the more money those people . . . the more their oath is worth then the more . . .

JENNY and CATHERINE: . . . your case is aired.

KATE: [Almost simultaneously]: Yeah.

JENNY: So, the thing is, if you've got . . . say the cow is worth 20 (25) shillings as it is here, if you can get that many people to swear that you are not guilty [Kate nods agreement], I suppose it is a sign of your innocence, I mean if you can get so many people to testify for you, on your behalf, of innocence.

KATE: [Looking at the pamphlet]: What's it go on to say later about (30) the . . . um . . .?

CATHERINE: That's . . . [inaudible and interrupted by Jenny].

JENNY: That's an eyewitness isn't it?

KATE: So it's . . .

What happened if Ethelred couldn't find enough people to swear (35) for him? . . . Presumably if he *did* find enough people to swear for him then that would mean he wasn't guilty.

JENNY: Well, he might not have been but . . .

KATE: [Over Jenny saying something similar]: Oh, well that shows the faith they had in . . . I mean the importance they attached to (40) God.

JENNY: Yeah.

KATE: Because it's . . . um . . . because it's the be all and end all, just swearing out loud.

[Pause – they gaze at their papers.] (45)

JENNY: What about the ordeal though?

KATE: That's because he couldn't find out . . . people to swear for him.

JENNY: So he'd have to go and . . . first of all he's judged in front of the people who lived there and all that sort of thing, and then he's (50) judged in front of God himself, isn't he, by these ordeals.

KATE: Amazing isn't it.

[All three laugh.]

JENNY: It's stupid. When you think about all this water business, I mean it's . . . (55)

[For a moment they all talk at once. Then]:

CATHERINE: What do you expect?

JENNY: You take for granted that you're going to float, aren't you? I mean, unless you tie a weight to yourself. You – you drown both ways don't you? (60)

[Pauses and looks at the others for their agreement, as she says]: So we've got it as superstition, haven't we?

KATE: [Inaudible – subsides.]

CATHERINE: Yeah . . . just a thought . . . leaving it to God.

KATE: [Interrupting Catherine]: I'm not sure whether it is (65) superstition though. I mean, I don't know whether that is the right word to use because . . . um . . . to them God was not a superstitious thing.

JENNY: It's just a religion isn't it? I mean, it's just such a strong religion that they've got nothing else. (70)

KATE: [Simultaneously]: I mean . . . if . . .

JENNY: I mean if you believe in something wholeheartedly all the time . . .

KATE: 'Cos today we tend to class . . . um . . . God and religion . . . or . . . 'specially people who don't believe in God, as a (75) superstitious thing but, I mean, people who believe in God don't think it's superstitious . . . so . . .

JENNY: [Interrupting]: So we'll just say it's a strong faith in God then.

CATHERINE: Yeah . . . and a belief in nature – that sort of thing. (80)

JENNY: [Simultaneously]: Yeah.

Really – and um . . . yeah . . . human nature. I mean, if somebody is good all their life . . .

KATE: [Interrupting]: In the . . . in the . . .

JENNY: To get these people to swear by them. (85)

KATE: [Almost simultaneously]: In the question it says 'Oath-Helping', so is oath-helping . . . um . . . oath-helping is all his friends, isn't it?

JENNY: Yeah.

KATE: So why do you think Anglo-Saxons used oath-helping? (90)

JENNY: Well, the oath-helping is character judgement of other people, isn't it? [Looks to see what response is.] I mean, by the people around you. I mean if you generally do things which aren't very socially accepted you're going to be like . . . you're not going to get anyone to come up saying . . . 'I'll help you . . . um . . .' (95)

KATE: [Simultaneously]: Presumably . . .
Also . . . um . . .

CATHERINE: Yeah, but that's not it. I mean, it depends on how much land you own. Suppose you're a poor person . . .

JENNY: No but it doesn't say that. The thing is that you don't have (100) to . . . [Looks at paper.] It's not that . . . I don't think it's the poor people and all that. I think it's just whether you can muster up the people to come.

CATHERINE: Yeah, but they're worth how much land they've got.

JENNY: [Points to paper]: No, look they're worth twenty shillings. (105) 'Cos the cow was worth 20 shillings you've got to get the amount of people to . . . er . . . make up that amount of money.

CATHERINE: [Reading from and pointing to the pamphlet]: But 'In Anglo-Saxon times a man's oath was worth a certain amount of money, depending on how much land he owned . . .' (110)

JENNY: Aah.

CATHERINE: '. . . or how important he was.'

KATE: So therefore if – er – you were – er – a poor Anglo-Saxon then you couldn't use your friends. You were all poor . . .

JENNY: [Simultaneously]: Yeah. (115)

KATE: So you had to get, so therefore if you were . . .

JENNY: So really it's judging before you've even started because the poorer people got off with the worst deal anyway.

KATE: Yeah, yeah . . .

Kate's first move is to make preliminary sense of oath-helping and ordeal by taking them as signs of the importance attached to God. Jenny (lines 7–10) makes another advance, attempting to show that in the circumstances this was not irrational. But the institutions are still seen as essentially superstitious, even after further exploration and a confirmation of the importance of faith in God. Despite Jenny's concise summary (lines 49–51) of ways in which sense might be made of what happened, all three sixth formers go through a further period of incredulity in which the ordeal by cold water is assumed to be fatal to all comers, and Jenny herself sums up 'So we've got it as superstition, haven't we?' (line 62). At this point Kate makes a new move (lines 65–8) 'I'm not sure if it *is* superstition though' and in an exercise of historical imagination attempts to distinguish the Anglo-Saxon point of view from that taken by the group (lines 74–7). Next Jenny tries to resolve the problem of how exactly oath-helping fits into this pattern (lines 91–5). (The implicit problem troubling Kate at line 90 seems to be why, if God is the arbiter, a simple oath by the accused person is not sufficient – see Excerpt 5 above.) Jenny begins to fit the institution into a social context, but is brought up short by Catherine (line 98), 'Yeah, but that's not it'. Jenny at first resists Catherine's interpretation, which makes wealth central, but after looking at the passage, concedes (line 111). From here to the end of the excerpt the group explores the implications of this further social dimension. (But note that there is still at least a vestigial amazement – even contempt – for the gullibility of the poor, as referred to above in the discussion of Excerpt 4.)

The relationship between the attempt to understand the problematic practices from the point of view of those who employed them, and the attempt to offer a 'deeper' explanation from our current point of view is difficult to capture in a few short excerpts. At one point Catherine's explanation verges on a conspiracy theory: '. . . the more important people get out of oath-helping' – meaning they find no difficulty in getting together an oath of sufficient value – 'and the ordinary people *don't* get out of the ordeal' (Excerpt 4 lines 8–10). The discussion of the first question ends in an illuminating exchange.

Excerpt 11:

JENNY: I mean . . . It's like er . . . judgement before man and judge-   (1)
  ment before God, isn't it?

CATHERINE: If you're innocent God will see you through.

JENNY: Yeah. But I don't think it is . . . [inaudible] the same myself.
  [Again inaudible] . . . hands and floating around in rivers, etc.   (5)

KATE: I think that . . . I mean it is totally . . . . You would have
  thought they would have been a bit more sensible about it.

JENNY: [Interrupting]: Yeah. But if you . . . I mean . . .

KATE: Or ask for a sign, like, say, striking down dead . . . if he's
  guilty.   (10)

JENNY: With a thunderbolt.
  [Jenny and Catherine laugh.]

KATE: I mean a couple of [inaudible].

JENNY: The thing is this is most probably made up by . . .

KATE: [Interrupting]: It's as if they're saying, you know, 'They are   (15)
  causing trouble, chuck them in the pond.' And . . . [peters out].

JENNY: [Continuing]: But if you look at it, it seems, like you said, it
  seems quite a rational way to do it. It's not until you start looking
  into it deeper that you can see that for those who have got more
  land and everything else they are able to sort of twist it for their own   (20)
  advantages, aren't they? So therefore it's there for their own
  advantages.
  [They all write.]

Jenny (lines 1–2) and Catherine (line 3) summarize the earlier attempts to understand what was going on; Kate, for all her sensitivity to points of view other than her own, still finds the whole business hard to take (lines 6–7). Jenny finally sums up what she sees as the deeper approach (lines 17–22). More light is shed on how the relationship between the two different ways of making sense of things is seen by the sixth formers when they discuss question three. Kate tries to fit the two together, but her efforts are not entirely understood.

Excerpt 12:

    CATHERINE: I think... I think... it's also how much you   (1)
    believed... you know... the will of God.

    JENNY: Yeah. Believes [inaudible].

    CATHERINE: [Agreeing]: Um...

    KATE: Um... I'm not sure about that... Um... I mean, it's   (5)
    probably the way the system is explained, not how it's interpreted,
    if you see what I mean.

    JENNY: No. I don't.

    KATE: Um... like they might have come along and said, 'Well, you
    see... um... we, er, we say to... um... we say to God because   (10)
    he knows', instead of us thinking, well, you know, God *doesn't*
    know. He, he would have explained if from his point of view, but
    then again [quickly correcting herself] he would have interpreted it
    from his point of view. It's the wrong way round.

    JENNY: Pardon?   (15)

    [They all laugh.]

    KATE: [Smiling]: I'm just mumbling.

Despite Kate's uncertainty about the words 'explain' and 'interpret', this is a remarkably sophisticated second-order point (that is, *about* the concepts in history, not simply employing them *within* history), the more so in that it arises spontaneously. Kate is distinguishing between the way an Anglo-Saxon might set about enabling an outsider to make sense of oath-helping and the ordeal by relating it to other Anglo-Saxon beliefs and values, and what *we* might want to say about both the practice and the Anglo-Saxon account of it. Our explanation might well go beyond the Anglo-Saxon account – which is just what the group does in suggesting that the system functioned as a form of social control in which the rich preserved themselves against the poor.

At primary-school level the discussion is in general much more concrete: indeed the pupils have to work through what seem to them anomalous details to their own satisfaction before they can even begin to tackle the questions asked. (We will discuss this exploratory activity further below.) But at the end of the extract Richard and Jane are using these concrete explorations to good purpose.

Excerpt 13:

    RICHARD: [Reading pamphlet]: 'If you swear an oath in court you   (1)
    are promising that what you say is true. In Anglo-Saxon times
    people swore on something holy (like a Bible or a saint's bones).'
    [They all laugh ruefully.]
    That's nice isn't it!   (5)

    MAY: A saint's bones! [They all show surprise.] How can they tell...
    how do you know... if they're buried whole, how are you going to
    get saints' bones?

    RICHARD: No... no... it means... um... like er... suppose you
    swear by the bones...   (10)

    MAY: It sounds like that though, doesn't it...

RICHARD: Suppose like you say 'On St George's bones I didn't do it'...

JANE: Yeah but how do you know... how do you know... er... 'cos... um... when... when... (15)

MAY: They have a whole Bible there, don't they...

JANE: When the people die and they don't usually know... when they're still alive they don't usually know they're going to become saints... so... and they've already been dead'n buried that means they must dig 'em up... bones up... (20)

RICHARD: [Has been looking at the pamphlet while Jane speaks]: You see this...

JANE: [Continuing her own thoughts]: Must be a book...

RICHARD: [Now getting the attention of the others, reads out from his pamphlet.] 'They swear on something holy (like a Bible or a (25) saint's bones). That meant they were promising God they were telling the truth.' For all they know he could be lying...

JANE: Yeah.

RICHARD: ...and then praying to God afterwards...

JANE: That proves... that proves they believed in God more than (30) what we do now... don't it, really.

An important part in the real progress made by these 10-year-olds towards making sense of Anglo-Saxon justice is played by the deployment of the children's own experience of promises. (See Excerpts 22 and 24 below.) Prior knowledge of other parts of the past can also provide a key for interpreting the unknown. Consider this discussion, in which the same group of primary children as in Excerpt 6 try to work out questions to set their classmates on the passage describing Spartan education.

Excerpt 14:

SARAH: Do you know what... why... you know... why, why (1) they trained so much?

GEORGE: It says something about 10,000 Spartans and 300,000 other people, why didn't they rebel against them?

SARAH: They didn't have the weapons. (5)

GEORGE: [inaudible beginning, then]: ...just fight with farm things.

MELISSA: Yeah, they had forks.

SARAH: No, I still don't agree with that, 'cos these Spartans, well, I think they, they had lived so much under these Spartans you see, (10) so many years, they'd grown to fear them, you know, they had nothing to fear at all because they were, you know, in numbers they were larger, and they could fight with really anything in those days.

GEORGE: Mmm...

MELISSA: Sticks and stones... (15)

SARAH: [Loudly to silence interruption from other two]: During the ages, during the ages they've got so used to being under the

Spartans, they can't, they can't think of living without them.   (20)

GEORGE: True ... mmm ...

SARAH: And ...

GEORGE: What about, what about this piece here ... look ... er.

MELISSA: [Whispers]: Say it louder.

GEORGE: Oh, not *that*.

MELISSA: [Whispers again]: Say it louder ... [inaudible] say it   (25)
louder.

GEORGE: [Reading and echoed by Melissa]: 'They chose 2,000 of
their best men, the Spartans marched them away, then they killed
them all.' [Looks at Melissa with a horrified expression.] They
tried to keep them [inaudible] though, I think that's because they   (30)
[inaudible] ...

MELISSA: [Interrupting]: Why did, why did they do that?

SARAH: It explains it there [pointing to text] ... um ...

GEORGE: They just wouldn't, they didn't want them to fight against
them and all that.   (35)

SARAH: Yeah, they ju ... they j ... they asked them ...

MELISSA: [Looking at George]: Did they kill them?

GEORGE: Yeah.

SARAH: Stupid!

GEORGE: It's not, it's horrible! [Grins ruefully at Melissa.]   (40)

SARAH: [Emphasizing her words by gesticulating with pencil]:
They asked them, you know, who ... who had served the
Spartans best, they chose the best ones, you know ... so they
would share the awards and so on ...

MELISSA: [Talking to Sarah]: Can you get off my thing [pulling   (45)
paper from under Sarah's elbow].

GEORGE: Who ... who?

SARAH: My s ... [then looking at George and solicitously answering his question]. I think it was to perhaps frighten them off.
[Pause.]   (50)

GEORGE: [Looking at paper]: What's all this?

MELISSA: [Reading]: 'From the age of 7 to 12 all boys and girls had
to run ... they had to run races and wrestle each other' [smiles at
George and then laughs].   (55)

SARAH: [Talking through laughter at first]: Make their race ...
Hitler did it ... Hitler did that to make his race better, you know,
he threw out all the Jews ... this is what they're doing ...

MELISSA: Why are they ... why are they wrestling ... ?

SARAH: ... you know, 'cos in those days, they, they, you know,
girls and boys, you know, they were practically the same, you   (60)
could wrestle and things, in wars and things, you know, if there's
going to be a war they're going to be the superior race.

MELISSA: [Turns to George]: You could put 'Why ... why ... why
did they run ... why did they ... make their children run races
and ... er ... wrestle?'   (65)

SARAH: [Inaudible.]

GEORGE: I've got to write . . . [confidingly] well, 'cos *they* don't know much about this . . . I'm going to write 'Why didn't they rebel?' . . . for a question, they don't know much do they?

MELISSA: But why . . . but why? (70)

SARAH: Yes . . . oh they weren't given that *training*! . . . you know . . .

MELISSA: [Reads from text to herself]: 'less than 10,000 . . .'

SARAH: We're given the training of freedom . . . right . . . we're given this ever since we grew up . . . (75)
[Melissa continues to read to herself under her breath.]
. . . we have had freedom . . .

GEORGE: [Listening to Sarah]: . . . Mmm . . .

SARAH: . . . In different ways . . . but these people never had freedom at all, so they can't imagine life without being sl . . . enslaves [sic] . . . right . . . they don't know what it's like, they'd be scared of it. (80)

GEORGE: True.

MELISSA: [Turning to George]: Could do sort . . . the question like that . . .

GEORGE: Mmm . . . (85)

SARAH: And . . . on the question of . . . um . . .

GEORGE: [Starts to write]: . . . shall have to write . . .

SARAH: . . . you know [taps pencil] . . .

MELISSA: You know that one about why did they . . . why didn't they rebel . . .? (90)

SARAH: . . . all these people . . .

GEORGE: [Writing]: This one's all wrong . . .

SARAH: [Sighs]: . . . I wond . . . I wond . . . I wonder . . . you know this Laconia . . . er, what's it called . . . (95)

MELISSA: [Talking to George]: Why did . . . Why didn't?

SARAH: [Continues, poking Melissa with her pencil to get her attention]: What's yer name . . . well . . . that's funny, it says that they got Laconia and Messenia, that's because of these, this training they're giving these children, right . . . (100)

MELISSA: [Interrupting]: What [inaudible] . . . So it says . . .

SARAH: [Refusing to be interrupted, and talking over Melissa]: . . . from an early age, right, so they grow up to fight, and they're going to want, um, you know, think of fighting for their country only . . . (105)

GEORGE: What's the name . . .?

SARAH: . . . they give 'em this training, since they were babies.

GEORGE: What's the name of the, um, Spartans' . . . What's the name of the Spartans' . . . enemy, that they attacked and conquered?

MELISSA: [Starting to read]: 'Spartans . . .' (110)

SARAH: Messenia and Laconia, and . . . [inaudible]

MELISSA: [Starts to read again, but is immediately interrupted by
    someone coming into the room. Tape stopped and then
    restarted.]   (115)
SARAH: And so, the same, the Spartans this is, were...
    they... they train their children from an early age to... to be
    perfect in all things, so if there was a war, they, they would be
    certainly the superior race.
GEORGE: Mmm...   (120)
SARAH: And that's why they put their babies – weak babies – on to
    hills and kept the strong ones... you know they used to put
    their... weak ones...
MELISSA: That's what...
SARAH: ...on to a hill and let them die. [Looks at George for   (125)
    reaction.]

In several places in this excerpt Sarah brings to bear an analysis derived from
what she remembers of other periods of history (for example in lines 55–7),
and also works out the difference in behaviour that is likely to follow different
ways of being treated (especially lines 9–14, 17–19, 74–5 and 79–82). The strategies made available by her analogies enable her to make sense of a range of
anomalies that for the other children seem to remain separate problems. Sarah
is able to provide a tentative context in which to set the anomalies, and to
display various elements of Spartan behaviour as being responses to the same
overall problem – the relation between Spartans and Helots.

With the Anglo-Saxon material, an important part of understanding oath-
helping and trial by ordeal is to see them as pointing to certain kinds of beliefs
about God. The first step is to redescribe the relevant practices in terms that
show what people thought they were doing – making an appeal to God. A
further step is to see how an appeal to God made sense in a wider framework of
beliefs and in the context of a particular way of life. Once things are understood
in this way it is possible to suggest explanations that go behind the Anglo-
Saxons' own account, and try to show (for example) how institutions of this
kind might serve particular interests, or have certain functions, whatever any
participant might have said about them. All three age groups (primary, third
year and sixth form) made the connection with beliefs about God, and the third
years and sixth formers tried to go behind this. But the third years made no
more progress in grasping the implications of the connection with God than the
primary schoolchildren. In fact the primary children explored the point of
giving oaths in more concrete detail than the third years, and came to the conclusion that 'if you swear an oath on God... then you probably would tell the
truth'. (See Excerpts 22 and 24 below.)

In schematic terms, there is a consistent pattern of response to the material
whether it is concerned with Anglo-Saxon justice or Spartan education. The
opening phase is one of astonishment, puzzlement, and cynicism. The
practices under investigation are taken to be simply absurd. This is followed
more or less rapidly by an exploration of the concrete details of the practice,
often leading up blind alleys. During this period interpretations are made that

provide a preliminary understanding, and sometimes these lead to attempts to explain the relevant institution from a historian's (as opposed to a contemporary) viewpoint. Suggested explanations are gradually refined, but this is not an even, progressive process, but something circuitous, proceeding in fits and starts.

(c) What makes a difference? (contributions to success or failure)

The transcripts in sections (a) and (b) show the spasmodic nature of each group's progress in making sense of the strange goings-on that they were asked to explain. They also reveal the children employing their experience and the information provided in a variety of ways in their search for understanding and explanations that satisfy them. Section (c) explores the contributions that particular elements appear to make to their success or failure.

Some knowledge of the details of the past social practices being studied and their particular context of life is required in order to redescribe the practices in terms of what the people at the time thought they were doing, or to go beyond this and fit them into the wider framework of their beliefs. The transcripts show our children acquiring many relevant details by picking out specific points from the information provided. Sometimes they simply locate and accept them without question or comment; almost as frequently they take time to sort out the meaning to their satisfaction (see, for example, Excerpt 9, lines 1–8). On a number of occasions aspects of the situation are clarified as a result of puzzlement – arising from either the material supplied or their 'second record' – being articulated and someone providing relevant assistance. In the excerpt below one third former raises a question and another immediately corrects the misconception that it reveals.

Excerpt 15:

> LINDA: The thing about . . . punishment, right? . . . and the way   (1)
> they were . . . but it says here they . . . they usually *knew* who was
> doing it and who was usually the honest ones . . . I mean, if they
> *knew* why did they deal the punishment on to all these people?
> MARY: Well, they didn't know. It was just a suspicion, wasn't it?   (5)
> [inaudible] . . . being no evidence.

All this seems to emphasize that children need access to information that gives them a realistic chance of gaining understanding and opportunities to explore it, preferably for at least part of the time with their peers.

The importance of imagination as supposal in the successful use of evidence is twofold: the children's exercise of imagination can indicate what has been understood and what not, and at the same time it is by trying to cash what is available to them that they make progress. Imagination may be relatively sophisticated, or it may involve working out concrete consequences of specific actions in specific situations. At one point in the sixth-form discussion Kate says (in a slightly disparaging tone) '. . . they didn't need to take evidence into account . . . . It was all God.' After a moment's thought she adds, 'But there again, if God is a person who sees all, knows all and . . .' (Jenny interpolates 'Does all'.) '. . . then he wouldn't need to look at the evidence, would he? . . . 'cos . . . 'cos he knows it all.' At primary level the supposal is likely to be more concrete, but plays an important role in the children's efforts to sort out relevant possibilities, even if in the end it is sometimes harnessed to something other than the question asked.

Excerpt 16:
   RICHARD: Suppose you were an Anglo-. . . er . . .   (1)
   JANE: Saxon.
   RICHARD: Saxon, and you did steal the cow, . . .
   MAY: I'd just try and make . . .
   RICHARD: [Very definitely]: You were Ethelred and you *did* steal the   (5)
      cow . . . now um . . .
   JANE: Ethelred's the one who owned the cow in the first place . . .
   RICHARD: No . . . Wul . . . Wul . . . Wulfric owns the cow. Ethelred
      . . . He thinks Ethelred stole it. Now suppose you were Ethelred,
      and you *did* steal the cow, how would you . . . how would you . . .   (10)
   JANE: Try and make up for it . . . make up for it any way I could . . .
   RICHARD: But supposing he was a real bad criminal . . . I mean
      suppose Ethelred had stolen many cows . . .
   JANE: Well, I'd cut . . . if I was . . . if I did do that . . . I would most   (15)
      probably skin the cow, and leave it in the ditch . . .
   RICHARD: [Laughing ruefully]: Oh, that's nice!
   JANE: Yeah!
   [All start to talk, then stop.]
   MAY: But they'd soon find the body though, wouldn't they . . .   (20)
   JANE: No, not if you'd eaten it . . . not if you'd eaten it. They'd just
      think the cow had wandered and rotted away. . . wouldn't they . . .
   RICHARD: No!
   JANE: They would . . . Must be . . .
   MAY: [Asks about finding the body: exact words unintelligible   (25)
      because Richard starts talking.]
   RICHARD: I couldn't steal a cow in the first place . . .
   JANE: Yeah – but if you did . . .
   RICHARD: How would you take it away? . . . How would you take it
      away?   (30)
   JANE: What do you mean, how would I take it away?
   RICHARD: Well Mr . . . Hang on . . . Wulfric has got all his cows in
      a . . . no, he's got two cows in a kind of a . . .
   JANE: Pen . . .
   RICHARD: [Almost simultaneously with Jane]: . . . pen thing . . .   (35)
      Right, now . . . Now Wulfric's indoors having his dinner and so
      Ethelfred . . Ethel . . . red says 'Ah, right, he's gone in, he's gone
      in, he's in the back room eating his dinner so I think I'll nick his
      cow', er . . . how do you take the cow away? You can't pick it
      up . . .   (40)
   JANE: No, you'd lead it away!

RICHARD and MAY: [Simultaneously]: No but... say 'Now come on'... [laughs] It would start mooing and making a noise...

RICHARD: Start mooing...

JANE: You'd tie a rope round her neck... (45)

MAY: No, but it would start mooing.

[Jane says something to May who says something inaudible to Jane while Richard carries on.]

RICHARD: Making a noise, making a noise so... so what, so what I probably think, was that the cow probably... fallen into a (50) ditch... or... or... um.

JANE: [Interpolates]: Or...

RICHARD: Wulfric... hated Ethelred and he wanted to get him into trouble so what he did is he hid his cow... Wulfric hid the cow and claimed that Ethelred had stolen it... (55)

JANE: Yeah.

RICHARD: [Continues]: ... to get Ethelred in trouble.

JANE: Yeah. That's most probably it, because... perhaps he was jealous of him because he had more... He had the prize bull or something like that. (60)

In this instance the evidence provided and imagination as supposal enable the group to sort out the concrete consequences of specific actions in a specific situation and to suggest a possible explanation of the particular theft described in the main source. The third formers also call upon imagination as supposal to get at quite basic details of the situation.

Excerpt 17:

MARY: [Looks at the paper and says]: And about the laws down (1) here... he could make the laws up as he goes along, King... King Alfred, couldn't he?

[Long pause, then]: And I suppose when one king dies and you get another one he made up an... another lot of laws... (5)

GINA: [Comes in]: He changed 'em, didn't he?

MARY: [Continues]: Yeah. 'Cos he can make them up as he goes on 'cos it says that... um... not all the laws were written down. You know, if...

[Linda meanwhile is writing during the latter part of this. Gina is (10) looking around and obviously thinking. She now says]:

GINA: Where does it say that?

[She immediately answers her own question]: Oh, there it is.

MARY: [Simultaneously]: Bottom of the laws [i.e. passage on the laws]. [Long pause, then]: So... if you had been caught stealing (15) *once* no one would trust you again...

After a brief digression sustained – though slightly fanciful – supposal is again in evidence with the third formers exploring further details of Anglo-Saxon law and order.[12]

Excerpt 18:

MARY: I suppose people learnt the laws that mattered so they didn't (1)
get accused of anything . . .

LINDA: [Talks inaudibly under Mary.]

MARY: . . . but I suppose any little thing that they'd done they'd get
accused of that 'nd all. And they couldn't argue with King Alfred (5)
'cos he'd say 'Well, I haven't written it down – it's true, you know'.

GINA: He could change it if he wanted to.

MARY: Yeah.
[Linda and Gina both write as Mary continues after a pause.]
So he . . . somebody could be just sort of . . . I don't know, writing (10)
something . . . and um . . . King Alfred could say 'Oh, I didn't say
writing. I said so and so'.

GINA: [Laughs appreciatively.]

MARY: [Continues]: He can make it all up as he goes along . . . which
is handy really, isn't it? (15)
He can put his enemies away an' all.

The use that children make of their present-day experience is another
important factor in making sense of past social practices. If they simply ascribe
contemporary dispositions and assumptions (or generalized goals and beliefs)
to people in the past independently of evidence about them then their experience is likely to be of little or no help. If, however, they consider both their
experience and the evidence provided in search of comparisons and contrasts
they are likely to increase their understanding of the situation, and consequently to find the past becoming more intelligible to them. Our transcripts
reveal all the groups making significant advances on several occasions as a
result of the effective use of contemporary experience. For example, in Excerpt
7 Mary's conception of current attitudes to law and order enables her to draw a
clear distinction between Anglo-Saxon behaviour and our own (see lines 7–9
and 22–7) and this in turn encourages Linda to think about Anglo-Saxon
practices from 'their way of thinking' (lines 28–30). A little later Mary's
reflection on past and present attitudes to miracles and the weather leads her to
infer that they must have worshipped God.

Excerpt 19:

MARY: [Looks thoughtfully at the papers and says]: It says here (1)
about miracles. Well, now we don't consider rain a miracle and the
rest of it, do we?

GINA: Sun. When we have sun.

MARY: [Laughs, says something inaudible and then]: Not rain. We (5)
don't think much of that nowadays. [Pause.] They must have worshipped him, and all that . . . God.

Unfortunately the girls fail to draw out the relevant implications (see Excerpt
9) but their later explorations do provide further evidence of the value of their
efforts to utilize the sources supplied and their present-day experience in search
of comparisons and contrasts. For instance, after Gina and Mary have

examined the information provided about the size of the Anglo-Saxon population, and drawn comparisons between village life then and contemporary life in a large school and sprawling metropolis, Mary reaches the conclusion that in an Anglo-Saxon village 'everybody knew each other there so it isn't like now' and 'it was all just like some big family really'.

The same strategy enables Mary to draw an analogy between stolen cattle then and stolen cars now. Analogies, whether derived from present-day experience like Mary's or from knowledge of other periods of the past, are important for a number of reasons. They can provide the teacher with useful evidence of understanding or anachronistic thinking. If explored thoroughly they can aid the reconstruction of a particular situation. Even at a relatively superficial level they can help to build up a tentative context of life that can assist children to make sense of a range of happenings which for others remain as separate and anomalous actions. Sarah's progress in Excerpt 14 illustrates this.

Sarah's progress also emphasizes that knowledge of other periods of history is another important influence on the attainment of understanding. All our recordings reveal at least one member of each group making use of prior knowledge of other periods of the past. Some like Sarah use it to good effect (see Excerpt 14, particularly lines 55–62. Linda, Mary and Gina are conspicuously less successful, but they do at least try to apply this important strategy on several occasions. For example, they endeavour to establish a link between something mentioned in the information provided and work they have done in school earlier on the feudal system. Unfortunately their knowledge of the latter is much too vague for them to make meaningful connections so this particular attempt peters out.

Excerpt 20:

GINA: That's what we got in history.   (1)
MARY: What?
GINA: Um . . . What's it called? . . . Um . . . The king came at the top and then the nobles, and then . . .
MARY: [Interrupting]: We done that in R S as well, didn't we?   (5)
GINA: [Continuing]: We got down to the peasants.
LINDA: [Simultaneously says something inaudible.]
MARY: Yeah.
GINA: And it's called something . . . I can't remember . . .
MARY: I can't remember what it's called. It was like a . . . a triangle   (10)
thing, wasn't it?
[Pause. They all stare at the papers.]
GINA: Something . . . system.
MARY: [Inaudible]: . . . system [and they all laugh].
[They stare at the papers again.]   (15)

The girls obviously need some substantive assistance if they are to convert their link into a more exact and detailed one. Our experience seems to suggest that the most propitious moment to supply extra information is when children are puzzled or confused about something. The sixth formers in Excerpt 3 are obviously confused about certain financial aspects of oath-helping. When they are told that no money changed hands and are given further information about wergild and kings, thegns and ceorls they quickly sort out their initial misconception. After doing this to their satisfaction they start on a detailed exploration of oath-helping (see Excerpt 10). Excerpt 23 below reveals that Mary and Gina are also confused about the money and want to know who received it. When told that an oath was worth a certain amount Mary immediately says, 'Oh, it's just an idea, is it?' When given the same additional information as the sixth formers she not only redescribes wergild as a type of compensation but also suggests that it is a good idea. Thus the extra data helps to advance her understanding of an important aspect of the situation (and also Gina's and possibly Linda's) and for the first time she expresses respect for an Anglo-Saxon practice.

Excerpt 21:

GINA: ... the poor man paid ten shillings each ... to who though?   (1)
[Looking at Mary]: Does it say?

MARY: Yeah. To who?

GINA: [Asking PJL]: Who gets the ten shillings?

PJL: Their oath is *worth* that amount but they don't actually pay it.   (5)
The idea is that those people ...
[Mary and Gina interrupt simultaneously but with different comments.]

MARY: Oh, it's just an idea, is it?

GINA: [Looking at Mary]: Oh.   (10)

PJL: ... the idea is that those people's oaths are worth ten shillings.
Here you are. There's something that might explain it out here.
[PJL points to desk with papers laid out. PJL feeds in information on thegns, ceorls and wergild. They all read the new information.
After a long pause Mary and Gina grin at each other and then   (15)
return to reading.]

MARY: That's like compensation, isn't it?

GINA: [Mumbles] Yeah.
[Long pause.]

GINA: What if they didn't want to pay the money, though? 'Cos   (20)
usually now you have to get courts to ... er ... to get compensation.

LINDA: [Mumbles something inaudible.]

MARY: [Says something inaudible, then]: Didn't want to pay it, did
they? ... the money.   (25)
[Long pause. They stare at the papers.]

MARY: *That's* not a bad idea. If you're badly wounded, you know,
like losing your arm, you'd get a large part of your ... er ... to
whoever done it. 'Cos it's not a ... you don't want to lose your
arm, do you? Or lose your leg or whatever. Your leg's sort   (30)
of ... your leg's better than money innit? Can't buy a leg?

LINDA: [Agreeing]: Umm.

Feeding-in supplementary information can have a profound and beneficial effect but timing is crucial. None of the pupils we have recorded discussing aspects of life in Sparta have made thorough use of the figures given in the first paragraph of the pamphlet ('Less than 10,000 Spartans were in charge of about 300,000 other people.'). When they are given, at what appears to be an appropriate moment, a piece of paper that states that the Spartans were outnumbered at least 30 to 1 by the helots it invariably has a considerable effect on their thinking. All the groups become very conscious of the fact that there were a great many more helots than Spartans and use this to explain the issue that is currently puzzling them. When the problem uppermost in their thoughts is the decision of the Spartans to stop attending games and festivals outside Sparta, or some of their rules regarding education, then the new knowledge proves very helpful. But sadly this is not always the case. For instance the children in Excerpt 6 are clearly unable to make sense of the Spartan decision to stop going to the Olympic Games. They need extra information. It is supplied as quickly as possible but while this is being done George articulates a new problem, 'Why didn't the helots rebel?' (His question contradicts information supplied in the pamphlet but this is overlooked.) The group seeks to link the new information to the most recent question and concludes that the helots must have been 'dum dums' because they had great numerical superiority but failed to stage a successful rebellion. Excerpt 2 shows that the children there also need extra information, this time on the size of the population and the scale of village life in Anglo-Saxon England. When given this information they link it to the ordeals instead of oath-helping as intended, and this leads them to wonder whether there were so few people at that time because of 'all these punishments'. Obviously additional information can be very influential but the timing is crucial if it is to help the development of understanding, not hinder it!

One effect of supplementary information is (frequently) to stimulate a new round of discussion, and interaction of this kind plays a central role in every aspect of the process of achieving understanding. This is not to say that discussion will always be successful or even fruitful. For example the interaction between pupils reported in Excerpt 20 fails to lead to a substantial advance in understanding, but on many occasions pupil interaction does lead to various features of the situation being sorted out and on some occasions it is instrumental in pupils achieving a major breakthrough in understanding. For example Richard, one of the 10-year-olds, confesses to his peers early in their discussion of question 1 that he does not understand why the Anglo-Saxons used oath-helpers and Jane agrees that it is a rather difficult question. Their written answers at this stage confirm their assessments. Richard has put 'I think that they used oath-helping and the ordeal to get money – so they could pay the working people.' Jane's answer reveals the same serious misunderstanding: 'The Saxons got money to pay the workers.' May has written 'To get more money', indicating that she is also very confused. By the end of a fairly lengthy exchange of ideas between the three children significant changes have occurred. Richard now appreciates that the oath-helpers were swearing to God, is convinced that they used oaths so that people would probably tell the truth and has added this to his written answer. This significant advance stems from Mary drawing on present-day experience and remarking 'They still swear on the Bible now, don't they?' Her rhetorical question leads Jane to think about a particular contemporary context ('Yeah, they still do it in court') and then they all start thinking about various oaths, possible subsequent happenings and how people might explain them.

Excerpt 22:

RICHARD: People . . . people . . . say, like . . . like . . . if you tell me (1)
this secret I swear on . . . so and so's life that I won't tell no one.

MAY: What? Cross my life . . . cross my heart.

RICHARD: Cross my heart, I hope to die if I ever tell a lie. Well, you
soon . . . soon tell a lie afterwards, don't you? (5)

MAY: No but sometimes it's you . . . let the cat out of the bag, by
mistake, don't you?

JANE: Yeah, you could.

RICHARD: [Immediately]: It's like you say 'I'll never cut bread
again.' You forget and go and cut the bread and cut your finger off, (10)
you know . . . 'Ow . . . What have I done?'

JANE: [Interrupting]: Could be something like that.

RICHARD: . . . Suppose . . . Suppose you've been really horrible to
somebody. Then you get on your bike and fall off. People say that's
God punishing you for . . . being horrible. (15)

All three children are confused at first but after discussing for several minutes they answer confidently and eagerly when they re-read the question.

Excerpt 23:

ALL READING: 'Why do you think the Anglo-Saxons used oath- (1)
helping and the ordeal to decide if someone was guilty of a crime?'

RICHARD: I think . . .

JANE: [Simultaneously]: Oath helping . . . oaths. You're swearing to
God that you weren't . . . (5)

RICHARD: [Simultaneously]: Why do you think they used oaths?
[Hastily]: They probably used oaths to make sure they were telling
the truth because you're swearing an oath . . .

Indeed Richard, who starts by saying 'I don't really understand the question', ends their discussion of this particular question defending his new point of view with considerable conviction.

Excerpt 24:

RICHARD: [Simultaneously with Jane who is inaudible]: So if you say (1)
that 'I swear on my mother's life'. . .

MAY: [Coming in]: I suppose like . . . [rest inaudible].

RICHARD: [Simultaneously]: Then you just *do* tell the truth
because . . . (5)

MAY: It's like with these oath-helpers, isn't it?

RICHARD: Yeah, so that's what I put there . . . [Reading his written
answer]: 'If you swear an oath on God . . . then you probably
would tell the truth.'

The transcripts show that pupil interaction also facilitates significant advances in the understanding achieved by the third-year girls and the sixth formers. When the third-year girls are given question two it has the effect of making them wonder about their original assumptions and interpretation (see Excerpt 7). Then after a long pause and some writing they begin to sort out various points of detail. In this phase they explore the passage and articulate a number of questions. Sometimes this activity leads to misconceptions being corrected, sometimes not, but over all it helps to clarify various features of the situation and context of life, a prerequisite of understanding such social practices. The sixth formers make even more progress as a result of a period of sustained interaction during which historical imagination is displayed (Excerpt 10, lines 74–7) and questions are raised about the practices (lines 35–6 and 58–60) and the students' own assumptions (lines 14–16 and 62). They also make use of the sources provided and their own experience to help them resolve such questions, to compare and contrast the use of oaths then and now (lines 11–16) and to settle a disputed interpretation (lines 100–10). Indeed their willingness to articulate their ideas, listen carefully, and learn from each other result in their progressing from a state of incredulity to one of making sense of the particular social practices from the point of view of those who employed them and then moving on to offer a further explanation from a current point of view.

Questions play a very important part in all these instances of interaction and progress. Our questions are the starting point of each discussion but the transcripts also reveal the importance of many of the questions that the pupils pose to each other. Their questions are both numerous and influential on many occasions.[13] In Excerpt 10 questions that overtly invite other members of the group to clarify specific details (lines 35–6 and 86–8) or to offer connections (line 46) have the effect of aiding exploration and the working out of various points. Early in the excerpt (lines 14–16) Kate manages to articulate as a question one of her assumptions about which she has doubts and this also prompts thoughtful discussion and clarification of the details of oath-helping. Later Jenny's attempt to summarize the views of the group ('So we've got it as superstition, haven't we?') leads Kate to try to distinguish the Anglo-Saxon point of view from that taken by the group (lines 65–8 and 74–7). Kate herself then asks a question that also prompts a particularly significant advance: 'So why do you think Anglo-Saxons used oath-helping?' This question encourages Jenny to try to fit oath-helping into the social context of the time and this in turn leads Catherine to offer a different interpretation, one emphasizing what people now might want to say about it. Even the least productive of their questions, those that amount essentially to confirming talk (lines 58–60), could have stimulated significant progress if someone had possessed the knowledge to correct the misunderstandings present in them.

Other exchanges between the members of the same group provide further evidence of progress achieved as a result of a combination of worthwhile questions, utilizing the evidence available and effective pupil interaction. One such exchange features questions whose purpose is to test the hypothesis upon which they have so far based their response to a particular question. It occurs when they are discussing how the Anglo-Saxons would have explained oath-helping and the ordeal and is initiated by Jenny saying 'Yeah, but they must have believed in it to let it carry on, mustn't they? I mean, if you don't believe in it then you don't let things carry on, do you?' Catherine is not convinced. She thinks that circumstances must have affected some people's beliefs and that if they all believed in God and the system then no one would have stolen the cow. Later in the discussion she returns to this point after Kate has raised a very different type of question, but one that prompts Catherine to wonder aloud whether people would have stolen things if they had the kind of strong religious beliefs that Jenny and Kate had claimed in their answer.

Excerpt 25:

KATE: I wonder how often that . . . that kind of situation would arise (1)
in . . . in England, you know? Whether it's a frequent thing that
cows disappeared?
[Kate and Catherine laugh.]
JENNY: I shouldn't think . . . It doesn't have to be, necessarily, a cow, (5)
sort of thing, does it?
KATE: No. No.
JENNY: I mean, just . . . anything.
CATHERINE: But then the thing is, if they had such a strong religious
belief they probably wouldn't do it. That's why I sort of question it. (10)
You know. . . . Because you have this idea of all being really
religious Anglo-Saxons with crucifixes round their necks, and that
sort of thing.

Jenny's first reaction is to laugh. Soon, however, both she and Kate concede that Catherine has raised an important issue and then all three girls make a further determined effort to try to work out what the Anglo-Saxons probably thought about the system.

Personal experience, the explicit and implicit evidence available, imagination or its absence, and the possibilities for fruitful interaction, all have an impact on the kind of thinking children display in tackling the strange behaviour and institutions of past societies. It will be evident even from the short passages of transcript material we have been able to reproduce here that children are often persistent, tenacious and thoughtful when allowed room to explore what seems problematic to them; moreover they raise and tackle serious issues. The more we listen in on children struggling to make sense of the past, the more we feel that what we see and hear has important implications for history in school.

III. SOME IMPLICATIONS FOR TEACHING

Only the wilfully ignorant could afford to ignore recent research into children's thinking in history. But while it is in some ways correct in stressing the limitations of children's thinking, in giving this as the whole story it is highly misleading, and potentially disastrous for teaching. It is not hard to find examples of children making assertions that conflict with part of the evidence given them, or that suggest they they are just at the beginnings of 'describer' thinking. But further investigation reveals a more complex scene. Written responses do not bear a straightforward relationship to the thinking displayed in discussion (something experienced teachers know only too well); the form of children's thinking cannot be treated independently of content and mode of presentation; and the strategies pupils adopt and the level of understanding they achieve both vary considerably in the course of their interaction with one another.[14]

The central point here for history teaching is that understanding is not an all-or-nothing achievement, and is not something teachers ought to wait for, but something to try to develop. The (true) statement that children's thinking is limited in systematic – if complex – ways does *not* entail statements prescribing descriptive and simple-minded history for primary or secondary pupils. Our work suggests that the Inspectorate is quite correct in deploring the way children's ability is underestimated.[15] Given even difficult problems to solve, children will make serious attempts to reach solutions, and enjoy the effort. They will make serious mistakes; their discussions will reveal a range of misconceptions, and at times fall into incoherence: but none of this means that what they are doing is not worth while. We might all do well to remember that very little of what we learn is mastered in one moment of enlightenment, and even less of what we learn do we commit in writing to notebooks. Exercise books represent an apparently objective record of what has gone on in class, so that teachers are tempted to make sure they are filled with clear and correct notes and answers, not with the untidy bric-à-brac of the *process* of acquiring understanding. The blind-alleys, wrong guesses and muddles of active thinking are not welcome in 'best books'. Examiners, parents, and senior teachers must share much of the blame for arid caution here. The issue is particularly acute with history for the 'less able'. Pupils with low reading ages and writing difficulties are not necessarily poor thinkers in history, where experience of personal and social relations counts so heavily. Such pupils can often make perceptive contributions to argument without being able to express themselves in writing. The tyranny of the written answer decrees that history for many of these children is mindless blank-filling, note copying, and cross-word puzzles. Even a slight shift in emphasis towards the spoken word, and increased attention to the process by which understanding is achieved, will allow a different assessment of pupils' capabilities in history.

In any case teachers need to know pupils' muddles and misconceptions. Children's talk, questions, and written responses can all help here, but the exercises set must demand genuine thinking. If the full potential of problem-solving exercises is to be exploited, certain conditions must be satisfied, one of which is that the problems must seem to the pupils to be worthy of their attention and hard thinking. Our recordings suggest that children's own questions can be complex and taxing, and that some pupils at least have a very clear idea of what makes a question worth asking. When, for example, three 10-year-olds were invited to read a passage on Sparta and to think of some questions worth setting to the other children in the class one of them quickly indicated to the others the main criterion that he thought a good question should satisfy.

> You need something for them to think about, so that they have to think. Otherwise it's no good if you just look it up in the paper. You have got to think for yourself.

Later he reiterated this criterion when he found it necessary to dismiss another pupil's suggestion. This time he gained support from his other colleague.

Excerpt 26:
> MARGARET: Now . . . something about the Spartans . . . What cities   (1)
>   they took over, because they are not going to remember . . .
> TERRY: [Interrupting]: Oh, no. It's not a question of remembrance.
>   It's a question of . . .
> ADAM: [Interrupting]: Finding out.   (5)
> TERRY: [Continuing]: Finding out things for yourself and using your
>   brain, your loaf. All the questions we ask have got to make the
>   children think, not try and remember.

Terry's injunctions compare interestingly with some textbook assumptions about what questions are appropriate for schoolchildren.

Asking children to devise good questions based on whatever sources they have been given seems to be one way of encouraging them to read such material carefully and to interrogate it. All the children in our (necessarily very small) sample studied their material very attentively in order to produce what they considered worthwhile questions. They also decided, without any lead from us, that they should check their questions for accuracy of content, doing this by looking at the source again. The same group of 10-year-olds, for example, checked every time a question gained their approval. In the extract below it is Terry who initiates the move, but at the start of the discussion it was Margaret, and in the later stages Adam.

Excerpt 27:
> ADAM: [Writing down the question they have been discussing and   (1)
>   saying it aloud]: Why were the helots only allowed to eat the left-
>   overs of food?
> TERRY: Where does it say that?
> ADAM: [Pointing]: It says here.   (5)
> TERRY: [Checking]: Ah . . . yes.

All the children were also concerned, again without any directives from us, to answer their own questions and made further use of the source material to help them in this task.

Excerpt 28:
> TERRY: Let's see if we can find the answer first.   (1)
> ADAM: Why *were* the Spartans so strict with the helots?
> MARGARET: Probably because . . . . They are going to be strict so
>   that they will learn that they are . . .

TERRY: [Interrupting]: I thought they would be really strict with   (5)
them so that they would know where their place was, that they were
not ruling, that the helots were not ruling. They wanted the helots
to know that.

MARGARET: Yes.

ADAM: Let's write that down. [Writing and talking]: 'Why were the   (10)
Spartans so strict with the helots?' [Referring to the pamphlet]: But
they're not strict in here. It doesn't say that they were strict in here.
Oh! Yes it does!

Pupils in our recordings seem more willing to articulate their problems and
seek clarification of difficult points from their peers than from their teachers.
Take this typical exchange:

Excerpt 29:

CATHERINE: If . . . um . . . er . . . if they're found guilty because they   (1)
haven't got enough oaths what happens to them then?

KATE and JENNY: [Almost simultaneously]: They have to go to the
ordeal.

CATHERINE: That's what . . . if he hasn't got enough people to swear   (5)
for him . . . that's what it means?

KATE and JENNY: [Simultaneously]: Yeah.

Many of the extracts in section II offer fuller examples of pupils bringing up
problems and basic unfamiliarities, investigating and sometimes settling
them; similarly they show hypotheses being set up, explored, and tested. Our
material strongly suggests that small group discussion of specific problems
facilitates communication of difficulties and enables pupils to help each other
make sense of the past.

Once children plunge into discussion of a historical problem, there is a
tendency to get caught up in the material before them, even when other
information is available. None of the pupils in our recordings asked us for
more material, even when they had been told of its availability at the outset,
and when it was ostentatiously laid out on tables near them, very obviously and
concretely present in the room. This remained true even when it was clear to
them that they had reached an impasse in discussing a particular problem. In
contrast a group of MA students considering why the Spartans stopped going
to games and festivals outside Sparta, organized themselves to examine every
piece of extra information available, in search of anything that cohered or
clashed with the explanation they favoured most. It is possible that part of
children's reluctance to ask for more material reflects a tendency to assume
that when a teacher sets a task, it will not be a 'catch' one, and there will be
sufficient basis in what they are given to make a reasonable attempt at 'the
answer'. There are in any case good reasons for not supplying too much
information at first. In our experience, when children are offered extra
material, they sometimes use it to test the ideas they are considering, or to
suggest new ones, provided it is introduced at the right moment. If it is
produced when they have started to puzzle over a different issue – and this can

happen very suddenly – it may increase misunderstanding. Timing is crucial, and since teachers cannot possibly know the appropriate moment for each child in a crowded room, ideally pupils should take the initiative. Many pupils may learn to do this if they are given extensive opportunities for small group discussion, and are actively encouraged to consult well-chosen resources.

The major concern of the transcripts reproduced here is children's historical understanding. Imagination is central in this: the pupils whose discussions are recorded in the transcripts made progress when they were able to cash information supplied in the material they were given, working out its consequences for people with different beliefs, values and goals from their own. If the argument in Chapter 5 is correct, one of the best clues to children's understanding is provided by work that demands historical imagination. None the less imaginative work is still regarded by some teachers as especially suitable for very young or less able children. Such a view rests on a simple-minded conception of historical imagination, and displays a failure of imagination on the part of its proponents: from the pupils' point of view any exercise demanding genuine historical imagination is far from being an easy option, and even a cursory consideration of the thinking involved would dispel this kind of assumption.

One reason for the inadequate role accorded to imagination in school history is that much that is traditionally characterized as 'imaginative work' is in fact a strange mixture of fantasy and regurgitation. Children asked to write about a day in the life of a villein seldom produce more than a catalogue of snippets from lessons on the medieval manor, embellished with personal details that are either atemporal or downright anachronistic, and are imaginative only in the sense that they are 'made up'. There is no pressure in an exercise like this to cash the information which must be the basis of a genuine historical imagination: the villein has no problem, no history, and no finite situation in which to act. There are no proper constraints. The best answers will tend to use classroom knowledge to provide some framework – the villein will tell a story (or take part in one) which stresses his dependence on the seasons and his lord. But because the teacher has – rightly – stressed the differences between now and then, the pupils emphasize the strangeness of precisely those elements of the villein's life that he would regard as inevitable, natural and unchanging. Even worse are questions that more or less fraudulently demand a double exercise of imagination: 'Imagine you are a villein visiting a medieval town – describe your day and what you see.' What comes back from this kind of exercise is again frequently a mixture of regurgitation (town layout, close packed buildings, a passage on the guilds) and the 'imaginative' topping (open sewers and 'Gardez-loo!'). This approach is at best confused and at worst fraudulent. It is fraudulent if the limitations of medieval public hygiene have been played for cheap laughs.[16] It is confused because in stressing how 'different' a medieval town was from the pupils' conception of urban life, and yet pretending that the baseline of the comparison is what a villein would have seen, it conceals the difficulties of understanding involved, and allows pupils to treat the past with sniggering condescension. The exercise fails to distinguish between the way (time-travelling) pupils would see a medieval town, and what a villein would have seen. Pupils giving a description of a town from their modern point of view in terms that mark it off as quaint and primitive are not exercising historical imagination. Still less are they doing so in giving an 'imaginative' account of being doused by refuse from above, conceived of from the point of view of someone accustomed to current standards of personal and public hygiene. Far from indexing or developing understanding, such exercises encourage precisely the attitude to the past displayed in the first reactions of the children in our transcripts.

It is only when the 'time-travelling' perspective and the viewpoint of contemporaries are distinguished that it is possible to move away from rejection and contempt for the past, or at best condescending smugness towards it. It may be that a 'time-travellers' visit to a medieval town is a valuable first move in getting children to grips with the subject. Their attitudes and their surprise can then (legitimately and unconfusingly) have free rein. Once they have picked out and commented on things from their own point of view, the teacher can make a crucial and difficult move in such a way that pupils have some chance of grasping what is going on. 'OK', he says, 'You've told me what the town is like. Now suppose you were one of the people who lived there: what would *he* talk about if he were showing someone round? How would it be different from what *you* talked about?' Of course it cannot be left like that. What sort of person is doing the showing, and what sort of person being shown? What would a villein visiting a town for the first and (perhaps only) time in his life actually notice, and how would he see it? What is he doing there anyway – what is his interest? The minute it is put like this, the difficulty of the task becomes apparent, and with it the need for a great deal of information to serve as a foundation for imagination. Imaginative work in history requires a firm basis, and sensible historical constraints on what may be imagined. New instructions for the cavalry in the New Model Army after Marston Moor; a letter from Zinoviev and Kamanev to Lenin on the eve of the October revolution explaining why any hasty move will be fatal; a warning from Ned Ludd to a stocking-frame owner (preferably a specific owner in a specific place, so that a detailed background is available): this sort of question, given the right preparation, is much more likely to engage genuine historical imagination.[17]

Children learning history find it difficult sometimes to make any sense of actions and institutions; teachers can compound the confusion by emphasizing the peculiarity and strangeness of the past. Pupils will naturally find many of the antics of our predecessors amusing, if not downright laughable. If a teacher builds upon the interest aroused by this amusement, using the surprise and puzzlement behind it to challenge pupils to think things out, their history will benefit. If, on the other hand, the teacher is content with easy jokes at the expense of the past, children will not only fail to understand the specific topic, but be left clueless as to the whole activity of history. Given time, the right information to work with, and a chance to talk their ideas through (among themselves or with their teacher) most pupils make serious efforts to resolve their problems. The thinking they display runs up and down the accepted stages and levels of cognitive psychology, and its place on a scale of such levels at any given moment varies according to familiarity with similar content, the availability of relevant experience, and the quality of interaction with other pupils.[18]

Children can and do think effectively in history. Frequently it is not the quality of pupils' thinking that sets the limit on worthwhile school history, but a failure on the part of some teachers to recognize the complexity of what they are attempting. Moreover the way to cope with this complexity is not to teach ever more simplified and simple-minded 'facts' in an endless round of description and regurgitation, with pupils classified as 'less able' compelled to spend their lessons filling in the blanks in anodyne and mindless sentences. We need sufficient flexibility of method to allow pupils room to show us what they find problematic, and enough imagination to offer work that utilizes those problems and gives pupils some chance of making progress towards understanding. Underestimation of children leads only to pessimism and history as child-minding. Recognition of what children can do licenses realistic optimism, provided only that we start thinking more carefully about what is actually involved in the tasks we ask pupils to cope with in learning and understanding history.

NOTES

1. See, for example, Hallam, R. N., 'Logical thinking in history', *Educational Review*, vol. 19, 1967.

2. See Dickinson, A. K. and Lee, P. J., 'Understanding and research', in Dickinson, A. K. and Lee, P. J. (eds), *History Teaching and Historical Understanding*, Heinemann Educational Books, 1978; and Booth, M., 'Inductive thinking in history: the 14–16 age group', in Jones, G. and Ward, L. (eds), *New History, Old Problems*, University College of Swansea Faculty of Education, 1978. For a more recent appraisal, wider in scope, see Shemilt, D., *History 13–16 Evaluation Study*, Holmes McDougall, 1980, especially ch. 5.

3. All this is, of course, intended as illustration by analogy. To the best of our knowledge there is no coherent account of race, let alone empirical evidence to support claims of intellectual superiority for one group or another. Our analogy is imaginary and meant as a warning.

4. For our previous work, see Dickinson and Lee (eds), op. cit.

5. In case anyone should think the children in the excerpts that follow in any way unusual, the following information may be illuminating:

   (a) The primary school children in these excerpts came from lower-middle and working-class backgrounds, and were of average IQ as measured by their local authority. (Our thanks are due to the staff of Canvey Primary School, Essex, and especially to Mr Michael Emery, for their help.)

   (b) The third and sixth formers were from an inner-London comprehensive and in the case of the third years were of average ability according to their teachers. The sixth formers were classified as better than average, but not outstanding in any way. (We are indebted to the History Department of Kidbrooke Comprehensive School for allowing us to work with their pupils.)

   (c) The novelty of the TV seems to play only a small role, and children rapidly get bored with it. Their performance remains roughly the same even if (as has happened on occasion) the camera turns out to have been faulty and the whole exercise is repeated the following week – something that understandably does not evoke much enthusiasm from the subjects.

   (d) Tapes from a variety of schools and age groups all conform to the patterns discussed in this chapter, and recent regular work with first-year (lower band, often remedial) children in an Essex comprehensive shows similar results. The latter material is in fact startling in its implications, because it suggests that children who can write only with great difficulty can discuss a historical problem for 40–60 minutes with great serious-ness and considerable insight. This material will be the subject of further publication at a later date.

6. We have decided not to include the full test-passages in this chapter. The principal reason is simply lack of space: our priority has been to exhibit transcription material in reasonable length, in the hope of giving some indication of how children come to terms with what they see as strange past behaviour, rather than to discuss the technical problems of this kind of research.

7. Later in the discussion the children were offered some information on punishment in Anglo-Saxon times. Richard's response to the offer (before he received the material) was immediate: a broad smile spread across his face. 'Oh great', he said, 'The ducking stool!'

8. At one point Jenny says 'It's like witches though.' There is strong evidence of the damage to historical understanding done by teachers who play strange customs for cheap laughs. We sometimes see this done by students, but more often students see it done by experienced teachers who ought to know better. Letting children laugh at what seem to be strange goings-on is one thing, but failing to see that history is about getting children through and beyond this reaction is quite another.

9. Plainly Sarah, for all her wide knowledge and enthusiastic reasoning, is still unable to assess wide spans of time. But then if she has no ordered information as to what has happened between ancient Greece and the current world, this is not a defect in her *thinking*.

10. It has been suggested to us that there is an intellectually defensive element in this, as though pupils are saying 'If we can't make sense of it, it must be stupid.' More importantly, children's reactions to unfathomable past customs are like people's reactions to immigrant culture: 'If it's not like us, we don't want anything to do with it – if it's different it's worse.' The latter analogy is important and illuminating, but the rejection is usually brief: children really do want to know what is going on, and struggle hard to find out. The threat posed by past differences seems much less immediate than that posed by the present, and there is rarely any withdrawal to a defensive position that refuses to contemplate the possibility of different behaviour making sense. (We owe both these suggestions to Mrs Rosalyn Ashby of the Bramston School, Witham.)

11. This is supported by a later incident. After speculating that life must have been a bit much to live through in Anglo-Saxon times, because thegns would have had to be obeyed, Mary says 'it's all different now innit?' Then she adds 'Say a policeman . . . we don't do what *they* want half the time, do we?' This is said with a mixture of bravado and regret, as if it represents a sad state of affairs. All three girls then sigh, and stare at their papers.

12. During the digression Gina commented that she preferred making notes to doing the test because for all her reading she had completed less than one page of writing. Both Linda and she were worried about all the material they had been given. ('All this paper. What are we going to do with all this? We've got hoards of it, haven't we?') Mary was alone in preferring the small group situation we had created.

13. This is in marked contrast to the pathetically small number of pupil-initiated questions related to learning (and not just procedural points) that Douglas Barnes found in his study of the role and frequency of questions in formal history lessons. See 'Language and learning in the classroom', *Journal of Curriculum Studies*, vol. 3, no. 1, 1971.

14. For a discussion of the effect of familiarity of content on success in logically isomorphic tasks, see Wason, W. C., 'The theory of formal operations – a critique', in Geber, B. A. (ed.), *Piaget and Knowing*, Routledge & Kegan Paul, 1977.

15. See, for example, DES, *Primary Education in England: A Survey by HM Inspectors of Schools*,

HMSO, 1978, ch. 6, section 6.19; and DES, *Report by HM Inspectors on Educational Provision by the Inner London Education Authority,* HMSO, 1980, *passim.*

16. See note 8. The damage is not in the initial laughter, but in exaggerating things and in leaving pupils with the idea that there is nothing more to it.
17. See the discussion of imagination in Chapter 4.
18. The experimental evidence is not conclusive, but there is much to suggest that styles of teaching may be critical here. A bottom-band first-year class in an Essex comprehensive, presented with an exercise in which it had to decide how (as Roman governor of Britain) it would treat the new province, soon teased out the problems involved in too harsh or too 'soft' a policy on weapons, religion, taxation and so on. The children were accustomed to having to think problems through in history, and also had some experience of archaeological work. The equivalent top-band class, without such a background, proved anxious and reluctant about the whole enterprise, asking where the right answers were to be found.

6. The Power of Visual Presentation

P. J. ROGERS

This paper is the second describing an experiment that attempts to show genuine historical enquiry to be a feasible objective for senior primary and younger secondary pupils. A fundamental aspect of the approach is that historical enquiry must sample – of course in a simplified and scaled-down form – the *sort* of procedures in which historians actually engage.[1] To teach history is to teach *history* and there can be no adequate, or even honest, teaching that ignores its genuine procedural character.

The first paper[2] described the experiment. The content covered with over 200 children aged 10–13 years was the Nine Years' War and the essence of the design was to contrast an orthodox teacher-centred approach with a programme of source-based materials involving some of the procedures characteristic of historical enquiry. Results showed superior test performance by children following the programme approach, and this indicated that the enterprise is practicable. The present paper repeats none of this but explains the rationale and design of the programme and how it engaged the children in some genuine enquiry.

I. A 'TECHNOLOGY' OF INSTRUCTION – BRUNER AND IKONIC REPRESENTATION

What was needed if the daunting but necessary task was to be undertaken was a relevant 'technology' of instruction adequate to connect child and content, and it was Bruner's central concern with this problem that made his work of special interest and value. A brief outline of his concepts of structure and spiral curriculum was given in the earlier article (see note 2) and the hope was expressed that the use made of the third main element of his work, the modes of representation, might be explained later. The present chapter attempts to do this and is concerned especially with ikonic representation. (Reference to the heavy use of visual materials was made in the earlier article.)

Bruner holds that

At each stage of development the child has a characteristic way of viewing the world and explaining it to himself. The task of teaching a subject to a child at any particular age is one of representing the structure of that subject in terms of the child's way of viewing things. The task can be taught as one of translation.[3]

The course of mental growth commences with concrete and palpable perceptions and gradually moves towards a grasp of more and more abstract and generalized principles. There are, according to Bruner, three modes of representation that serve this progression: enactive, where content is coded in some pattern of physical activity; ikonic, where it is embodied in some visual representation; and symbolic, where abstract principles with no concrete referents may be meaningfully coded by means of abstract symbols such as language.

Ikonic representation at first sight confines an agent to a limited world since it seems to confine him to interpretations and judgements based upon surface appearances rather than upon 'such invisible and silent factors as relationships'[4] that cannot be visually represented. This is particularly true of theoretical concept formation. Bruner gives as an example the impossibility of representing ikonically

Clausewitz's famous dictum that war is a continuation of peacetime policies. The two do not look enough alike. It may be true that a picture is worth a thousand words but if the object is to locate its functional equivalent in another context then perhaps a word is worth a thousand pictures if it contains the conceptual key.[5]

In short, the difficulty with ikonic representation according to Bruner is that its strength (perceptual vividness) often cannot focus upon those features of what is represented that are crucial – what is *per*ceptually vivid is often not what is *con*ceptually important.

The general truth of this seems indisputable but unless qualified, it may well lead to an undervaluing of ikonic representation. First, it is important to realize that the three modes, enactive, ikonic and symbolic, are not discrete. Of especial relevance to the present concern with ikonic representation is the example of 'Three degrees of pictorial literalness' where a picture of a battery, switch and light bulb grows, by successive redrawings into a (still visual) generalized statement of the relationship of which battery, switch and bulb are a particular instance.[6] What is happening here, of course, is that ikonic *form* is being charged with more and more generalized content – that is, it is becoming more and more 'symbolic' in its *function* – without ceasing to be visual.

Two important points follow from these examples. First ikonic representation is not, perhaps, so incapable of carrying non-literal content as the earlier arguments suggested. Indeed, the possibility is raised of a representational continuum within which the three modes, enactive, ikonic and symbolic, might be variously deployed to represent a wide range of content at varying levels of generality which gradually lead the learner, by translation among them, towards a comprehensive understanding.

The feasibility of such a continuum is enhanced when it is realized that none of the three modes is quite discrete and homogeneous. We have just seen how ikonic representation can be accessible to symbolic content. The same relation holds in reverse in that language can be more or less visual in its impact. One thinks of Shakespearian metaphor – *Macbeth* is particularly full of examples[7] – where the profundity of what is said is carried in large part by the imagery the words evoke. And a similar Protean flexibility may well characterize enactive representation too.

Secondly, the concept of 'translation' among the modes is not only that, in so far as it is remembered, it preserves ikonic (and enactive) representation from wrongful (and wasteful) neglect, but that it provides a powerful means for subjecting 'visual aids' to critical scrutiny. To be valid – to be an *ikon* – a visual representation must genuinely carry whatever message is at stake and this criterion shows that the conventional 'visual aid' may fall far short of realizing the true potential of ikonic mode. As its name, 'aid', suggests, it typically consists of a picture or diagram merely illustrating some aspect of the written work, not a fully articulated representation of the concept or information concerned. Visual representation is thus treated not as a code of communication (perhaps) analogous to language, but as a mere adjunct to it. Indeed, in so far as the items chosen for illustration form a relatively trivial aspect of the written material (as is often the case), the illustrations, in proportion as they are effective, will weaken the learning by diverting attention away from essentials. The indiscriminate and undiscriminating use of 'visual aids' thus greatly undersells the potential of ikonic representation both by the naivety of its form that typically underestimates its conceptualizing and relational power, and by its unplanned and ill-considered selection of the features to be illustrated.

Both these possibilities were (it is hoped) tested in the present experiment. The use made of the 'representational continuum' was, admittedly, confined to ikonic and symbolic modes,[8] but with that limitation, every effort was made to establish linkages between the codings and to exploit different levels of concreteness and abstraction in both of them. Printed sources (symbolic representation) were chosen sometimes for their strong visual suggestiveness so that linkage to concrete imagery was easy, and sometimes for their summarizing expression of a principle that had already been extensively experienced with visual and simpler verbal sources. The visual sources (and other visual materials) on the other hand were always verbally explored, translated and combined both by and with the children. In particular, no visual material was included that was *merely* illustrative. It had to be something from which by inference, cross-referencing, etc. some significant aspect of reconstruction[9] could be undertaken. It had, in short, to be an ikon, not a mere 'visual aid'. (This possibly rather cryptic paragraph is explained in section II, by means of examples, when the programme is described.)

II. THE PROGRAMME DESCRIBED – IKONIC REPRESENT-ATION

With its rationale (I hope) clear, the programme may be described. It consisted of four assignments, each of which was a fortnight's work except for the last which extended over three weeks. Assignment I dealt with Ulster before the Nine Years' War – the nature of Gaelic life, connections with Scotland and English attitudes to this most Celtic (and virtually uncontrolled) province. Assignment II put the war in context by relating Ulster to the Spanish threat which made firm control of Ireland imperative from an English point of view. Assignment III dealt conceptually with the war, seeking to explain why it went on so long, in terms of the terrain and the equipment, strengths and weaknesses of the two sides. Finally, assignment IV covered Mountjoy's final campaign, bringing out its rationale and strategic brilliance in the light of the difficulties studied in assignment III. Each assignment except the third (which was entirely visual and is, therefore, of especial interest) consisted of a pack of 'documents' (see below) and a set of slides reproducing contemporary maps and pictures together with additional pictures and diagrams designed by us. The children were asked to perform certain operations believed to represent, albeit in scaled-down form, genuine historical activity, and for the first three assignments every class had a worksheet of questions whose answers had to be worked out from the sources. However, 'open-ended' inquiry was also encouraged in that the children were asked to jot down any (*literally any*) question that occurred to them during their study of the sources, and then to search for answers to it (or qualifications for it) in other sources. The printed sources were recorded on tape so that children could listen as well as read. This was obviously intended to help the poor reader, but also – and more central to the purpose of the experiment – it was intended to promote a further basic feature of historical inquiry – namely the use of sources for their overall significance, and the inferences that can be drawn from them rather than the naïve face-value acceptance and rummaging for details which is all 'source-based work' in schools often amounts to. The recorded sources, it was hoped, would encourage this process; since the pupil *had* to keep up with the (admittedly slow) pace of the recording he could hardly focus attention on details but must strive to make sense out of the *overall* message – an operation assisted initially by the questions provided on the worksheet. Manifestly, this very sophisticated skill takes much time to develop, but its quite fundamental importance means that it cannot be neglected.

Examples and discussion
Examples may now be given from the Nine Years' War project to clarify the various points just made, and the earlier paragraph concerning the interlocking of symbolic and ikonic representation and the nature of an ikon (p. 155 above) may be further explained.

Several detailed, and very concrete, printed sources spoke of clan battles, cattle raids and the seizure of a castle and the children knew, from visual sources, what (for example) soldiers of the time looked like (so that terms like 'kerne' and 'gallowglass summoned up clear and powerful images). The precision and concreteness of the sources enabled them to be used for inferential reconstruction of the reality of sixteenth-century life in Ulster. On the other hand, at the end of a (visual and simple verbal) study of the strategic importance of waterways - and, indeed, of the concept of 'strategic importance' as such - they were presented with, and asked to explain, the following abstract passage, referring back at will to the simpler materials (largely visual) that were, of course, concrete referents of it, and whose study had familiarized them with the places named.

> Besides the Erne is so necessary to Connaught, as the joining of it to the province excludes them from aid and hope. It is the convenientest place of garrison to hold the people of both sides to obedience; a straight between those countries; and at all times, if the Kingdom were in rebellion, it may be victualled.

> [For summary by visual means see below p. 159][10]

(Obviously the teacher would help by simplifying the language but more especially by referring the source to the relevant visual - the map of Lough Erne and its surrounding districts with all appropriate physical features shown (or added as discussion proceeds). The interplay of ikonic and symbolic, and their 'translation' one into the other, is well shown here. A relief model would be even better.)

These two examples illustrate the concrete and the summarizing aspects of the verbal sources (see above, p. 156) and also the possibility of reading for overall significance (above, p. 157). For what was interesting was that the strong imagery and concrete detail of the passages greatly facilitated reconstruction through inference. It seemed that it was the reiterated accounts in the source of battles, cattle raids, participation of Scots and English and so on, each somewhat different in the richness of its details, but nevertheless isomorphic with every other, that built up conceptual understanding of pre-war Ulster.

The use of visual materials in combination with verbal and the ikonic slant given to many of the latter by their concrete nature has already shown the importance attached to ikonic representation. However, even given their richness in vivid (and, it was hoped, exciting) detail it was anticipated that the 'documents' would be less attractive than the visual materials if only because of their unexciting physical appearance (solid blocks of print). If any significant learning (that is genuine reconstruction) was to take place, it was therefore mainly the visual materials that would be expected to bring it about, and in this respect the experiment was a test of the power of ikonic representation. For this reason examples of the use of visual materials will be given from assignments I and II, and assignment III (entirely visual) will be described in full. Assignment IV, though heavily visual and in some respects the most interesting, is unfortunately too long and complex for summary here.

It was suggested above that recording the documents went some way to eliminating the disadvantage of the poor readers. Pre-eminently is this true of the visual sources. Exactly the same inference-drawing use was made of these as of the documents. One example may be given. In assignment I the set of slides included one of a raid on a farm. From earlier slides the children had learned much about costume and weapons and could, therefore, identify the nationalities of the people shown in the raid slide. One of the questions they had been asked to consider was whether the implication in some Irish sources that all the Irish were united against the English was true. The slide in question shows clearly that victims and attackers are, alike, Irish. Certainly internecine strife does not disprove unity against an outsider, but it corroborates certain passages in the documents and prompts further cross-reference to them. (One document actually refers to an Irish chief's alliance with the English against another.) The pictures, and the use made of them, thus promote the detective work of piecing together a vanished past.

Assignment I also contained another important use of visual representation. Instead of using supplied visual materials, the children had to *construct* a visual. As the very last item in the fortnight's work the pupils were asked to use the information in any of the source materials to make

a big map showing the geographical relation of Ulster (a) to the rest of Ireland and (b) to Scotland. Mark, and name in *black*, all places and districts named in any source. Print the names of the various *CHIEFS* (like that) and of their TENANTS (like that) over their territories. Use a different colour for each chief and mark his tenants in the same colour. If a tenant has more than one chief, use the colours of all his chiefs in printing his name.

When completed, with appropriate pictures such as of 'gallowglass' optionally added, the map constituted a master chart summarizing much the greater part of what assignment I had been concerned to teach. It constituted a skeleton file, so to speak, of learnings, reference to which might reactivate the reconstruction of which it is a digest. For example, if McQUILLAN is printed in more than one colour that prompts recollection of the complexity and potential fragmentation of the clan system (with political and military advantages from the English point of view); ships plying between Ulster and Scotland, perhaps with gallowglass on board, and the bonfire on the Antrim coast, remind the pupil of the close links with Scotland – and so on. (The exercise was popular, though the teachers reported that it was also very time-consuming.)

The slides of assignment II tried to bring out the Spanish threat to England and the Low Countries by a developing series of maps of Western Europe with movable pieces showing all salient features including English intervention in the Netherlands and Spanish in Ireland. Again this prompted cross-reference to accompanying documents, but the slides seemed much more powerful for explaining the conceptual (strategic) issue involved, even though the documents contained constant (English) references to the strategic threat, and frequent (Irish) contacts with Spain, including the (reported) explicit argument of the Irish 'ambassador' in Madrid that 'Ireland once possessed, Scotland, England and Holland might with very little difficulty be assailed and conquered by Spain'.

As has already been stated, assignment III was largely visual – it contained no pack of documents as did the other assignments. It was also by far the most popular assignment (see below) and will now be described in some detail. Its aim was to explain the course, nature and duration of the war. The essential problem was to relate the geographical and technical facts of the case – how the nature of the terrain and the weapons and logistics of the two sides shaped the conduct of the war. In a word, it was an attempt at a reconstruction of late six-teenth-century reality by valid inference from evidence.

This was attempted as follows. First, the nature of the terrain was examined. A scholarly article, which utilized all the original sources relevant to the subject, was broken down into a set of definite statements about fairly precise areas and the source of each noted. Each of these was printed on a separate sheet. A large-scale map ($\frac{1}{2}''$ to 1 mile) of Ulster was prepared and mounted and then cut up so that each piece represented the area covered by one source sheet. The information was then 'translated' into visual form, forest or bog or pasture, etc. being painted on to each piece. Like the article, the representation was done on a county-by-county basis, and the whole work thus formed a jigsaw of Ulster. County by county, the children had to reconstruct historic Ulster by matching sheets and pieces – no fitting together was allowed until the matching was complete. The reconstruction was thus carried out through the use of sources of which the pieces were an ikonic translation. The pieces, and ultimately the counties, were then fitted together and a complete reconstruct-ion of historical Ulster was the result.

Attention was next turned to the equipment of the two sides. Each side was subdivided into infantry and cavalry, and the attempt was made to re-create, in a set of slides, the precise details of the conditions under which a typical member of each sub-group campaigned, and then to draw out the implications of this, given that the war was fought over the kind of terrain already discov-ered from the jigsaw. Together terrain and logistics constitute the 'enabling knowledge' necessary to empathize[11] with our soldier and, to some extent, with commanders as their plans and decisions are set in the re-created context of their problems seen from the inside. For reasons of space, only one of the detailed inquiries will be given here, but the other three sub-groups were similarly treated. (The entire programme was presented in the form of slides.)

The investigation of the English infantry began with a contemporary print of 'A captain of pike'. The picture is interesting and vividly illustrates armour and weapons of the period. The attempt was then made to turn this *illustration* into an *ikon* by drawing out its latent significance in the context of the Nine Years' War. A copy drawing of the picture was presented with items of armour named, followed by pictures of the pieces of armour, front and side views. By discussion the children gathered the elementary point of *weight* (especially in contrast to the Irish soldiers similarly investigated). The question then arose 'How heavy?' A slide of a letter to the writer from the Tower of London was presented giving the weights of the various items, which the children added together. A further slide presented a letter from an English commander com-plaining first of the lack of cart-horses and then of its consequence. Since the soldiers had to carry their own supplies and could only carry about a week's food, their mobility was greatly reduced. The next few slides presented inform-ation from sources about a man's rations for a week. The weight of this was added to that of the armour and the total found to be about that of a small child. The point of this was driven home by slides of a chase over boggy ground in which an adult pursuer carried a child of the right weight on her back. The slide of her collapse was immediately followed by a drawing of a contemporary soldier in the same posture, and, finally, an extract from a further contemporary letter was shown:

> The road was a broken causey beset on both sides with bogs where the Irish might skip but the English could not go.[12]

This highly successful (see below) assignment was almost entirely visual in its presentation. It is true that at crucial points in the sequence a slide of a document (i.e. a written material) was introduced, but this does not weaken the claim that the assignment was essentially visual. What was at stake was a reconstruction that will explain the course and duration of the war and this was achieved by inferences drawn overwhelmingly from visual sources, the verbal interpolations (such as the reference to the lack of cart-horses) being items of information that gain significance solely from this visually derived context. Certainly, they can contribute importantly to its articulation, but this does not alter their essentially subordinate role; it merely provides a good example of the interplay of verbal and visual elements within the 'representational continuum' explained above.

Since the means of achieving reconstruction are here essentially visual, and since reconstruction must involve reaching below surface appearances to draw out their implications, the attempt, on a strict Brunerian view, should be difficult; for 'inference and implication' are of course examples of just the 'silent and invisible' factors with which (Bruner holds) visual representation is ill-designed to deal. However, Bruner does not seem to consider sufficiently the inferential suggestiveness of visual representation; its power to point, articulate and summarize at any rate some forms of 'silent and invisible' content. In the foregoing example two visuals, one showing an armed soldier, the other marshy and heavily wooded terrain, can perhaps change from discrete pictures into a powerful ikon for the reconstruction of a past reality because in combination they vividly, though inferentially, encode the 'hidden and silent' *significance* of what, singly, they palpably show. Certainly language, especially discussion, may play a large part in effecting this transformation (the interlocking of symbolic and ikonic codes has, after all, been insisted on throughout the chapter) but when inference is what is at stake visual materials have an advantage. Unlike verbal materials, they do not have to be held in a mind simultaneously busy with attempting to think or talk about them. In the present case the various pictures can stay on the screen together for as long as is necessary while their significance in combination is extracted from what they individually show. And what may stay in the mind is the visual encoding of that significance in concrete form – the final picture of the soldier stuck in the bog which may be filed as a summarizing ikon, reference to which can, on subsequent occasions, refresh the memory and reactivate understanding of the entire sequence that it summarizes and, hence, of the rationale of the course and conduct of the war.

III.   PUPILS' ATTITUDES – POPULARITY AND POWER OF IKONIC REPRESENTATION

The main object of the experiment was to test for differences in performance attributable to the different teaching strategies rather than to differences of presentation, verbal or visual, within the programme approach it-self; consequently, no overt provision was made for assessing the different contributions to learning of visual and verbal elements respect-ively. Yet it is obviously desirable that some estimate of this should be obtained, and this was done by ascertaining the *popularity* of the various materials in the programme. Since 'affective' and 'cognitive' aspects of learning are closely connected, especially in the younger pupil, it is surely reasonable to attribute any success he may achieve mainly to the form of rep-resentation for which he expresses a preference (if he does). Accordingly, at the end of the experiment every child was asked to fill in a questionnaire indi-cating which parts of the work he had enjoyed and which he had disliked. It will be recalled from the previous article (1978) in which test results were reported that experience of the programme (the 'structured inquiry' approach) had a very marked effect upon test performance. If the measure now proposed (children's preferences) should indicate strong liking for the visual materials, then the programme's effect in boosting test scores must surely be largely attri-buted to its visual components. This is all the more so in that the test sources from which questions had to be answered contained no visual materials. Pupils who had enjoyed, and (when they could in the classwork) learned from, the visual sources thus had to apply their visually derived learning to a verbally coded test – in short to 'translate' from ikonic to symbolic representation. In so far as test results showed that they could do so, this demonstrates the effective-ness of the ikonic coding in that it not only taught the content at stake but did so in a way that was readily translatable into an alternative (symbolic) coding (written answers to printed test questions).

In fact, the children's preference for visual representation can only be described as overwhelming. For each assignment the various elements of the work were listed and the children indicated preferences by numbering them 1, 2, 3, etc. Combining the votes for assignments I, II, and IV (assignment III is excluded as it contained no verbal element and therefore cannot be used for

Table 6.1   Comparison of visual and verbal materials

	Most liked	Least liked	Visual or verbal type of material
Slides	309	12	Visual
Documents	59	17	Verbal
Tapes	30	15	Verbal
Answering worksheet questions	24	18	Verbal
Giving written reasons for answers to questions	0	277	Verbal

this comparison), the extent of the preference for visual materials can be seen in Table 6.1

There is reason to think that the preference was even more marked than the figures in Table 6.1 suggest. First, only items such as slides and documents that figured in all the assignments used (I, II and IV) were included. This meant that several visual items – notably the summary map for assignment I (see p. 159 above) – were excluded and did not affect the voting. Some of these items were known to be highly popular, and would undoubtedly have boosted the visual preference score.

The children were also asked to indicate which assignment, and which three single items in the whole programme, they had enjoyed most. Unfortunately some of them misunderstood the wording of this request and their responses had to be discounted, but from those that were unambiguous assignment III (the entirely visual one) was by far the most popular with eighty-nine (valid) votes. The other three together totalled only fifty-seven among them. As to individual items, the five most popular were all visual. The jigsaw was the most liked by every class except one (where it was second most popular). The big (campaign) map in assignment IV or the summary map in assignment I – which was not always clear – followed by the slides to assignments II and I and II in that order were the next most liked.

The children were also invited to add any comment they wished about the experiment and, in particular, to say whether they had preferred the control or programme approaches. Seven of the eight classes preferred the programme approach and the voting of the one apparent exception (as is shown below) cannot be taken at face value. Given the present advocacy of ikonic represent-ation and of a 'forms of knowledge' approach, the children's *reasons* for preferring the programme and for favouring the visual elements within it are even more significant than the mere fact that they did so. Their dawning and intuitive, but genuine, apprehension of the nature of history emerges clearly from the comments of the grammar school girls particularly in their stress on the importance of evidence and on 'getting inside' the reality they are re-constructing.

'It made history more interesting. I enjoyed working out the answers.' 'Tremendously interesting . . . I really enjoyed going deep into the documents to find English and Irish methods of warfare; [making the map from the documents in assignment IV] . . . made us think things out for ourselves using our own judgement.' The secondary pupils were equally explicit if less fluent. One mixed class of modest ability was particularly favourable to the programme, including (surprisingly) the documents. One boy wrote 'I like history better this year because of the docnents [sic].' Another agreed: 'If history could be like this all the time with slides, tapes, papers, etc. it would be far more interesting than the tax [sic] book.' Even more explicitly one grammar school girl wrote 'The work gave us a glimpse of the job historians do.' She liked 'imagining we were the actual person rather than an onlooker' and many of her peers agreed. In short, reconstruction *by* empathy and *from* evidence is coming to colour the pupils' consciousness and the process seems intriguing and enjoyable to them.

The children's comments are just as informative about the power (as well as the popularity) of visual presentation. One 10-year-old wrote 'I liked the slides better than talking because it [sic] showed it happening and it puts a better idea on your mind.' Another primary child maintained that 'We learned as much from the slides as we did from the sources [i.e. documents].' Grammar school girls put exactly the same point more fluently. 'The slides were a great help [with the worksheet]. It [the visual presentation] made it easier to imagine the difficulties they had to face.' From the visual sources (especially jigsaw and big map), 'one could *see* how the English started to capture [sic] around Derry whereas the papers just seemed to be names and dates'. Most telling of all, perhaps, is the letter written by one girl in the less-able grammar school class:

> I enjoyed this work very much. It is a lot more interesting than ordinary classwork. When we done [sic] ordinary work I hated coming to history because it was so boring but the new type of work is great. I have learnt an awful lot more from these slides, tapes and maps. The slides were very interesting to look at as you could see what the real-life looked like without just listening. I hope we get more of this work to do next year.

We turn now to a more detailed examination of the responses of the oldest and ablest class in the sample, class C, which was unique in expressing a strong preference for the control (orthodox teaching) approach.[14] Two points are of especial interest: the nature of the preference itself – how far it can be taken at face value – and the very strong preference for visual materials that class C share with all other pupils.

There can be no doubt whatever on this latter point. Despite the 4–1 adverse vote on the programme, twenty-four pupils (out of thirty) made favourable comments on it and twenty of these, sometimes very favourable indeed, refer to visuals. By contrast, of the thirty unfavourable comments – sometimes de-vastatingly so – only one refers to visuals and is relatively mild – the slides 'got boring after a good start'. Even the pupil who wrote 'For the most of it I found it very boring and a complete waste of time' found the campaign map 'enjoy-able' and allowed that the slides were 'sometimes interesting'. The visual/verbal contrast was really pointed by the young lady who wrote 'All interesting and different. I wish we could always do it, except those question-naires [she means the worksheets] are a *menace*. The question "give reasons for your answer" is awful'; and by her class-mate who felt she could 'even bear those papers if we had lots of other things like jigsaws, maps, slides, sketches, etc.'.

It seems that the heavy anti-programme vote is, first, an anti-worksheet, and to a lesser extent, an anti-document vote. (It seems to have been the use they were required to make of the documents rather than the printed source-based work *per se* that upset the pupils. One girl, for example, liked assignment IV because it had no worksheet and the documents could be used 'by them-selves'.) But this is not the whole explanation, for all other classes shared the hatred of worksheets; yet, without exception, they voted for programme approach because of their enjoyment of its visual and manipulative elements. The second explanation of class C's anti-programme vote involves a consideration that weighed heavily with them but (as far as can be judged from the questionnaires) not at all with the other children. Again and again (fifteen overt references) C's responses reflected doubt and anxiety concerning the *value* of the programme work. For example, 'We had no notes to revise from'; 'I need notes'; 'Time was wasted . . . we have very little to show for the work. I can remember very little.' Several pupils seemed to feel almost guilty at enjoying the (visual) programme. One girl who 'really enjoyed' the campaign map concluded rather sadly that she 'learned more the ordinary way' and voted for control approach. Even the pupil who by her comment that the tapes and slides fitted together 'to [let us] actually see and think what it was like many hundreds of years ago', and voted for the programme approach, was uneasily (?) aware that 'we learned more the old way'.

What is revealed here, of course, is the consequence of too sharply diverging from pupils' expectations. Underlying the opinions quoted (and the many similar ones) is the tacit but unquestioned assumption that history is simply a connected body of facts – to be understood, certainly, but then to be memorized and held available for recall at examination time. References to 'learning more the old way' seem to mean that more ground was covered and that the information gained was safely garnered in notebooks. To cover only ten years in a term, and to have, at the end, no permanent record of the usual kind, clearly pointed at the type of examination to which they are accustomed, and left many pupils in a position of considerable insecurity. I suspect, though I have no direct evidence, that parental attitudes may be significant here. Few parents are likely to understand the rationale of the programme approach and those of 'high flying' grammar school pupils are likely, *on average*, to be both more involved with their children's studies and more inclined, and able, to express an adverse opinion than those of the other children.

There are grounds, then, for thinking that class C's vote cannot really be taken at face value as evidence of hostility to the programme approach as such. In so far as the vote reflects dislike of the worksheet and, in particular, of having to 'give reasons' it was not unexpected and poses no serious problem. The worksheets were present solely to give reasonable uniformity of treatment (given that this was an experiment) so that 'programme approach' could confidently be assumed to mean a uniform thing. They could easily be done away with or drastically modified so as to remove their most objectionable element (giving written reasons). In so far as the objection relates to the worksheets it is easy to remove.

The second objection – pupils' doubts as to the value of programme work, despite their liking for it – is more intractable, for the really fundamental question underlying this practical dilemma is, of course, the epistemological one with which we began. What *is* history? That is, what are the distinctive features which (or some of which) must figure in any practical programme with pretensions to validity? This question cannot be pursued in this short chapter[15] but the present example is an interesting illustration of its importance. The pupils' expectations no less imply an answer, albeit tacit, than does the programme, and the incompatibility of the two cries out for resolution. *No* practical course can avoid the question – even the teacher who ignores it does not *avoid* it: he is merely uncritical (or unaware) of his assumptions – and makes his pupils so also. A *reasoned* approach cannot but involve its judicious consideration. The general epistemological issue applies to all subjects and concerns all teachers: it is the essence of the 'forms of knowledge' argument. Immediately, however, we are concerned with a possible solution to the practical dilemma that must be sought in compromise. I would suggest dividing the three terms of the school year between programme (source-based) and orthodox (teacher-based) approaches using the latter in the Spring term to connect two in-depth programme-type studies in the Christmas and Summer terms. (Or the balance could be reversed, or could alternate from year to year.) In this way epistemological requirements, pupil anxieties, and parental perceptions might well be harmonized.

It seems that class C's attitude to the programme is in fact favourable, or could easily be made so. What is quite beyond dispute is the unambiguous and overwhelming vote in favour of the visual approach. In this respect class C's preferences scarcely diverge from those of the other children and the efficiency of the visuals for learning already strongly inferred (see p. 162 above) receives further overt support.

IV. CONCLUSION

All in all the present experiment suggests that a 'forms of knowledge structured inquiry' approach would be popular and feasible. The test results presented in the previous article[16] showed that the programme was effective in implementing a 'forms of knowledge' course with children of varying levels of ability over a three-year age range, while the evidence of the questionnaire very strongly indicates that it was the heavy use of visual presentation that was responsible for the popularity of the programme. It must surely be concluded, then, that visual representation was effective for learning – for otherwise the highly superior test results associated with the programme strategy must be attributed to items viewed with indifference or hatred. Specifically, the stress laid on *reconstruction* (which was entailed by the nature of history, given that this was a 'forms of knowledge' approach) surely indicates that ikonic representation is not always tied to surface appearances. For many of the component skills of reconstruction, such as inference forming or assumption finding, are by definition invisible and non-palpable. Ikons, can, it seems, sometimes reach silent and invisible factors: when visual and verbal representation were placed to some extent in competition in assignment II the visually biased treatment proved more effective for reconstructing the relevant (strategic) reality. What is *con*ceptually important can sometimes be made *per*ceptually vivid – or at least perceptual vividness is not necessarily an obstacle to conceptualizing, but may be a valuable prop to its development: when solely (or almost solely) visual means were used in an attempt at an explanatory reconstruction (assignment

III) the attempt was both successful and highly popular. And, finally, since the test was entirely verbal in form the results mean that the children could 'translate' their visually based learning into symbolic notation, so that the stress laid on 'translation' in the programme – the 'representational continuum' – was productive and justified.[17]

NOTES

1. For a detailed defence of this claim see Rogers, P. J., *The New History – Theory into Practice*, Historical Association, 1979, especially ch. 1.
2. Rogers, P. J., 'An experimental test of a "forms of knowledge" approach to teaching', *Educational Research*, vol. 20, no. 2, February 1978, pp. 130–6.
3. Bruner, J. S., *The Process of Education*, Harvard University Press, 1960, p. 33.
4. Bruner, J. S. *et al.*, *Studies in Cognitive Growth*, John Wiley, 1966, p. 26.
5. ibid., p. 29.
6. ibid., pp. 8–9.
7. One thinks of the raven hoarsely croaking Duncan's fatal entrance; of Heaven peeping through the blanket of the dark; of Pity, like a naked new-born babe; of the stealthy pace of withered murder as he moves, ghost-like, towards his design; of the brief candle, lighting fools the way to dusty death.
8. For two attempts to use enactive representation, see Rogers, P. J., and Aston, F. M., 'Play, enactive representation and learning', *Teaching History*, no. 19, October 1977, pp. 18–21; and Rogers, P. J., 'Play and enactive representation in teaching mathematics', *Scottish Educational Review*, vol. 11, no. 1, May 1979, pp. 29–41.
9. For reconstruction as the essence of history, see Rogers, '*The New History*', op cit., ch. 1, section 2.
10. Extract from a letter sent by Sir Calisthenes Brooke to the Privy Council in 1595.
11. Empathy is, of course, a very important aspect of reconstruction. See Chapter 1 of this volume.
12. The last three paragraphs are taken from Rogers, *The New History*, op. cit. They are an integral part of the present argument.
13. It should be realized that Northern Ireland retains a selective system of post-primary education.
14. Voting was 4–1 as opposed to a general reverse preference of over 2–1 – which, incidentally, underestimates the degree to which the programme was preferred. (The justification of this is as follows. First, in at least one primary class it was obvious from the accompanying comments that several 'anti programme' votes were really merely 'anti worksheet'; secondly, another primary class were taken on a visit to a castle during the summer term – when, as it happened, they were following the control approach. The result may be imagined. The visit preoccupied them and the 'pro control' vote (a bare majority anyway) was really a 'pro visit' vote.)
15. For the present writer's view, see Rogers, *The New History*, op. cit., especially ch. 1; and Rogers, P. J., 'History', in Dixon, K. (ed.), *Philosophy of Education and the Curriculum*, Pergamon Press, 1972, pp. 75–134.
16. Rogers, 'An experimental test of a "forms of knowledge" approach to teaching', op. cit.
17. The nature of the visual materials used makes their reproduction in this book impracticable. However, copies of the slides are available, and anyone interested should write to Dr. P. J. Rogers, Department of Further Professional Studies in Education, The Queen's University, Belfast BT7 1NN.

7. Understanding the Past: Procedures and Content

D. THOMPSON

I. INTRODUCTION

This chapter is divided into four sections, including this introductory section, but it is hoped that the reader will regard them as parts of a coherent whole, the basic theme and concern of which is the kind of historical understanding and awareness that teachers should be concerned to develop. The two areas of generalized discussion clearly have a strong connection and can, in an important sense, be seen as complementary. The specific analysis and example with which the chapter concludes arises directly from the analysis that precedes it.

The opening two sections contain some reflections on two major recent developments in the approach to history in school, both of which have had considerable impact on classroom practice and arose out of a widespread concern about many aspects of traditional school history. More specifically, it was felt that these defects made it difficult to present a forceful and valid case for the continued existence of history in the school curriculum at a time when what should be taught was coming under increasing scrutiny, and new subjects such as sociology and politics were advancing their claims. The two developments are, first, the move to a concept of history that emphasizes the methodology of the subject and requires the extensive and developing use by the pupils of sources as evidence, from which they reconstruct a picture of the past; and secondly, a concern with analysing the development of central aspects of the pupils' thinking and understanding in history based on how they respond to and comprehend actual historical situations. These areas reflect the two basic interpretations of what history means – what actually happened in the human past and the historian's reconstruction, from the remaining evidence, of an intelligible and significant account of what happened. That there was a past that is separate from and independent of the historian is clear, just as it is that we can only come to know that past as a result of historical inquiry. It will be argued here that both elements should make a significant contribution to the justification of the study of history, that both should be regarded as important in any school history course, but that while a knowledge of the process of inquiry is essential, the encouragement of an understanding of and response to actual historical situations and developments remains the fundamental justification for the study of history in school.

The final part of the chapter examines a specific example of the causal analysis of an 'important' event in English history – the Peasants' Revolt of 1381. The example itself has no particular significance, but this type of explanatory causal framework, dealing with developments over a period of time, is frequently used and is important in history teaching, and it is hoped that the example will shed light on some of the common elements in this type of analysis.

II. THE 'NEW' HISTORY

Of all the suggestions for change in the purpose and nature of school history in the last fifteen years, the most fundamental and radical, both in theoretical terms and in its implications for what should be done in the name of school history, is the argument that its central concern should be developing an understanding of the methods or process of historical inquiry. The focus of study in schools should not be on the past as such and what has happened, but rather on how we come to acquire our knowledge of that past. Contact with and response to the *product* of historical inquiry, actual situations and developments that occurred, becomes secondary to the *process* of inquiry, to the methodology (or important aspects of the methodology) by which that knowledge is acquired. At its best this is to be achieved by the pupils making extensive, guided, thoughtful and increasingly demanding use of the sources of history as evidence. Such activity is clearly the central and unique characteristic of the 'new' history.[1] Seminal works in the early 1970s advocating such an approach were Lamont,[2] albeit in the context of a critical evaluation of traditional history examinations, and a moderate and limited advocacy by Edwards.[3] These were followed by a number of books and articles that extended the arguments and often the claims for the new history, the philosophy of which was a key element in the theoretical underpinning of the Schools Council History Project.[4] Its philosophical case in the context of the nature of historical knowledge was impressively presented by Rogers in 1979, along with an analysis of some possible ways in which it might be applied in the classroom.[5] Whereas earlier attempts to encourage an evidence-based approach to school history stuttered and failed in terms of their general acceptance,[6] it can now reasonably be said that the recent advocacy has generated a widespread response at all levels in the secondary schools, to the point where some are already referring to it as the new orthodoxy. Its acceptability is clearly demonstrated by, but not restricted to, the number of schools using the Schools Council Project *What is History?* units, and, to a lesser extent, those following the Project's O level and CSE courses, and the AEB's pilot scheme for A level.

The new history has brought a dimension to the nature of historical study and understanding that was completely absent from traditional school history. As is well known, sources of any kind were rarely used in that context, and to the extent that they were, it was almost invariably to illustrate or embellish an already identified or established historical 'fact' or event.[7] In the traditional framework, that we knew about the past was taken for granted and questions related to how we knew were regarded as having no place in school history.

A further major argument supporting the new history is that it must, by definition, do much to counter the fundamentally false view of the nature of history that much traditional teaching did and still does inculcate – that it is a body of established and indisputable facts and that things happened as they did with almost complete inevitability. The whole nature and procedure of the new history approach is the opposite of such a view, for encouraging pupils to re-construct their own accounts from evidence must highlight the problems, difficulties and uncertainties that relate to historical knowledge. The danger in this instance – and it could, with poor teaching, be a serious danger – is much more that the pupils will either develop an excessively subjective picture of the past, or the whole possibility of any sound historical knowledge might be questioned. Further, the new history is by definition a 'reconstruction' activity that lends itself very easily to a problem-solving approach, at the centre of which are the pupils' own ideas and analyses, and where there is considerable scope for the teacher to set up the discussion and evaluation of them. In this context, one of the principal benefits claimed for this approach is the contri-bution it can make to a more reasoned and critical examination of the actions and decisions of people, and of the basis upon which they can be known. The pupil is involved in the reconstruction of particular situations in the past within the framework of a careful and critical use of evidence. Central to the new history will be the development of a more penetrating and discerning use of sources as evidence – of the identification and interpretation of relevant evidence; the relating of separate pieces of evidence and an awareness of possible conflict between them; recognition of what the evidence will carry and that it may be inadequate to support a definite conclusion; assessing the reli-ability of evidence – for example, bias; arriving at judgements or 'accounts' on the basis of the sources and defending these by reference to the relevant evidence in those sources. The pupils are not being asked to accept an author-ized account or opinion of people in the past, but to formulate and justify their own account, to present a reasoned argument for their statements and views and to develop an appreciation that at times it is difficult to be certain of our understanding of historical situations and that there is room for a variety of views. It is argued that such a study of the behaviour of people in the past should encourage a more discerning and thoughtful examination of con-temporary human affairs, and that in a world where new issues and develop-ments are constantly emerging, it is the way of looking at them that matters, a questioning approach that will show a concern for supporting evidence and an evaluation of the arguments in terms of it. If the way history is studied in school encourages such an approach to the understanding of contemporary affairs, then the case for its inclusion in the modern curriculum is that much the stronger.

All the above arguments amount to a powerful case for the new history, yet there remain serious grounds for concern if it is suggested that this approach should form the basis of history in schools. Important though the development of reasoned and critical thinking in relation to human activity is, it is extremely doubtful whether this of itself could ever amount to a sufficient justification for the study of history. Neither the new history nor the more enlightened and demanding study of actual historical situations and developments (which is argued for later in this chapter) have any exclusive claims in this area. Specifically, the selective and critical use of evidence to understand human actions and intentions could be encouraged by the study of fictional situations that were purpose-built to develop and reinforce those aspects of the assessment of evidence thought to be important, free of the constraints and difficulties that might apply to the use of evidence in history. Indeed, in the first of the Schools Council case studies in *What is History?*, Mark Pullen admirably demonstrates this.[8] Many pupils and teachers seem to find this a more satisfactory exercise *for these purposes* than some of the 'historical' examples that follow. But it may well be argued that it is the reality of history that makes its study important (which implies that we can establish that reality), and therefore that we must examine what actually happened, what people actually did, or rather the evidence for what they did, and that artificial constructions can never be a substitute for historical work. Why, then, not study contemporary events or those of the very recent past, where the additional argument of the subject matter having more immediate 'relevance' to the present world and experience of the pupils might be invoked? Clearly it is impossible to make any sense of contemporary events or the recent past without a knowledge of their history and further, the extent of our understanding of the significance of current developments lacks the perspective of time. Both these points are a part of the central concept of hindsight, but the importance of this relates not so much to the procedures or methods of the subject as to an awareness and understanding of their product, namely what has happened in the past. It is this that enables us to put our present world in its historical perspective.

The writings of some of the advocates of the new history seem to suggest that the only alternative to that approach is the transmission of a mass of teacher-centred, useless and inert historical information which will suffocate any worthwhile pupil activity, inquiry or understanding.[9] This was not true even of good 'traditional' teaching, but it certainly is not the case when teachers are freed from the requirement to cover such vast amounts of history, when ideas of how to exploit the study of actual historical situations in a more active and demanding way have been more carefully thought out, and when the purposes of studying the past are radically different from those that underpinned traditional school history. The manner in which history was often presented in the classroom and the limited demands made on the pupils in terms of their thinking and ideas has been quite rightly rejected, but the baby will have disappeared with the bath-water if the values that can come from a thoughtful and positive response to the study of the historical past, a study concerned to develop an insight, awareness and evaluation of how and why people in the past acted as they did, are underplayed or discarded. The time is right to reassert that it is the nature of the subject matter of history – its concern with understanding a variety of human actions and behaviour in the past, of examining situations and problems that were faced and lived through, the dimension of change in human affairs over time – that is the fundamental justification of historical study, and that this can offer a particular perspective and insight into the present world and experience of the pupil. The challenge of history teaching is to stimulate children to put themselves in the position of people in the past, to think about what the human past was like, and from that many important aspects of cognitive and affective development can be encouraged, including the important areas of historical imagination and empathy.[10] The critical factor is, as always, how the teacher encourages the pupil to respond to and think about past situations, how the past is made to work, but there is every scope for the use of more pupil-centred, problem-solving methods, for individual and group work, and for creating a classroom atmosphere where what matters is not 'covering the ground', but the development of the pupils' understanding of that piece of history, and the opportunities for them to express and work out their own ideas about it. Studying the 'content of history' does not have to be a mindless and inert process.[11]

This does not mean that the importance of giving children insight into how we know about the human past is rejected. Rogers's point that we cannot talk meaningfully about historical knowledge without the dimension of some understanding of how that knowledge is arrived at, is indisputable,[12] and at the level of classroom practice, the benefits of working with sources as evidence have already been outlined and are well established. But it does mean that studying the procedures of history should not form the basis of the school course, because this would too severely restrict opportunities for the pupil to examine and think about actual historical situations. Dickinson, Gard and Lee have clearly indicated that the dichotomy between 'content' and 'method' cannot be sustained, and that historical use of sources as evidence requires contextual knowledge.[13] It might be that advocates of the new history, recognizing the force of this argument, would accept the infusion of some contextual knowledge as a necessary element in the appropriate historical use of sources. But this would be inadequate and very limited both in usage and above all in purpose, because its function would clearly be no more than to allow of the better use of evidence. Still less would the position of Rogers, that one could build up contextual knowledge from the sources[14] be acceptable, because this would again mean concentrating on the use of sources as evidence in a way that would have a very limiting implication for the analysis and understanding of 'content'.[15] The contention here is that the study of events and developments in history are central in their own right, but that within such a study, the teacher should build in the use of a variety of sources as evidence for reconstructing the past, and thereby develop an understanding of that essential element of historical knowledge. Indeed it might be argued that the best possible understanding of the place of evidence in the process of historical inquiry would come from using it in such a way, within a sound knowledge and understanding of the historical context to which it relates. Perhaps the concept of the 'new' history should be broadened out from a concentration on procedures and methodology into an approach that recognizes the importance of studying the past in 'new' ways, ways whose basic concern is to develop children's understanding of and response to the position of people in the past, and within which the use of sources as evidence would still be seen as an important element.

III.   CHILDREN'S THINKING IN HISTORY

The growing interest in analysing and evaluating children's thinking in history in recent years has been one of the major influences encouraging the more thoughtful and stimulating examination of the 'content' of history that has been advocated here. It is worth re-emphasizing that the purpose of this approach is to encourage an understanding of and response to past situations, the antithesis of imparting an indigestible mass of inert information. As is well known, much of the early research and many of the ideas in this area were strongly influenced by work on the general development of children's thinking by Piaget and Peel, and two recent substantial contributions, which have taken our knowledge in this area a good deal further, have made direct and to some extent conflicting observations on this connection. Dickinson and Lee question the extent to which the work of either Piaget or Peel can make a significant contribution to the study of children's historical understanding, a fundamental point in their critique being that the procedures and observations of both are based on and relate much more closely to problems and reasoning that are characteristic of science rather than history.[16] There is undoubtedly much in this for, as they indicate, important areas – a covering law type of explanatory framework, a concern with the common and classifiable aspects of situations, and in particular Peel's application of the process of equilibrium, tension, change to human affairs – are basic features of scientific thinking, and to impose such a pattern on history could result in a serious distortion of the subject and to the values of studying it. It remains true that 'the first and vital stage in research into how children think in history should be a careful examination of what is meant by historical thinking',[17] rather than starting with the procedures and criteria of any general work on children's thinking, and hoping or assuming that history will fit neatly into that pattern. This is the justified concern of Dickinson and Lee and the basis of their questioning the value of Piaget and Peel in the context of thinking in history.[18] It is possible, however, to accept that there are major differences between the subject matter and procedures of science and those of history, and agree that the characteristic feature of a historical view of the past is a concern with human activity in particular situations and at particular periods in time, without rejecting the value of the respective frameworks of thinking that Piaget and Peel suggest, and that is the most general outcome of their work. This is the view of Shemilt, who has studied a fund of evidence from work undertaken in the context of evaluating the Schools Council Project, and who has a more sympathetic view of the contribution that Piaget's developmental analysis might make. 'Despite all the problems, it is possible to feel optimistic about the applicability of Piagetian genetic epistemology to children's learning of history. But a version of this theory specifically tailored to history must be devised.'[19] The importance of the rider should not be underestimated, but nor should the basic premise – that these ideas can provide a basis from which those interested in historical understanding can derive value, initially of a background and general character that will require adaptation and application to historical thinking.

The general outcome of the work of Piaget and Peel, the notion of a broad framework of levels of thinking that are followed through sequentially (the essential features of Piaget's concrete and formal stages of operational thinking and Peel's 'describer' and 'explainer' categories are broadly comparable) and the general criteria by which these levels are identified, can offer insights into how children will approach and deal with historical problems and situations. The indication that at one level children will tend to be restricted in their thinking about a variety of problems by a concentration on the immediate information and evidence[20] in a reasoned but fairly straightforward way whereas at a higher level they will appreciate the limitations of the information, will tend to think through and beyond the immediate evidence in a disciplined manner, hypothesize and consider possibilities not immediately stated or apparent, is a general but useful distinction. Two brief examples of its application to history will serve to indicate the possibilities, the first of which relates to a central aspect of the pilot study of Dickinson and Lee on the Battle of Jutland.[21]

Recognition that the information given or known about any historical situation may provide only a limited basis (or no basis at all) for coming to conclusions, that is questions relating to the adequacy of that information or knowledge and an awareness that there may well have been other factors influencing the situation that it is necessary to know about, is a central concern of the Jutland study and one of the important elements in the general levels of thinking identified by Piaget and Peel. Asking questions of the information or evidence and what it will support, not simply taking it at its face-value, and a realization that there are other possibilities that might explain a situation, are central features of formal operational and explainer thinking. The example quoted by Peel of responses to the story of Alfred and the cakes,[22] though not a question that historians would be interested in, establishes this in principle very clearly. It is not possible to conclude that Alfred could not cook; there may well have been other factors that affected him in that *particular* situation.

It may well be that interventionist strategies that guide pupils towards a consideration of such matters, both in classroom discussion and in written work (as in the Jutland study), have an important contribution to make to developing this kind of understanding and should form a much more important part of the history teacher's technique.[23] It is only when pupils have accommodated this into their own thinking, when they typically approach information and evidence in this kind of way, that it has clearly become a part of their way of seeing such problems. Only then is it possible to talk of higher levels of understanding being established and consolidated.

The second example is concerned with the complementary activity to appreciating the limitations of the information and evidence, namely how well pupils are able to exploit it, how much they can make it work and contribute to their understanding. Essential aspects of this activity are the ability to identify and consider connections between different aspects of the historical situation being examined,[24] the drawing of inferences and consideration of possibilities that will rest on an understanding of these connections and that can be substantiated by reference to the information or evidence given. In an example quoted elsewhere,[25] children of different ages were given some information about the background of William I which gave a broad context or background to the Domesday Survey and were then asked why they thought William had the survey carried out. There were those answers that clearly showed an appreciation of the connection between aspects of the contextual situation – the significance of his being a new king who had only recently established his authority and who would want to know what his wealth, income and entitlements were – and further, which went beyond the immediate evidence and considered the usefulness to a king in that position of knowing who else was powerful and wealthy in the land and who, by inference, would be important to him. The understanding shown by that sort of response clearly demonstrates important aspects of formal/explainer thinking, which 'allow of a deeper level of insight into William's motives in undertaking Domesday'. In order to achieve this it was essential to go beyond the evidence directly concerned with the survey, to relate it to the contextual information that indicated that William had acquired the crown by conquest and had taken time to establish his authority throughout England, and to consider the connections and implications which that relationship suggests. Other responses were very much restricted to what was immediately obvious in the passage, and listed the kind of information he had asked for in the survey. They could clearly be categorized as 'content dominated' or concrete operational – they had not made the vital leap of connecting that information to William's position and considering how such knowledge would be *useful to him in his position at that time*. Again, interventionist strategies by the teacher, both oral and written, that are designed to push the pupils beyond the immediate evidence and encourage them to make connections between all the important aspects of a situation, could make an important contribution to developing understanding. Such strategies would give teachers valuable feedback as to how pupils saw that situation and should give ample scope for them to work out and discuss their own ideas.

The central focus of the earlier work of Dickinson and Lee is on appreciating the position of people or agents in the past in order to understand the actions that they took in a particular situation, and also to identify how those actions might be seen subsequently (by the historian) and how they were seen by the people at the time. This, though challenging, is undoubtedly a central element in historical understanding and it is also a matter of considerable importance in the wider context of the justification of the place of history in the curriculum, as discussed above. It concentrates attention on history as a study and re-enactment of human behaviour and on the need to appreciate the position, problems and decisions of people in the past. The pilot study on the Battle of Jutland (and additional material in this volume) gives some indication to teachers of possible ways in which such understanding might be encouraged, but above all it raises and illuminates this whole area as one of central concern to history teaching and historical understanding.

At the same time, at the level of classroom practice, it raises two important and related questions – first, the probable complexity and amount of content required in 'providing much more information than usual'[26] about the position of people in the past; secondly, and a direct consequence of the above point, the level of generality of the treatment of historical topics in school history, and the scope and range of historical situations to which the pupils might be exposed.

The pilot study was, of course, a research exercise, but it clearly highlights the problem, central to any such approach, of the amount of information or evidence that pupils might need to handle in order to see a situation in anything like the way it confronted people in the past. Dickinson and Lee clearly recognize this,[27] but within the exercise as set out, which is already complex and requires the holding in mind of a considerable amount of information, it could be argued that there is important additional information that the pupils need in order to understand why Jellicoe acted as he did. On the 'technical' side, for example, the accuracy and speed of torpedoes, the manoeuvrability of the ships in turning away; on the 'personal' side, the sort of man Jellicoe was and how he was likely to react in the kind of situation that confronted him. Was he the sort of man likely to be aggressive or to chance his arm or had he become imbued with caution and a defensive outlook, as one section of the information suggests?[28] To the extent that this is the case, it highlights a major problem: that even where one is dealing with 'a relatively "simple" historical situation in which an agent or groups of agents could be regarded as having a limited range of possibilities for action',[29] the amount and complexity of the information may be excessive in terms of what the pupils can handle and use effectively. It is valid criticism of school history that pupils are often asked to give answers to questions on the basis of very inadequate information. It is, however, necessary to recognize that there has to be an important activity of selection and simplification on the part of the teacher, invoking considerable professional judgement, of what it is reasonable to present to the pupils if they are able to take it fully into account and use it effectively in working out their ideas. Teachers might regard one element in the definition and identification of progress as a gradual reduction in the extent of simplification necessary and, correspondingly, a higher level of historical understanding on the part of the pupils. This may appear to be a statement of the obvious, but it commits the teacher to a clear emphasis on encouraging pupils to put themselves in the position of people in the past, of giving them increasingly demanding contextual information to do this more adequately, of encouraging them to work out their own ideas and responses, and of evaluating and developing understanding.

A second important consideration arising from the analysis is the level of generality at which history is taught in schools.[30] It has been argued that within the teaching of any historical topic, the level of generality of that treatment must be reasonably consistent if distortion or misunderstanding are to be avoided.[31] The Battle of Jutland study is a highly detailed and specific examination of one decision taken in a major naval battle in the First World War, and such an analysis was essential for the purposes of study. At the other extreme, history teachers do sometimes operate at a very high level of generality, when for example dealing with the background to a new area of study or the summary treatment of a major topic which might cover a long period of time. Within the framework of the purposes and outcomes of studying history and of children's understanding of history, it seems not only possible but necessary that pupils should examine the past at different levels of generality, but that consistency of treatment and selection should be maintained *within* those levels. Considerations such as the concern of history with change and development over time, the intelligibility and significance of particular situations both within themselves and in the wider framework to which they relate, the importance of bringing pupils into contact with a variety of human experience and activity, all indicate the value and contribution that a range of levels of generality might bring to the overall study of history.

In order that the Jutland exercise should be intelligible, the information given had to include the wider context of the First World War, the role of the navy in that war and the general naval strategy of the time. Such highly detailed in-depth studies of very specific situations confronting individuals or groups in the past, and a careful analysis of why they acted as they did in those particular circumstances, ought to be a part of the strategy of all history teachers, and they can be built into the treatment of a broader unit of teaching that would give them the necessary historical context. It would be straightforward, for example, to incorporate into a general study of the First World War a specialized examination of Jutland, a particular army action, etc. That teachers should make use of such studies is essential in the sense of the particular dimension they bring to an understanding of the past; how frequently such an approach was used would reflect the importance that individual teachers attached to the outcomes of such studies. The contribution their systematic use might make to the development of a central element of historical thinking, of creating an insight into the uncertainty surrounding the eventual outcome of the human past, and of giving a particular dimension to history, is considerable.

The history teacher will find himself more usually operating on a broader or more general level of treatment than this, but though the perspective will be different, the concern to foster understanding and to encourage pupils to work out their own ideas and interpretations of historical situations should remain fundamental. The final section of this chapter outlines and discusses some of the implications and possibilities of one particular type of a more generalized causal analysis.

IV. AN EXAMPLE OF CAUSAL ANALYSIS

History is concerned with the study of change and development in human affairs over time – indeed, it might be argued that this is one of the more distinctive elements that the study of history has to offer and that it should be an important consideration in school history, certainly throughout much of the secondary age range. To the extent that this is true it will usually mean operating at higher levels of generality and from a different perspective than that of a detailed analysis of particular events, and will bring its own learning challenges. Such an approach to history, if change and development are to be in any sense intelligible, must involve the identification and examination of causal connections between events and actions. There is some evidence to suggest that this is not well done in the classroom and that teachers often make dubious assumptions about the pupils' understanding.[32]In bad 'traditional' teaching, of course, this sort of analysis, which must involve judgement and discussion in relation to relevant evidence or information, was often dealt with in exactly the same way as the hard external events of history – cut and dried, and indisputable. The causes of the First World War were presented as being of the same order of 'events' as the fact that war was declared between Britain and Germany in August 1914. Such teaching would create or reinforce the kind of misunderstanding in relation to cause in history that Shemilt discusses, and if improvement is to be achieved teachers must be prepared to invest time in the careful study of causal connections and giving pupils enough opportunity to work out their own ideas and thinking.[33]

The whole area of the nature of historical explanation and the concept of cause in history is problematic and the subject of a considerable body of discussion, aspects of which have been taken up and examined in the context of their implications for history in schools and children's historical understanding.[34] The scope of this brief analysis is modest; it sets out to examine and discuss some of the implications of an established approach to the problem of presenting and examining change over time in an intelligible fashion and within a particular framework of causal connections. In school history it appears in a variety of contexts, but perhaps is demonstrated most clearly when teachers seek to get children to understand the analysis and explanation of a major 'event' in the period being studied. Typical examples might be the outbreak of the First World War or the English Civil War, or a major new development – such as the rapid spread of industrialization in late eighteenth-century and early nineteenth-century England. With hindsight, historians and history teachers often see factors at some distance from an event or development as being of major importance in understanding why things happened – and the notion of 'real', 'fundamental' or 'underlying' causes begins to emerge. As against this, the particular or immediate factors that brought things to a head, that ignited the bonfire in the case of wars or rebellions, and that are themselves often (but not always) to be understood as manifestations of or responses to the longer-term influences, are seen as the immediate or short-term causes. In certain situations it may be possible to identify critical changes happening over time, which are a central consideration in the overall explanatory framework.

An example of such a causal framework in relation to the outbreak of the Peasants' Revolt of 1381, together with some observations on the nature of the

responses of pupils of different ages, concludes this chapter. The questions set
were designed to test understanding of the different causal categories implicit
in the information that was presented. The example chosen (see Apendix I) is
reasonably typical of this type of analysis, and was originally used as part of a
small-scale empirical inquiry, which influenced its particular format and
presentation. There is no reason, however, why it could not be altered or
adapted to meet other circumstances – for example, made to fit into a unit of
teaching that had already dealt with the relevant aspects of medieval society,
such as the manorial system and feudalism.

The exercise was given to some 150 pupils in two schools, approximately
sixty of 12 + years of age, sixty of 14 + years of age and thirty in the lower sixth,
17 + years of age. They were asked to read the information in the introduction
and passage carefully, and then to answer the questions using that information. They were given as much time as they needed and if the meaning of any
individual word was not understood it was explained. The information
contained in the exercise was deliberately kept brief to give a generalized but
very directed analysis of developments that were clearly but not explicitly
related to the outbreak of revolt in 1381. The information was presented
chronologically and worded to bring out how a long-established situation
began to change and break down. The first two paragraphs sketch out in
summary some essential elements in the position of peasants and townspeople,
indicating clearly that these had been the normal pattern of things for a long
period of time. The third paragraph indicates the critical element of a fundamental change taking place in the position of some, but not all, peasants and
towns over time, namely that they obtained freedom from the lord. This information relates very directly and crucially to the information about what the
peasants did in 1381. The fourth paragraph introduces an important specific
factor – the Black Death – which reinforces the difference between those
peasants who had obtained freedom from the lord and those who remained
unfree, but which did not initiate the change. The final paragraph introduces
certain happenings in the ten years preceding 1381 – the 'immediate' factors
that would highlight discontent and hardship and led to the march on London.

The information was, therefore, deliberately presented in a way that fits the
pattern of causal analysis discovered earlier. No explicit connections are made
between the developments as outlined and the outbreak of revolt in 1381; it is left
to the pupils to think out what they regard as significant in the information and
the connection it might have with the revolt. The questions were specifically
designed to bring out the extent of the pupils' understanding of the different
elements in such an explanatory framework and whether they could establish a
consistent overall pattern of causal connections. The first two questions give
'background' factors that are necessary conditions, but clearly have existed for
a long time and cannot be a sufficient explanation; the third question introduces a critical change in the position of *some* peasants over time and question
four an event, the Black Death, that affected the implementation of that
change; question five highlights immediate causes of discontent in a very
specific manner and the final question relates to whether the lack of freedom of
some peasants and towns, in the light of what happened in 1381, might be

identified as a major cause of the revolt.

This is one type of exercise, set up as a small empirical study, whose basic focus is on children's understanding of change over time within a particular and established explanatory framework. There are many alternative, interventionist strategies, more or less damanding, that any teacher concerned to identify and develop the understanding of change over time could use with value and that could be built into his normal teaching programme; the essential starting point is a commitment to this as an important dimension of the value of studying history. A selective and limited analysis of some typical responses to questions one, three and six will provide some notion of the levels of understanding of change over time within this particular causal framework that this small sample of pupils showed in their written answers. It will also indicate how the pupils' own ideas and thoughts can provide an invaluable basis for further work and discussion to develop that understanding.

A typical sixth-form response to question (i) was that of Dawn (17 years 4 months):

> The hard life that the peasants led is quite important as a cause of the revolt, but it cannot be considered to be the most important point, because although their lives were hard, to them they were usual. For hundreds of years these people had not revolted because of their hard lives and this shows that other things must have contributed to the causes for the outbreak of the revolt.
>
> Perhaps one of the reasons of the revolt was that over the hundred years before the revolt, their hard lives had been eased a little for some, and others now realized how hard their existence was, and therefore the revolt took place to help the conditions of these people.

This clearly shows an awareness of the significance of the change and improvement in the position of some of the peasants in the period before the revolt, and of the fact that the harsh conditions were themselves not a sufficient explanation. Such understanding was characteristic of the great majority of sixth formers but not all. Murray (17 years 8 months), in the same class as Dawn, answered as follows:

> The harsh life of the peasants was an important factor in the cause of the Peasants' Revolt. The peasants and poor townspeople had only just about managed to remain alive. For hundreds of years they had been very badly treated and most of them expected to die before they reached the age of thirty. It is not surprising that the peasants finally revolted as they wanted to be treated fairly like normal human beings and they wanted to be able to live longer in decent conditions.

This response indicates no appreciation of the significance of the changes discussed by Dawn; the final sentence shows anachronistic thinking and ignores the information that a harsh life and low life expectancy were usual. This level of answer, though usually briefer and more directly tied to the wording in the passage, was typical of the majority of third-form responses, illustrated by Gary (14 years 2 months):

The main reason why pesants revolted was that their conditions were very bad. The people worked hard for very long hours and they didn't get enough food to keep themselves alive and because of this many of them would die before they reached thirty years of age.

However, a significant minority of the responses at this age, approximately 24 per cent, showed an understanding that the harsh conditions had been in existence for a long time, were usual, and that therefore of themselves could not account for the revolt. Nicky (14 years 5 months) is a slightly unusual example:

The passage seems to imply that the hard life (long hours, little food, etc.) was not directly responsible for the revolt as much as the lack of freedom – obviously the harsh life had something to do with it but don't forget that some of the peasants became better off. Even if something is usual (in modern times going to school) some people show a sort of revolt by playing truant.

In the first year sample of sixty pupils, virtually all, with varying degrees of thoroughness and clarity, indicated that the harsh life must have been a major cause of the revolt and made no reference to the fact that it was usual and accepted. Jackie (12 years 7 months) is representative:

I think that the importance of the harsh life was that they got fed up with the lords and so they decided to revolt. This was because they were leading terrible lives and would die before they was 30.

Question (iii) is more direct and precise, being specifically related to the major change in the position of some peasants over the 100 years before 1381 and what the significance of this might have been. The range of responses between the different age groups was more limited, reflecting perhaps the scope and nature of the question. Responses that were typical of virtually all the sixth formers stress the importance of the fact that only some had obtained improved conditions and obtained their freedom, contrasted this with the position of the others, and indicated that many towns and peasants remained unfree in 1381. This was then related to the immediate factors that would increase discontent and strengthen the demand for freedom. Typical is Ken (17 years 8 months):

The peasants revolted because it was only the position of *some* that had been improved over the hundred years prior to 1381. It had taken a long time to bring about these changes, and many of the peasants were still suffering very harsh conditions and still under the control of the lords in 1381 – their position was different, they may have felt jealous of their free counterparts and wanted their freedom, which incited them to revolt. The bad harvests and the Poll taxes before 1381 would have brought this discontent to a head, and the peasants therefore demanded freedom and an improvement in their conditions.

The answers of some 40 per cent of the third-year group, though not so well phrased and fully developed, expressed substantially the same points. The great majority of the remainder indicated that improvements were slow and only affected some, but did not develop the implications of these points or refer to the immediate causes of discontent.

Geoffrey (14 years 2 months):

> I think the revolt still happened because although conditions had improved for some of the peasants over the last 100 years or so, because it was slow and many of them were still under the lords' control even after 100 years, they were getting fed up.

This follows very closely the information as stated in paragraph three with very little development of the implications. Such an answer was typical of almost 40 per cent of the first-year responses, though some 11 per cent produced answers in substance equivalent to that of Denise (12 years 4 months), whose sophistication of language matches the quality of her thinking:

> Although some peasants' lives were being improved a majority still had to work hard for the lord. Probably only the richer of the peasants were able to buy their freedom, the poor could only get their freedom by rebelling. It may have been that as other peasants had earned their freedom others were impatient for freedom so when they got a leader they rebelled.

At the other extreme was Robert (12 years 5 months):

> Because in the ten years before 1381 there was bad harvests and the king was short of money so he made them pay a poll tax, which made the peasants poorer and the king richer.

This centres completely on two of the immediate influences and makes no reference to the improvement in the conditions of some peasants that the question asks him to consider. Some 25 per cent of the first-year responses were similarly restricted, whereas this was true of only 9 per cent of the third-year sample.

The final question was designed to provide some evidence of the extent to which pupils could identify any common grievance between the peasants and towns in the revolt and how far they would see this as a basis for identifying the main causes of the revolt. Compared to questions one and two this is again rather more specific, but it does require making the connection between the demand of those involved in the revolt to be free from bondage and developments during the century before 1381. Some 85 per cent of the sixth formers brought out this connection with fully developed reasons. Dawn (17 years 4 months) again provides a particularly well-thought-out example:

> Both the peasants and towns which revolted were presumably held in bondage by the lord and likely to be poor. Neither, most probably, experienced the freedom that other towns and peasants had – or if they did it was probably taken away after the Black Death, when people were needed to work on the land. Also both peasants and towns would be suffering from bad harvests and the Poll tax, which brought their discontent to a head.

These similarities between the towns and peasants suggest that perhaps the most important cause of the revolt was that the peasants and townspeople wanted to be free of their lords like some others were. They wanted to shake off the restrictions of the lords' control.

My reasons for this statement are that people who see freedom given to and enjoyed by other people and who have grievances against their lord, will also wish for this freedom. Also some of the peasants may have been made to work again for the lord after the Black Death and they would resent this.

In the third-year sample, almost 40 per cent of the pupils identified the basic points, though usually not drawing out their significance so fully. In the first-year group 20 per cent of the responses stressed the importance of the lack of freedom, but gave only a limited development of the point. Michael (12 years 7 months) is typical of these:

The towns and peasants that revolted were probably the ones that had the worst lords, the lords who stopped them from being free and this is why they demanded an end to bondage – others had got it so why shouldn't they.

Space does not permit a fuller discussion of how the pupils tackled the considerable challenge that this exercise deliberately posed. Sufficient indications emerged from the responses of the third- and first-year pupils to suggest that if they were given the encouragement and opportunity to work out, discuss and refine their own thoughts and ideas, they may be capable of much more understanding than is often supposed. How far would interventionist strategies directly concerned to make children think about aspects of change over time improve the quality of their understanding in this area of particular importance and concern in history? In all the age ranges referred to above a variety of responses offered teachers considerable scope to use the ideas and arguments of the pupils in developing a better understanding of the causal framework on which the passage was based. If they are prepared to recognize the importance of such areas of understanding from the early years and devise exercises (which can be less complex and demanding than that discussed above) that stimulate the pupils to work out and express their own ideas, it may well be that levels of thinking can be achieved that many teachers would find surprising.

APPENDIX I

The Peasants' Revolt 1381

Introduction
In June 1381 some peasants and towns of England rose in revolt. The rioters attacked the houses of the rich, the places where the records which told of their *bondage* were kept and they demanded to be free. Wat Tyler and John Ball led a march on London.

bondage – not being free to leave their lord or his land, and having to work for him and make him payments.

Read the passage below carefully

Peasants and poor townspeople had led a hard life for hundreds of years. They worked long hours to get enough food to keep alive – even so, many of them would die before they were thirty years old. It is difficult for us to understand what a hard life they had, but for them it was usual.

Most peasants were not free – they could not leave their lord or his land. They had to work on his land and give him part of their crops and produce. In return, they had a small piece of land to farm for themselves. Towns also belonged to a lord and had to make him payments. This also was what the people had been used to for a long period of time.

Life got better for some peasants in the hundred years or so before *1381*. They were allowed to pay money each year instead of work and some managed to buy their freedom, which meant they could leave their lord and move around freely. Some towns also bought their freedom. But these changes were slow and there were many peasants and towns still under the lords' control in *1381*.

In *1348* a plague called the Black Death killed one-third of the people of England. Because workers were scarce some lords tried to force the peasants to go back to work on their land even though they had agreed to a money payment instead. Others, however, continued to let peasants buy their freedom or pay money instead of work.

In the ten years immediately before *1381* there were bad harvests and therefore less food; the English were fighting the French and they lost several important battles; partly because of the war and the bad harvests the king was short of money, so in 1377, 1379 and 1381 he made everyone pay a special tax called a Poll tax. Also at this time a priest called John Ball became well known around London. He told the people how poor and miserable they were and how wealthy and comfortable the rich were.

Answer the questions below as carefully as you can

(i) What was the importance, if any, of the harsh life of the peasants (mentioned in Paragraph 1 of the above passage) as a cause of the revolt?

(ii) Could the fact that the lords had controlled the lives of the peasants and towns for a long time be a cause of the revolt? Give reasons for your answer.

(iii) Why do you think the peasants revolted when the position of some of them had improved over the hundred years before *1381*?

(iv) Is there any connection between the Black Death *1348*, and the revolt? Give your reasons for saying there is or is not a connection.

(v) 'The events of 1371–1381 decided only the *time* of the revolt – they were not its real cause.' What does this mean and do you agree with it? Give your reasons.

(vi) What do you think the particular peasants and towns that revolted in

1381 might have had in common? Does this suggest the most important cause of the revolt? Give your reasons.

NOTES

1. It might be argued that there are a number of elements that make up the 'new' history (see Chapter 9 in this volume), but clearly the fundamental aspect is the pupils working with sources as evidence to reconstruct a picture of the past.
2. Lamont, W., 'The uses and abuses of examinations', in Ballard, M. (ed), *New Movements in the Study and Teaching of History*, Temple Smith, 1970.
3. Edwards, A. D., 'Source material in the classroom', in Burston, W. H., and Green, G. W. (eds), *Handbook for History Teachers*, Methuen, 1972.
4. Schools Council, *History 13–16 Project: A New Look at History*, Holmes McDougall, 1976.
5. Rogers, P. J., *The New History – Theory into Practice*, Historical Association, 1979.
6. See Chapter 9 of this volume.
7. Gard, A., 'The nature of historical evidence and its use in the teaching of history', unpublished MA dissertation, University of London Institute of Education, 1977.
    A typical example of this is the treatment of the manorial system of feudalism with younger pupils, where the rights and duties of the villein to his lord having been discussed and established, one or two actual instances are used to illustrate the point and to 'bring it to life'. As Gard has pointed out, there is a sense in which to use sources in this way runs counter to working with them as evidence to establish or reconstruct 'facts' or events.
8. Schools Council Project, *What is History?* – 2: 'The mystery of Mark Pullen'.
9. Lamont, op. cit., seems to suggest this, but modifies his position in his *The Realities of Teaching History*, Chatto & Windus, 1972.
10. See Chapter 4 in this volume.
11. It must be accepted that this will mean a drastic reduction in the amount of 'content' that can be covered and will create additional problems of selection and the criteria that should influence that. The central concern, however, has to be developing the pupils' understanding, and the use of methods that will encourage that.
12. See Rogers, op. cit.
13. See Dickinson, A. K., and Lee, P. J., *History Teaching and Historical Understanding*, Heinemann Educational Books, 1978, ch.1.
14. See Rogers, op. cit., p. 40.
15. This is not meant to imply that Rogers argues that context can *only* be built up from sources in this context, but clearly far more significance is attached to procedures than to studying their end product. In Chapter 2 of this volume, 'Why Teach History?', he suggests that our positions on the respective importance of procedures and content is, if not the same, much closer.
16. See Dickinson and Lee (eds), op. cit., pp. 95–9.
17. Thompson, D., 'Some psychological aspects of history teaching', in Burston and Green (eds), op. cit.
18. Work produced by both B.Ed. and PGCE history students in recent years indicates that in the area of teacher training there is a real danger of over-simplification, distortion and excessively categorical and sweeping statements in this context. It would seem to be an area where a little knowledge could be an exceedingly dangerous thing, in that the expectation of pupils' achievements could be pitched too low.
19. Shemilt, D., *History 13–16 Evaluation Study*, Holmes McDougall, 1980, p. 50.
20. Throughout this section, evidence is used in the broad or loose sense of anything that might be used to answer a question – rather than the narrower and more precise methodological meaning it has in the context of the 'new' history. The distinction is clearly established by a

comparison of the way sources are used as evidence by Rogers in *The New History* and the way in which information is used by Dickinson and Lee in the Jutland study (see note 21). In the latter, what actually happened is taken as *given*, what the pupils are required to do is to try to understand, on the basis of the information they have, why Jellicoe acted as he did. They are not asked to use sources as evidence in the way that I conceive to be central to the 'new' history.

21. Dickinson and Lee (eds), op. cit., pp. 99–107 and 112–18.
22. See Thompson, op. cit., pp. 23–4.
23. Some small-scale empirical research of my own suggested that even students of 17 + doing A level history, when asked to consider whether evidence given in a passage was sufficient to allow particular statements about the situation to be made, tended to find reasons why the evidence could provide an adequate justification (often showing very subtle and sophisticated thinking), rather than recognizing that it did not, and that additional information was required. This may well be a reflection of how they had been taught history, how they had come to see the subject as a result of that teaching and what their expectations were. Interventionist strategies (and the critical use of evidence in a methodological context) should help to eliminate this.
24. Historical situations can be complex and demanding or they can be relatively simple, direct and readily related to the pupil's experience.
25. See Thompson, op. cit., pp. 31–3.
26. Dickinson and Lee (eds), op. cit., p. 100.
27. ibid., p. 106.
28. ibid., p. 113.
29. ibid., p. 100.
30. This does not refer so much to whether the perspective is world, national, regional or local, but rather the level of detail that is gone into within any particular perspective – one can have, for example, a more or less detailed study of local history.
31. Burston, W. H., *Principles of History Teaching*, Methuen, 1972, pp. 103–5.
32. Shemilt, op. cit., pp. 30–2.
33. The particular example here may well be thought difficult and demanding, but the whole area of causal connections can be developed in much simpler ways and historical contexts where this is appropriate.
34. See, for example, Burston, op. cit., chs 4 and 5, and Dickinson and Lee (eds), op. cit., ch. 5.

8. Assessment, Examinations and Historical Understanding

A. K. DICKINSON

I. INTRODUCTION

A paradoxical situation has existed for many years in which teachers and examiners have vied with each other in condemning mindless regurgitation of historical information while blaming each other for its remarkable persistence. The fundamental aim of this chapter is to encourage further thought and action about some of the things that can be done to change all this and to use assessment – including examinations – to *aid* significant learning and understanding.

The main theme of section II is the constructive role that in-school assessment can play in improving the quality of teaching and learning in history. Emphasis at first is on the clues that assessment can provide about each pupil's learning and the kind of activity most likely to assist him or her. Space permits the inclusion of only one detailed example. This empirical study, though limited in scope, shows clearly that assessment can provide illuminating insights into how children cope with understanding certain kinds of historical actions and how their understanding may be advanced. The section continues with a brief look at some other ways in which in-school assessment can help teachers and learners. Several problems are also emphasized – principally, two major constraints on the development of wide-ranging and useful diagnostic assessment programmes, work-load and public examinations. Section III begins with a short critique of various public examination practices. Within this context there is some discussion of the implications for these examinations of the possibilities raised in section II. The chapter ends with an outline of some opportunities for improving teaching and examining arrangements in history.

The approach favoured throughout is in the deliberative tradition.[1] Public examinations are a feature of every formal educational system and there is a high level of interest and activity in all aspects of assessment.[2] It is assumed here that we should do all we can to improve our capacity, both individually and collectively, to make sound pedagogical decisions and, without necessarily accepting their legitimacy, respond to examinations and other aspects of assessment by trying to turn them to advantage. We should search for ways of using them to improve the quality of teaching and learning.

II.   POSSIBILITIES AND PROBLEMS OF ASSESSMENT

Schools are very busy and demanding places in which to work but teachers must spend time on assessment because it is a necessary condition of effective teaching. One cannot claim to be seriously involved in teaching unless one intends to bring about learning, and this must involve some sort of check on one's successes and failures. The first part of this section provides a detailed example of how carefully planned assessment can provide valuable insights into the range of understanding, puzzlement, confusion and teaching opportunities existing in a history class.

It is based on some work done with BL2, a class of sixteen girls and fourteen boys aged between 12 years 6 months and 13 years 5 months. They were asked to read a pamphlet about the Battle of Jutland and then answer some questions in writing. The text began by emphasizing that Britain depended on her navy to protect the country, her colonies and supplies. Later paragraphs (plus three diagrams) outlined the various stages of the battle from the first skirmish of the opposing battle-cruisers to the return to port of the German fleet. A key section stated that at the height of the battle the German destroyers laid a smoke-screen and fired twenty-one torpedoes, Jellicoe temporarily turned the British fleet away, at least eleven torpedo tracks were seen and all were avoided. It also reported that some time before the battle Jellicoe had been told by the Director of Naval Intelligence that the Germans had successfully concealed their torpedo tracks, but this turned out to be false information.[3] Five questions were given separately, each probing a particular aspect of the children's understanding of why an agent, Jellicoe, acted as he did. (The questions are given in Appendix I.) Peter Lee and I have discussed elsewhere the mechanics of the test, its rationale and some of our findings.[4] The intention here is to show how such an exercise can help one to work out how far each pupil has grasped certain things during a learning episode (formative assessment) or at the completion (summative assessment), his or her strengths, weaknesses and reasons for difficulty (formative or summative diagnosis), and the effectiveness of the programme (formative or summative evaluation).[5] Also, a number of responses are quoted in full this time in order to give as detailed a picture as possible of the thinking of individual pupils in relation to this test.

Each set of five answers was treated as an overall response and scored as such. Category six (see Table 8.1) was the highest level in the system we used to evaluate the responses. The essential characteristics of such a response are that the subject redescribes the action being studied in terms that show understanding of the agent's particular intentions and his own view of the situation, distinguishes between the latter and what we know with hindsight, grasps the vital considerations that demanded his attention in the extended as well as the restricted context *and* integrates them successfully.[6] Approximately a third of the sixth formers we tested did all this. Kate was one of them (see her answer below). Although none of the pupils in BL2 produced such a response it is possible for children at least as young as them to think at this level. One 13-year-old from a different class who did so was Brian. (Names are invented to preserve anonymity but indicate the sex of each pupil.) The extracts below

Table 8.1   Key features and categories for the analysis of children's understanding of why an agent acted as he did

Key features of responses	Categories of response where particular features predominate					
	1	2	3	4	5	6
(a) Information available frequently misconstrued in elementary ways. Fails coherently to grasp the agent's intention or situation so action not understood.	×					
(b) Action explained by reference to the agent's intentions and situation but without getting at the *particular* intentions and view of the situation.		×	×			
(c) Use of information as in (b) *plus* perception of problematical aspects of the action without recognizing what the agent could and could not have known.				×		
(d) Information available utilized so as to uncover the agent's particular intentions and view of the situation in the context of the description under which the action requires explanation.				×	×	×
(e) Response shows awareness of the considerations which demanded the agent's attention in the wider context.					×	×
(f) Successful integration of the rival considerations which demanded the agent's attention in the limited and the wider context.						×

show his appreciation of the agent's view, awareness of the wider context and ability to reconcile conflicting goals. (Key indicators in answers have been italicized.) Admittedly Kate refers immediately to the wider context.[7] She also develops certain points more than does Brian and employs knowledge from outside the pamphlet (her reference to pre-war decisions), but the answers of both pupils contain the essential characteristics of a category six response.

Brian (13 years 5 months):

1.   Jellicoe turned the fleet away because he had information from the Director of Naval Intelligence that the Germans had successfully concealed their torpedo tracks. *Thinking this could practically wipe-out his fleet, or present danger to it*, he saved his fleet from casualties.... He thought that if he temporarily turned his fleet away *he could still attack the Germans* ...

5.   Jellicoe was trying to wipe-out the German fleet *with as little damage as possible to his own fleet so Britain could look after its colonies*, etc. There is plenty of evidence to show this:
(a)   He called many meetings for the defence of the fleet. He and all the officers met to discuss tactics.
(b)   He turned away from the German torpedoes to save his fleet from damage.

Kate (17 years 6 months):

1. The British naval fleet was vital to the British war effort, *providing protection against invasion plus protecting the importation of food and raw materials*, which because of her position as an island could make or break Britain. British industry had to be maintained to supply arms and ammunition. Therefore *it was necessary that Britain keep her advantage over Germany* just as the politicians had decided when building up the navy in competition before the war.... This obviously influenced Jellicoe, who knew that to loose [sic] too many ships would be a disaster. He was also under the impression that German torpedo tracks could not be seen and therefore *had no knowledge of the number of torpedoes that had been fired, for all he knew there may be many more than the eleven that were visible.*

5. ... This was just the situation Jellicoe wanted, *the maximum destruction of the German fleet with the minimum risk* from the German guns, or topedoes. As it was important that the British sustain as little damage as possible, enabling them to *continue their protection of imports, and their naval supremacy* ...

Andrew came closest to this level of understanding in class BL2. His response shows that he has grasped Jellicoe's intentions to a considerable extent and has distinguished the agent's view of the situation from that of a person who has the advantage of hindsight (see 4a below). His final answer reveals awareness of the extended context, but over all he fails to deal effectively with certain problematical aspects. It is a category five response. If he could integrate the rival considerations that demanded Jellicoe's attention he could achieve 'explanatory equilibrium' in category six.[8] He mentions Jellicoe's concern for the safety of his ships and his desire to get a decisive battle. Careful questioning centred around these apparently conflicting goals may help him – and students in the same category – to reconcile them and so advance their understanding further.

Andrew (12 years 10 months):

1. Jellicoe turned away from the Germans because of the torpedoes. He had received information telling him the Germans had managed to conceal the trail left by the topedoes *so he (thought) it might be too dangerous to stay if he could not see them.* But the information was incorrect.

2. *It seems funny* that anyone should *run away* – if the Germans had done the same thing the obvious thing to do would be to follow them.

3. I think he would have been more likely to achieve what he wanted if he had followed – he would not have got anywhere otherwise.

4a. The battleships turned away together and the destroyers laid a smoke-screen at the same time as they were firing their torpedoes. The information I got from the admiralty was incorrect about the Germans having concealed their torpedo tracks but *I did not know this at the time.* So I turned away because *we could not avoid torpedoes we could not see.*

4b. We could have followed them but we would have been prone to the

German torpedoes. We could have split up and gone in. We would
have been safer from the torpedoes from the ships but we did not know
if there were any submarines lurking around so I turned away thinking
it was safest for my ships.

5. Jellicoe was trying to get a decisive battle so they would have the seas as
a free dominion to the British. He also wanted to beat the Germans *so
they could transport all the necessary raw materials* to the army and as much
food back to England as was needed to boost the war effort on land (but
not yet in the air).

Nine pupils produced category four responses, explaining the turn away by
reference to Jellicoe's particular intentions and his view of the situation but
without fitting it into a wider context. The responses of five of them suggested
that they were very firmly in this category. Most of them – like Delia below –
indicated that they were *not* puzzled from their second answer onwards.

Delia (12 years 9 months):

2. *Nothing puzzles me* about Jellicoe's turning away because if he had stayed
he *might* have lost a lot of ships because of the torpedoes. Also he was
only turning away *temporarily*. He wasn't retreating from the Germans
completely.

Ken's answer seems to suggest that he – like another boy in the group – was
puzzled when answering questions 2 and 3 but eventually succeeds in decisively eliminating the alternative course of action that appealed to him earlier.

Ken (12 years 11 months):

1. Jellicoe turned the fleet away from the Germans to stop being hit by the
German torpedo attack. He did this because he had been told that the
Germans had successfully concealed their attacks, but this was false information.
2. Surely Jellicoe should not have turned away because *the British wanted a
decisive battle, whatever happens*.
3. Jellicoe surely should have followed the Germans in order to get a
decisive battle . . .
4a. When the Germans fired their torpedoes I remembered what I had
been told about they had successfully concealed their torpedo attacks,
so I turned away in order not to loose [sic] any ships.
4b. I considered turning towards the Germans and clashing in the middle
but then *this could end the battle and possibly cause our side to loose*, so I turned
away.
5. When he sighted the Germans he meant to get a decisive battle and win
a good fight for the British. When he turned around he only meant to
turn away until the Germans stopped their torpedo attack.

The responses of all these pupils revealed a sound understanding of Jellicoe's
view of the situation. This group could, therefore, be an invaluable aid to their
teacher, helping to convince those who have not grasped the distinction
between the agent's view and our own that there are indeed certain important

things that we know now but Jellicoe could not have known at the time. If they are to achieve a higher level of understanding themselves their attention must be drawn – orally, using a map or diagram, or with a brief written reminder – to the wider context. After that the problem is to get them to integrate this and the turn away. Probably the best way of facilitating this development is group discussion of specific issues. This should encourage an exploration of their ideas about the situation – and the agent's intentions – and may lead to a significant increase in their understanding.[9]

The other four eventually achieved equilibrium after saying that they were puzzled (question 2), but their responses suggested that two of them were close to leaving category four whereas the other two had only just attained it. The first two showed a good grasp of the agent's view of the situation and eliminated various courses of action, but there was also some evidence that they still believed that a superior course of action was available and one of them made a brief – though unsuccessful – attempt to link the turn away with the wider context. Some encouragement to pay more attention to the extended context might enable these pupils to advance further. The first priority with the other two, however, is to consolidate their position in category four. Julia's first sentence (see below) shows awareness of Jellicoe's view of the situation but her third one gives an unusually early indication of problems. The rest of her response reveals considerable puzzlement about Jellicoe's intentions (see 2, 3 and 5 below) and confusion regarding some aspects of the situation. Her answer to question 2 suggests that she has not realized at this stage that the turn away reduced the effective speed of the torpedoes – an understandable gap in her 'second record'. Her answer to 4b, however, seems to indicate that she has sorted out this misunderstanding herself, but provides evidence of a new misconception, that the British were not firing.

Julia (13 years 1 month):

1.   Jellicoe turned the fleet away because he saw about 11 torpedo tracks coming straight for him and he had also been told that the Germans had managed to conceal their torpedo tracks and so *for all he knew there could be lots more as well*. In the pamphlet it does not say what state the British ships were in when the attack came – if they were badly damaged there would be more reason to turn away. *Although I cannot see where it would have got him to do so.*

2.   *It puzzles me* why Jellicoe turned away just then, after all *the torpedoes would still hit the ships*, the only difference would be instead of hitting the front they would hit the side or the back. Also the British were winning at that time and so he should have just kept on going.

3.   I cannot answer this properly as the pamphlet does [not] explain exactly what Jellicoe wanted to do in the first place. If he wanted to win the battle he would not have turned away at all and I do not think that he really wanted to retreat.

4a.   At the moment the Germans launched the torpedoes there was confusion on the ships because they had to put up a smoke screen and we could not see what was happening but when it cleared a bit we saw torpedo tracks, 11 of them.

4b. I could have just carried on going regardless but I did not think it was a very good idea because they would have battered us to pieces. Or I could have opened fire on them, but we were not really close enough so I chose to turn the ships away and *so get out of the range of fire.*

5. *I cannot see that he was trying to do anything.* It was the Germans who lured the British into the battle not the other way round. The British just took the bait and had to fight it out.

Julia needs assistance to sort out certain misunderstandings that adversely affect her thinking. Her initial puzzlement seems to be caused by a failure to grasp certain physical relationships and this leads to puzzlement regarding Jellicoe's intentions. The mode of presentation is such an important factor that some variation in this might be helpful.[10] Drawing diagrams – pencil and paper, blackboard or overhead projector – or manipulating representative objects, plus appropriate exposition, should help to clarify key physical relationships and the outcome of actions consequent upon them. This in turn would aid her understanding of both the situation and Jellicoe's intentions. Julia's difficulties emphasize several major problems in learning and teaching history. Historical investigation differs fundamentally from those studies where it is often possible to manipulate physical objects in search of answers and then to observe the consequences of such actions. In science a visual demonstration can often end a dispute quite conclusively but in history learners must rely mainly on logical tests, not empirical ones. Also the situations they have to study are often complex. Consequently, although it may be equally important in other areas of study to be critically aware of one's assumptions, reflexive thinking is particularly demanding in history.[11] The search for equilibrium and understanding of Jellicoe's turn away is likely to be fraught with difficulties for many pupils even though it is a relatively 'simple' historical situation in which the British could be regarded as having a limited range of possibilities for action. Pupils will usually need some assistance and, as the examples given above clearly show, if teachers are to provide this effectively they must be able to pinpoint individual problems, another far from easy task.

Four pupils produced category three responses. Thinking in this category is characterized by the perception of problematical aspects of the action and an inability to achieve equilibrium in category four due to a failure to grasp the agent's particular intentions and to differentiate between his view of the situation and what we know with hindsight. The subjects' notion of the agent's intentions includes an important 'conventional' element. This consists of an amalgam of personal projection, stereotyped ascriptions of dispositions, and assumptions based on 'merely conceptual' understanding of intentions and situations. Thus they assume that an admiral's main goal is to win, or at least fight hard, and do not pay sufficient attention to the evidence of the particular agent's intentions. Consequently the action is not understood, subjects remaining convinced that some alternative action is more appropriate. Carol's response is typical of this group, all of whom said they were puzzled when answering question 2, asserted that there was a superior course of action open to Jellicoe, and maintained this view to the end.

Carol (13 years 5 months):

1. Jellicoe turned the fleet away because he had been wrongly told that the Germans had conclead [sic] their torpedo tracks. Also he temporarily turned the fleet away to avoid the torpedo attack.

2. Yes, I think it is a bit silly to turn away from the attack as the British fleet was supposed to have more ships and more guns to fire at the enemy and a better position as well.

3. Yes, I think Admiral Jellicoe could have stayed where he was and fought hard.

4a. *I was amazed* when the torpedoes started being fired and couldn't act quick enough. Fortunately the Germans were too far away to do as much harm as possible but it was still quite bad. I thought it best to retreat for a while, then attack again when they were 'tired'.

5. Jellicoe was trying to overpower the Germans (which they thought would be fairly simple because they were much stronger) at the beginning, he knew they were stronger and if – he thought – they fought until one fleet retreated they were sure to win.

Carol's answers indicate her lack of understanding of Jellicoe's particular intentions. However, the 'he thought' in her fifth answer is interesting and her first answer suggests some awareness of his intentions and possibly also of his view of the situation. She has not exploited the point about concealed torpedo tracks, but as she has mentioned it she may need only a little encouragement to work out its implications. She could then bring to an end the conflict inherent in her answer and so advance her understanding significantly. Indeed there are good grounds for feeling optimistic about increasing the understanding of the four pupils in this category. They all showed some signs of awareness of the agent's view of the situation and intentions amid their puzzlement and confusion. It looks as though they have the ability to make inferences about Jellicoe's view of the event but either find difficulty in doing it consistently or do not see the need to do it.[12] We may help such pupils considerably if we encourage them to work out what Jellicoe could and could not have known and to comb the passage for information about his intentions. The latter activity can significantly aid those whose thinking has been constrained by a 'merely conceptual' grasp of intentions. Alternatively we may assist them by feeding in some carefully selected information. Such intervention can have a dramatic effect, particularly if pupils have been worrying at a problem and are not satisfied with their answers.[13]

Ten pupils gave category two responses. They did not show awareness of the agent's particular intentions or his own view of the situation. Their answers also implied that they had ignored or failed to perceive problematical aspects of the action and so had 'achieved' temporary equilibrium. Karen's first four answers below suggest that she is probably firmly in this category. Her final answer, however, indicates some awareness of Jellicoe's intentions and it is possible that her earlier and rather brief answers may belie her real level of understanding.

Karen (12 years 6 months):

1. He turned away from the Germans because of the torpedo attack.
2. *No, nothing puzzles me.*
3. No, I can't think of anything else except attack from the air to warn the Germans off.
4a. It was awful out there, what with the German's [sic] smoke screen, and then their torpedo attack. We could not see where they were coming from, but we knew where they were heading. It was awful trying to dodge the attacks, they kept on coming – just as one finished, the next one started.
4b. –
5. He seemed quite concerned *to save the fleet* more than to fight and tried not to get involved with any battles that might cause the *loss of his fleet.*

All the pupils who produced category two responses could have improved their answers significantly if they had made better use of the material provided in order to get at the agent's intentions and view of the situation. Their answers suggested that they had relied on their own ideas and not made careful use of the material supplied. Seven of the ten pupils in this category in BL2 even made statements that contradicted information in the pamphlet. However, there were again some encouraging signs. Something in the responses of six pupils suggested at least an inkling of Jellicoe's view of the situation or his intentions, or both. The understanding of pupils in this category might be increased considerably by asking them to talk through the battle in small groups, preferably using models and diagrams, and encouraging them to utilize the information provided as well as any relevant experience and prior knowledge of the past in their possession.[14] Each group could be asked to decide what else Jellicoe could have done, whether he would have given the same explanation as them and whether there is anything that they know about the battle that he would not have known at the time. Alternatively they could be given a statement by Jellicoe himself and asked whether they want to change their answers in the light of this new information.

The responses of six pupils indicated very serious problems. They all made a number of basic assertions that contradicted explicit information in the pamphlet or treated the action as unintelligible. The thinking of one girl was seriously affected by her assumption that some of the German torpedoes hit the British ships although the pamphlet stated that all were avoided. The answers of another girl were dominated by the mistaken belief that Jellicoe wanted to prove that the Director of Naval Intelligence was wrong although not a scrap of evidence was presented to support this assertion. A third girl assumed that the German torpedo attack was successful. She centred on this point, presumably having misunderstood the key sentence, 'Some time before the battle Jellicoe had been told by the Director of Naval Intelligence that the Germans had successfully concealed their torpedo tracks, but this turned out to be false information'. Another pupil simply copied great chunks from the pamphlet. She wrote copiously and most of it was accurate, but eventually it became clear that she had mixed up the order of events and really had great difficulty making any sense of Jellicoe's action. Obviously all these pupils needed to make much better use of the material provided. We can help such children immediately by identifying and correcting their substantive errors but the fundamental need is to do all that is possible to equip them to make better use of any potential evidence. This includes doing our best to discourage pupils from simply copying information. Extensive copying is widespread and persistent.[15] It obscures both understanding and learning difficulties. Experienced teachers know how difficult it is to get some pupils to summarize sources, penetrate their meaning and express their ideas in their own words, but we must strive to help them master these important skills.[16]

Two pupils (a boy and a girl) found the turn away completely unintelligible. David (13 years 2 months):

1. *I do not know why he turned away*, the last thing said in the pamphlet was he was informed that the enemy had concealed their torpedoes. It could have been that he was just *coward* but it does not say.

   So I would like to have known what Admiral Jellicoe said to the critics such as the one demonstrated in the pamphlet.

2. *The thing that puzzles me* is exactly the same as the statement of the Admiral in the pamphlet.

   It looked as if he had the battle in his hand with the Germans being weak.

3. He could of persued [sic] the Germans *southwards* and called out any odd armoured ships from ports on the east coast to sandwich the Germans and split them up.

4a. We were heading *south east* when the torpedoing started. It was at 7.10 p.m. We had taken the bait of a German trap. But being *night* we lost the Germans but then they reappeared travelling *north east*.

4b. This is hard to answer, so again as in question 1 we would need a statement from Jellicoe because we need to know his thoughts. We only now [sic] the one he [sic] took from the pamphlet.

5. As fas as I can tell *he was got into the situation by the Germans* in the first place. So I suppose on the whole he was trying to destroy the German fleet and stop them returning to their bases, again we need Admiral Jellicoe's statement.

David's first two answers reveal that he is totally mystified and the final one suggests that even after responding to a number of questions designed to make him think about Jellicoe's intentions and the situation his understanding of what Jellicoe was trying to do remains very limited. There is no indication that he is able to work out the considerations that Jellicoe had in mind. But the final sentence of his first answer and the first sentence of 4b both suggest awareness of the need to find this out. Thus there are some grounds for optimism. His puzzlement and confusion may be ended if he is encouraged to work out the implications of the second part of his first sentence, or given a statement by Jellicoe as he requests.[17] His answers, like those of all his peers, reveal both problems and possibilities, for those intending to develop understanding of such actions.

We found a wide range of understanding and problems – both procedural and substantive – in all the classes we have tested in this way. (Table 8.2 shows the categories achieved by this and six other classes.[18]) In order to maximize the quality of teaching and learning it is necessary to know, for example, whether each pupil is aware of various procedures, is able to utilize them, and has an adequate grasp of relevant 'meaning-making' concepts, working concepts and substantive events. Unfortunately it appears that many teachers in both secondary and primary schools lack accurate knowledge of their pupils' capabilities. The commonest fault is expecting too little of them and setting work that is insufficiently demanding.[19] There is also evidence that teachers' expectations have a considerable effect on pupils' attainment[20] and that many pupils of all ages and abilities – including sixth formers – underachieve.[21] All this emphasizes the need for more teachers to incorporate carefully devised assessment schemes into their work.

Table 8.2   Distribution by category, age and school of scores on the Jutland test

Year	Mean chronological age	School	Category (score for subject's total response)						Total
			1	2	3	4	5	6	
2nd	12:11	Technical High	6	10	4	9	1	–	30
	12:11	Comprehensive A	3	13	8	2	–	1	27
5th	16:1	Technical High	–	1	10	6	4	–	21
	16:0	Comprehensive A	1	3	3	4	4	4	19
6th	17:10	Technical High	–	1	1	6	1	4	13
	17:1	Comprehensive A	–	–	–	4	2	2	8
	18:1	Comprehensive B	–	–	2	4	3	4	13

However, it is important to be mindful of the limitations and problems as well as the possibilities. One must not claim too much for any individual test. Jutland, for example, is *not* a general test of historical thinking. It is concerned with just one aspect of thinking in history, that part of historical explanation that involves understanding why some agent acted as he did. This is its strength, and its limitation. Another reason for caution is that pupils may not communicate all they understand. Young children in particular tend to give short written answers that do not bear a straightforward relationship to the thinking displayed in discussion. Even lengthy written responses may not provide a full picture. One boy – aged 14 – wrote a great deal about the Jutland situation but provided no evidence that he had grasped the agent's view of the situation and made no mention of the wider context. He was not puzzled and his written response suggested category two understanding. A post-test interview with his teacher, however, indicated that he was at least aware of the information about concealed torpedo tracks and, as the extract below shows, had some grasp of the wider context (although it is still not clear whether he could utilize this information).

T: Would it really matter if his fleet was badly damaged?

P: Yes, because the Germans could then send troops to England.
T: Was the German fleet so important to the Germans?
P: Yes, because they had to keep trade routes open just like the British.[22]

One must also appreciate that the level of understanding achieved by each pupil is linked to the subject matter and mode of presentation. Johnson-Laird and Wason have shown that performance can be dramatically improved on certain tasks if they are related more closely to the subjects' experience. Difficulty, it seems, is not so much intrinsic to the logical structure of a task but to its content and mode of presentation.[23] We did not find a statistically significant difference between the scores of all the boys and girls who did the Jutland test but readers will have noticed that five of the six pupils in category one in the class discussed above were girls. They all said, when answering a questionnaire before the test, that they had not read about or seen a film or TV programme or done anything for themselves *outside school* concerning the First World War. Twelve boys said they had done something on the war, including six on naval aspects, two on the Battle of Jutland and one on the actual turn away.[24]

Assessment, if done with perception and sensitivity, can help teachers to diagnose how far each pupil has understood certain things, locate factors restricting understanding and make reasoned guesses about the sort of further teaching appropriate in each case. Paradoxically it can, if mishandled, have serious effects on pupils' attitudes, attainment and view of a subject. Assessment can lead to concentration on a limited range of easily measured abilities, thus laying stress on an unfortunate view of the essence of history. Achievements of imagination may be turned into nothing more than exercises of comprehension.[25] A stream of low marks, harsh comments or page after page of aimless ticks are likely to breed hostility, particularly if the authors thought the work was good.[26] Ideally assessment is used carefully and thoughtfully with teachers showing interest in what pupils write and say, encouraging them to try out new ideas, and not judging them too hastily or simply in terms of what they are capable of doing themselves.[27] At departmental level colleagues cooperate in evaluating their courses, sharing information and ideas, and regarding pupils as the responsibility of everyone, not just the person allocated to teach a particular group.[28] But there are two great restrictions on the development of wide-ranging, effective and worthwhile in-school assessment programmes. The first is time. Sadly, very few people are aware of the number of hours per week that teachers are likely to have to spend on preparation, assessment, and the minutiae of institutional life rather than actually teaching. If an average secondary school teacher has direct responsibility for 200 pupils and spends just five minutes per week reading, evaluating and responding to each pupil's work outside the classroom that amounts to almost two and a half hours per night, seven days per week. A recent report by HM Inspectors stressed the importance of increasing teachers' awareness of pupils' abilities by developing a greater capacity and willingness to assess their performance.[29] The same report talked about the 'comparatively *low* [my emphasis] proportion of time teachers were spending in contact with their classes', 75 per cent of the teaching week, and concluded that there was considerable room for improved efficiency in deployment of staff.[30] Certainly extending understanding of children's capabilities can help to improve the effectiveness of teaching, but to assume that this can be achieved while increasing the number of lessons – and pupils – taught by a teacher smacks of hyper-optimism, or something worse. If society genuinely wants improvements in the quality of teaching one corollary is that teachers must be given time each week – not just an occasional in-service course – to plan their teaching and to carry out effective in-school assessment.

The other great constraint is the influence that public examinations may exert. The following extract from a spontaneous discussion, which arose after some fifth formers had done the Jutland test, shows some of these effects.

Pupil 1: 'We've just been . . . sort of been instructed to put down basic facts [in lessons and examinations] and . . .'

  2: [Interrupting]: 'Yeah. That's, that's what really history is.'

  1: [Continuing]': . . . and I think, I think the reason we're finding this interesting is because we've never done it this way before.'

  2: 'Like we were given information. . . . It was something, something really to build on. Before we were just told *facts, facts, facts* [his emphasis].'

Others: 'Yeah.'

  3: 'I've learned more about the battle of Jutland today than what I ever knew before.'

Others: 'Yeah.'

  3: [Continuing]: 'I . . . I always thought it was a straightforward victory for us but now I look down I don't think it was . . . because they [and he starts to explain his new view] . . .'

Their regular teacher was in many ways outstanding. When perceptive, able, caring and well-respected teachers decide that the most appropriate strategy for success at 16 + is to supply pupils with facts, train them to reproduce these in examinations and not spend time on exploring actions in detail, discussing causes and consequences, and imparting an appreciation of the discipline of history there is something seriously wrong. But is it fact or myth that the best way to prepare pupils for public examinations is usually to concentrate on knowing 'that' rather than trying to build up understanding of the past and the attitudes and procedures of the historian? And what are the implications for public examinations of the possibilities raised above?

III. PROBLEMS AND POSSIBILITIES OF PUBLIC EXAMINATIONS IN HISTORY

Prior to the mid-1970s most GCE O level and CSE Boards did little or nothing in practice to encourage teachers or pupils to devote considerable time to making sense of the past and building up awareness of the main characteristics of history although sometimes they expressed pious hopes in their regulations and reports. If pupils are to acquire understanding of past human actions they need time to explore them in various ways.[31] They need time to sort out situations that are open, complex and unfamiliar, grasp what considerations were borne in mind and what weight attached to them by people whose goals, intentions and values may have been radically different from their own, locate events in their historical context, establish their meaning and work out what connections existed between them in order to establish their significance. Time is also important if they are to achieve some appreciation of the nature of historical inquiry. An understanding of the ongoing activity of historians requires, for example, that pupils should have some grasp of what historical evidence is, gained through experience of working with evidence themselves. But learning to use such evidence involves a continuous process of handling historical material under supervision and in a wider context of historical knowledge. Understanding of evidence must go hand in hand with acquisition of knowledge of the historical context that produced it and is not something likely to be acquired quickly and easily.[32] For decades the breadth of many examination syllabuses – and the examining techniques favoured by the Boards and the range and wording of the questions – encouraged teachers and pupils to believe that what really mattered at 16 + was the acquisition of extensive information and the ability to communicate it under examination conditions.

Facts and myths about the marking guidelines issued to examiners reinforced the conviction that Examination Boards generally placed insufficient emphasis on historical understanding. Teachers employed as examiners were told – rightly – that full justice should be done to any candidate who honestly endeavoured to answer the question set. Most were also told that a bonus of one or two marks could be allowed for a suitable introduction or conclusion to an essay-type question. This too was a sound directive, but many of them were told that the same one or two marks, *not* a further bonus, could be awarded if an answer showed signs of really good historical understanding. Some Boards even instructed their examiners that they should not search for possibilities of awarding such marks.[33]

Instructions such as these were – and are – formulated because Examination Boards have always been very concerned that their teams of examiners should be fair and consistent in their marking and have assumed that they are more likely to agree about the accuracy and extent of factual detail than the level of understanding or the quality of an introduction or conclusion. It is understandable that the Boards have been anxious to achieve a high level of marker reliability. It is also understandable, given the breadth of most syllabuses, the range of possible questions, the kind of marking instructions issued to examiners and the high priority accorded to public examinations, that so many teachers have decided that the best way of equipping their pupils for these examinations is to concentrate primarily on the topics and questions thought to be favoured by examiners and the kind of answers that they think the majority of their candidates can produce to gain a pass. But the price of maintaining these policies, of increasing marker reliability in the way described above and concentrating in the classroom on the accumulation and memorization of historical factual detail, needs to be spelt out. It includes the sickening persistence of dictated notes and regurgitation and many teachers abandoning the careful promotion of meaningful learning at the start of the examination years. It also means that history is treated – and regarded – as a body of received information.

Other conventions have also helped to ensure that factual detail is frequently highly rewarded in practice, even when examination papers and guidelines to examiners appear to suggest otherwise. For example, examiners at 16 + have usually had to make clear where they have awarded marks 'by placing a tick boldly at the precise point where each mark is awarded'. This procedure has encouraged examiners – intentionally or otherwise – to award marks when they encounter accurate information. A more overt problem facing examiners has always been the substantial number of candidates who pay little attention to the precise wording of questions, particularly essay-type ones, and simply deposit as much factual detail as possible.[34] Traditionally there has been a widespread reluctance to fail them at 16 + ; the number would be so large and would include many candidates whose answers reveal extensive information and earnest endeavour. Therefore criteria have been fudged and Assistant Examiners encouraged to award marks for any facts that can be said to be relevant. Answers displaying both relevance and substance – a small minority – have been given a top grade. But teachers and pupils have found good passes have been given to those candidates who showed some understanding by focusing on the questions *and* those who revealed relatively limited understanding but extensive information. Indeed very detailed but loosely focused answers may be given a higher mark than better focused but much briefer ones. All this has helped to confirm the widespread belief that the best way of preparing most candidates for public examinations at 16 + is to concentrate on the acquisition and regurgitation of extensive information. It has also helped to sustain some regrettable practices.

Pupils are the main losers in such a situation. A proportion of them gain useful grades but too many suffer from lost opportunities in the classroom. Recent investigations have confirmed that many lessons continue to contain extensive copying and dictated notes.[35] Although students may enjoy the undemanding nature of such work they also censure it.[36] Their main complaint concerns the tedium and some have also criticized the lack of intellectual challenge and stimulus.[37] Even more worrying, however, are the effects upon their view of history and their historical conceptualization. The work that many pupils do in the examination years initiates and reinforces the belief that history is a compendium of pre-existing and inalienable facts and concerned essentially with description, not explanation. They are given the impression that their main task is to accumulate as much factual detail and received opinion as possible, memorize it and regurgitate parts of it when required. Many pupils acquire only a very limited understanding of the events they have studied. They miss opportunities to explore the intrinsic interest of the subject. They also learn little or nothing about the ways of exploring and making sense of human activity employed by historians, about how knowledge is arrived at in history. Consequently they lack what Rogers has called 'the *right* to be sure', because if they are always simply provided with information then they have no reasonable grounds upon which to base their knowledge apart from saying that this is what the book or the teacher told them.[38]

All the Examination Boards have made changes at 16 + in recent years. Some of these have arisen from genuine efforts to rethink examination aims, objectives and procedures and amount to real improvements. The Southern Regional Examinations Board, for example, deserves praise for its efforts to evolve better examination techniques and channels of communication. It has experimented with allocating one block of marks for grasping the implications of a question and another for the production of supporting evidence; it has published marking schemes, sample scripts and examiners' reactions to them, and sought to foster a genuine dialogue between teachers and examiners.[39] Some of the other Boards also have real achievements to their credit. They have, for example, reduced the proportion of the examination that invites answers involving recall and little else and improved communications between teachers and themselves. But some changes have been merely cosmetic because in practice there has continued to be too much concentration on factual recall and inadequate rewards for thinking. Others have produced a plethora of alternative objectives, periods, topics, examining techniques and procedures. The creation of the History Working Party of the GCE and CSE Boards' Joint Council in response to the Secretary of State's invitation in 1980 to submit for consideration its recommended 16 + National Criteria for History provided an opportunity not only for some pruning but also for developing and extending the rational elements in examining at that level. Unfortunately the 1982 report of the Working Party has left many important matters in the air. It contains a welcome emphasis on evidential skills and understanding, including 'an ability to look at events and issues from the perspective of people in the past'.[40] But most of the statements of assessment objectives need to be squeezed in order to make them more precise. Brief statements of objectives can easily be interpreted in different ways by Examination Boards and lead to totally different practices with significantly different real effects on teaching and learning. On the theme of assessment techniques the report recommends three techniques that it thinks should be included in any scheme of assessment. One of these is 'questions requiring responses in a variety of forms to given historical evidence', but each Board is left to decide whether historical evidence should be related to the context of a particular syllabus or not.[41] The report states that there should be the opportunity for a school-based element, but not whether it should be compulsory or what precisely ought to be its relationship with other components. The report also neglects to emphasize the need for more open government on the part of Examination Boards and the importance of weighing up the strengths and weaknesses of different assessment techniques, particularly their possible effects on teaching and learning.

Examination syllabuses and procedures have profound consequences for teaching and learning because teachers – and pupils – adjust their goals and methods to meet the demands of examinations. They are the nodal point. In the past many of their effects have been unfortunate at 16 + although some teachers, to their great credit, have worked out ways of achieving good examination results and ensuring that their pupils gain considerable understanding of some of the content of history and the historian's mode of inquiry. Many more candidates might be able to deal effectively with challenging questions about the content and methodology of the subject if given more opportunities in lessons to explore connections between events, build up awareness of their meaning and significance, and to make extensive and developing use of sources as evidence. More teachers would be willing to devote time to this if syllabuses encouraged it and they were convinced that answers showing some understanding of the past and awareness of the procedures and concepts of history would receive higher grades than those revealing more factual detail but less understanding. .

Of course one must not underestimate the difficulties for teachers and pupils of making sense of the substantive content of a syllabus or building up awareness of the attitudes and procedures of the historian. The problems that each pupil will encounter cannot necessarily be predicted and it is not immediately obvious to either teacher or learner whether or not understanding has been achieved. But there is growing documentation of the impressive things that children can achieve in history provided they are given appropriate encouragement.[42] The main burden of section II above was that teachers can help their pupils considerably by means of thoughtful planning and careful assessment, although neither can guarantee success. It was also implied that greater use should be made of criterion-referenced tests that focus on what pupils have learned rather than on whether they have learned more or less than others, and that teachers and examiners should focus on the essence of an answer and be prepared to tolerate some inaccuracy in relation to relatively unimportant points. Probably the most important implications for examinations, however, arise from the fact that pupils' thinking is significantly influenced by – among other things – the subject matter of a question or problem, the mode of presentation and the availability of relevant experience. This means that in order to be as fair and accurate as possible reliance on a single end-of-course examination should be replaced by sampling candidates' abilities in as many relevant areas and ways as practical. This in turn implies greater use of internal assessment (plus external moderation). But teachers need time to plan, assess and provide opportunities in school for pupils to advance their understanding as well as their knowledge. It will also help them considerably if Examination Boards make crystal clear that hard thinking and understanding are not only highly desirable in theory but will *in practice* be properly rewarded.

In 18 + examinations good grades have always been awarded to those candidates who reveal a sound grasp of the implications of questions and the ability to deal with most of them. Candidates who reveal some – though limited – awareness of the thrust of the questions and just about enough factual detail to support a satisfactory answer are treated as borderline cases, and those who show very limited understanding of what each question is about fail decisively. Many other qualities are taken into consideration, including organization, presentation and wide reading, but understanding, knowledge and sound handling of evidence are of crucial importance. The Boards have also shown some willingness to prune syllabuses to enable teachers and students systematically to build up understanding of the period being studied and the mode of inquiry of the historian. Several of them have started publishing their grade criteria, some encourage teachers to comment on the questions after their pupils have sat each paper, and at least one now sends a fairly detailed report on some aspects of each candidate's performance to both the student and the school.[43] Techniques for assessing candidates' use of sources as evidence have been developed, and it is pleasing to see that the questions set have usually gone far beyond mere comprehension. They have encouraged candidates to cross-examine the sources supplied, fit them into their context, and to think hard about what conclusions – if any – their available evidence will carry. This bodes reasonably well for the new situation created by the agreement on a common-core in A level history which means that consideration should be given during each course to the methods of the historian and that all the Boards will assess the ability of candidates 'to evaluate and interpret source material as historical evidence and to demonstrate facility in its use'.[44] Some Examination Boards have also introduced extended essays to give candidates an opportunity to formulate a topic or question of interest and historical validity, establish its relation to existing research and knowledge, and construct within the word limit an essay that is well organized, coherent and contains adequate evidence to support the main lines of argument. The essays have proved to be a very worthwhile activity but teachers have been slow to take up this option. In 1983 fewer than 2 per cent of candidates at 18 + were doing such work. It is also regrettable that teachers have been more ready to enter pupils for two outline papers rather than one outline plus a special subject paper, and that this trend is increasing. The most distressing feature of all, however, is the persistence at A level of lessons that contain extensive copying and dictated notes and other indications of much slow, narrow and unchallenging work.[45]

It is tempting for examiners and teachers to blame each other for the persistence of unsatisfactory teaching and the deserts of turgid irrelevance in some candidates' answers. What is needed, however, is a wider vision, a general appreciation that the quality of examining, teaching and learning are closely related, and a willingness on the part of examiners and teachers to strive together to remedy weaknesses and to begin a rational process of development. And their primary objective should be to replace the emphasis on information, which has continued to characterize too much teaching and examining, with a concern for making sense of the past and building up awareness of the propositional, procedural and conceptual character of history. Information has an important role to play in history but it is vital that obsession with 'know that' be replaced by concentration on understanding and 'know how'.

IV.   CONCLUSION: SOME SUGGESTIONS FOR EXTENDING GOOD PRACTICE

Although public examinations are expensive to operate and have neglected various important abilities they do have the potential to make a profound contribution to improving the general quality of teaching and learning in history. The future of these examinations and the quality of education in our schools is inevitably uncertain but there are a number of factors that encourage some optimism.[46] If this opportunity to make further improvements is to be exploited fully it is vital that teachers and examiners co-operate and think hard about developing and extending good practice. In the past uninformed criticism and a tendency to blame each other for the persistence of unimaginative teaching have helped to sour relations so the task is formidable. But it is not impossible. The following seem to be the minimum number of things that need to be done to produce rational examining arrangements.

1. There must be openness to eliminate confusion. All Examination Boards should periodically publish their instructions to examiners, guidelines for teachers and examples of scripts with examiners' reactions to them. They should also talk to teachers about their examining techniques, marking schemes, and aims and objectives harnessed to specific content.
2. Assessment objectives should focus on understanding whatever has been studied and awareness of the propositional, procedural and conceptual character of history. These objectives should be spelled out in detail in relation to each part of a course and candidates who achieve them must be properly rewarded.
3. The practice of relying totally on a single end-of-course examination should cease and no papers should be set containing an indiscriminate jumble of straightforward and challenging questions.
4. Extreme care is needed regarding content. A crowded syllabus is likely to hinder significant learning but both breadth and depth of study can aid understanding. Detailed thinking, therefore, is necessary about criteria of selection – and the demands made by questions.
5. The strengths and weaknesses of various examining techniques must be weighed up with particular reference to their likely effects on teaching and learning.
6. There must be machinery for systematic consultation between teachers and examiners so that examiners are kept informed of the impact of examinations on teaching, teachers are fully aware of what examiners are striving to do, and a sense of partnership is developed.
7. There must be opportunities for experiments in terms of both syllabuses and examining techniques, and provision for further changes when the necessity arises.

There are no easy solutions to the problems of assessment and examinations. Even this limited programme will demand considerable adjustment, hard thinking and co-operation, although some of the points are familiar features of the work of some Examination Boards. Many people will prefer to avoid such demands and one can understand the reasons for their attitude. But the consequences of maintaining the *status quo* will be profound. School history should build up children's understanding of those parts of the past that they have studied and their awareness of how we come to acquire our knowledge of the past and the nature of that inquiry and knowledge. If obsession with 'know that' continues to dominate the activities of many examiners and teachers then large numbers of school-leavers will go on associating history with the regurgitation of inert historical information and saying to each other, 'Yeah. That's what really history is . . . *facts, facts, facts.*'

Public examinations rule much of the curriculum . . . .
So why not a Magna Charta for Assessment?

APPENDIX I

Questions

1. Why did Jellicoe turn away from the Germans? Give as many reasons as you can.
2. Does anything puzzle you about Jellicoe's turning away at this stage of the battle? If it does, explain why.
3. Can you suggest anything else Jellicoe might have done which you think would have been more likely to achieve what he wanted?
4. Imagine you are Jellicoe talking to a sympathetic listener the day after the battle.
   (a) Explain in as much detail as possible what the situation was at the moment the Germans launched their torpedoes.
   (b) Explain what different actions you considered and what made you choose the one you did, and why you rejected the other alternatives.
5. Explain in as much detail as you can what Jellicoe was trying to do at the Battle of Jutland (not just the turn away – the battle itself).

NOTES

1. Reed, W.A., 'Deliberate approach to the study of the curriculum and its relation to critical pluralism', in Lawson, M. and Barton, L. (eds), *Rethinking Curriculum Studies*, Croom Helm, 1981, pp. 160–87, considers in some detail the assumptions and potential of this approach to curriculum studies and problems.

2. Further interest and activity have been stimulated in recent years by issues of accountability and evaluation. Central government created the Assessment of Performance Unit in 1975 principally to identify any significant changes in overall levels of performance. (For details of the creation and work of the Unit, see Satterly, D., *Assessment in Schools*, Basil Blackwell, 1981, ch. 10.) Local authorities, led by Cheshire, Hillingdon, ILEA, Lancashire and Surrey, have introduced evaluation schemes. (For some examples see McCormick, R. (ed), *Calling Education to Account*, Heinemann Educational Books, 1982, pt 2.) Regulations making the annual publication of public examination results compulsory from 1982 were introduced in response to public pressure and have stimulated considerable debate. (For evidence of the mixed reaction to this requirement, see Plewis, I. *et al.*, *Publishing School Examination Results: A Discussion*, Bedford Way Papers no. 5, University of London Institute of Education, 1981.) There has also been growing emphasis on illuminative evaluation and the teacher as researcher. (See, for example, Stenhouse, L., *An Introduction to Curriculum Research and Development*, Heinemann Educational Books, 1975; Lawton, D., 'Curriculum evaluation: new approaches', in Lawton *et al.*, *Theory and Practice of Curriculum Studies*, Routledge & Kegan Paul, 1978; and Lawton, D., and Lacey, C. (eds), *Issues in Evaluation and Accountability*, Methuen, 1981.)

3. The complete text is in Dickinson, A. K., and Lee, P. J., 'Understanding and research', in Dickinson and Lee (eds), *History Teaching and Historical Understanding*, Heinemann Educational Books, 1978, pp. 112–17.

4. ibid., pp. 99–107.

5. Satterly, op. cit., includes an extensive glossary of assessment terms – and informative chapters on the purposes and modes of assessment. See also Rowntree, D., *Assessing Students: How Shall We Know Them?*, Harper & Row, 1977.

6. The essential characteristics of all the categories are eventually outlined here. A fuller and tabulated description is provided in Dickinson and Lee (eds), op. cit., pp. 86–8 and 102–4.

7. Kate's set of answers was one of the most impressive we received. At her comprehensive school she got disappointing marks for timed-essays, spent most of her time in band two and got a grade E at A level. However, she gained admittance to Cambridge and achieved a second-class degree.

8. Equilibrium as we use it is a much less sophisticated concept than Piaget's. Basically if a set of answers contains a great deal of inconsistency, conflict or internal contradiction we regard the subject as being in a state of disequilibrium and the response is scored in one of the odd-number categories. If these features are absent because problematic aspects have been ignored (category two), partially reconciled (category four) or more permanently resolved (category six) then we say that the subject has achieved explanatory equilibrium. Thus it can be achieved at different levels in our tests. We use the term 'puzzlement' in relation to subjects who feel that they have not understood something and 'confusion' when they feel they understand but in fact have misunderstood various things.

9. Barnes, D., *From Curriculum to Communication*, Penguin, 1976, argues that 'explanatory' talk is very important for learning. See also Bullock, A. (Chairman), *A Language for Life* (The Bullock Report), HMSO, 1975; Edwards, A. D., 'The language of history and the communication of historical knowledge', in Dickinson and Lee (eds), op. cit., pp. 66–8; Schools Council, *Learning Through Talking 11–16*, Working Paper no. 64, Evans/Methuen, 1979, pp. 36–40; and Chapter 5 of this volume. Shemilt, D., *History 13–16 Evaluation Study*, Holmes McDougall, 1980, p. 52, suggests that children seem to learn best by solving problems, particularly those 'which emerge from the working out of their existing ideas in the context of historical problems arising from the prior application of these selfsame ideas'.

10. See Chapter 6 in this volume for a discussion of how the interplay of verbal and visual elements can aid learning.

11. Shemilt, op. cit., pp. 41–4, suggests that the difficulty of thinking reflexively may account for much of the instability that he has found in the level of adolescents' historical thinking.

12. See pp. 108 above for detailed discussion of these possible explanations.

13. Some evidence in support of this assertion is provided on p. 121–2 above.

14. The impact that the use of personal experience, prior knowledge of the past and explicit and implicit evidence provided by the teacher can have on children's thinking and understanding is emphasized and illustrated in Chapter 5, section II (c), of this volume (pp. 136–45).

15. Extensive copying is not limited to the examination years. One survey revealed that the average number of words written by each child in the sample in the first year of secondary schooling was 33,879, of which 15,920 had been copied or dictated. See Robertson, I., *Language Across the Curriculum: Four Case Studies*, Schools Council Working Paper 67, Methuen, 1980, p. 77.

16. Watkins, O., 'Active reading and listening', in Sutton, C. (ed), *Communicating in the Classroom*, Hodder & Stoughton, 1981, suggests some ways of encouraging active interrogation of a text. See particularly pp. 71–3. Many pupils may need considerable help with such reading. Dolan, T., Harrison, C., and Gardner, K., 'The incidence and context of reading in the classroom', in Lunzer, E., and Gardner, K. (eds), *The Effective Use of Reading*, Heinemann Educational Books, 1979, report that in the history lessons observed

the average time spent in reading in each forty-minute period was four minutes (top juniors), six minutes (first-year secondary) and 6.4 minutes (fourth-year secondary). Most of this reading was done in very short fragmented bursts.

17. Three of the six pupils in this category stated explicitly that they needed more information to give a definite or proper answer, and specified what information they wanted.

18. Only one class was officially mixed-ability. Table 8.1 seems to suggest that there may be a wide range of ability in terms of understanding in all classes, including examination groups, though the weighting is likely to vary considerably.

Pupils' scores could be entered quickly into classroom or school records. For a concise discussion of the value and problems of such records, including a critical look at their possible role in accountability, see Becher, T., Eraut, M., and Knight, J., *Policies for Educational Accountability*, Heinemann Educational Books, 1981, pp. 81–7. McCormick (ed), op. cit., also contains good coverage of various conceptions of accountability and ways that institutions might respond.

19. DES, *Primary Education in England: A Survey by HM Inspectors of Schools*, HMSO, 1978, ch. 6, section 6.19, claims that the work observed in history was matched to children's capabilities in less than half the classes observed. In almost all the cases where the standard was not appropriate the ability of pupils was being underestimated. DES, *Report by HM Inspectors on Educational Provision by the Inner London Educational Authority*, HMSO, 1980, sections 4.27, 6.23, 7.27 and 21.7 also says that too many teachers in both primary and secondary schools seem to expect too little from pupils, including sixth-formers.

20. Rosenthal, R., and Jacobson, L., *Pygmalion in the Classroom*, Holt, Rinehart & Winston, 1968. See also Rosenthal, R., *Experimenter Effect in Behavioural Research*, Appleton-Century-Crofts, 1966; Rosenthal, R., 'On the social psychology of self-fulfilling prophecy: further evidence for Pygmalion effects and their mediating mechanisms', in *Module 53*, MSS Modular Publications, 1974; and Martin, M., 'The philosophical importance of the Rosenthal effect', *Journal for the Theory of Social Behaviour*, vol. 7, no. 1, April 1977.

21. See, for example, DES, 1980, op. cit., sections 4.27 and 21.7.

22. I am grateful to Colin Johnston for this example, and to Richard Aldrich, Peter Lee, Joan Lewin, Vivienne Little, Peter Rogers and Douglas Thorburn for their criticisms of the first draft of this chapter.

23. Johnson-Laird, P. N., and Wason, P. C., 'A theoretical analysis of insight into a reasoning task', in Johnson-Laird and Wason (eds), *Thinking : Readings in Cognitive Science*, Cambridge University Press, 1977, particularly pp. 151–2.

24. The points made in this and the previous paragraph seem to the author to have important implications for teaching *and* examining.

25. Bryant, M., 'Documentary and study materials for teachers and pupils: part 2 theories and practices', *Teaching History*, vol. 1, no. 4, November 1970, p. 276.

26. Benton, P., 'Writing: how it is received', in Sutton (ed), op. cit., provides some evidence of this.

27. The Bullock Report, op. cit., p. 167, contains the excellent suggestion that a teacher's first response to a piece of written work should be personal and positive.

28. Lawton, D., *The End of the Secret Garden? A Study in the Politics of the Curriculum*, University of London Institute of Education, 1979, pp. 22–4, sketches some of the things that should be done in terms of assessment at regional, institutional and departmental level. More detailed suggestions are made in Harlem, W. (ed), *Evaluation and the Teacher's Role*, Schools Council Research Studies, Macmillan, 1978; and Shipman, M., *In-School Evaluation*, Heinemann Educational Books, 1979.

29. DES, 1980, op. cit., sections 21.17 and 7.27.

30. ibid., section 7.13.

31. Ideally they need time for careful reading and for oral exploration of points of detail,

connections and possible explanations with both peers and teachers. See Chapter 5 in this volume.

32. See Dickinson and Lee (eds), op. cit., particularly pp. 15–17.

33. It would be a breach of confidence to quote chapter and verse here but such instructions have been issued to some examiners for many years.

34. Lambert, W. R., *History and Economic and Social History at Advanced Level*, Oxford Delegacy of Local Examinations, pp. 4–6, reports in this short but useful memorandum to teachers that it is also the most common weakness of candidates at 18 + .

35 See DES, *Aspects of Secondary Education in England: A Survey by HM Inspectors of Schools*, HMSO, 1979, ch. 10.

36. Shemilt, op. cit., pp. 54–5.

37. loc. cit.

38. Rogers, P. J., *The New History – Theory into Practice*, Historical Association, 1979, p. 5.

39. See *Explorations* produced jointly for the Southern Regional Examinations Board and the *History 13–16 Project*, and available from SREB, Avondale House, 33 Carlton Crescent, Southampton SO9 4YL.

40. GCE and CSE Boards' Joint Council for 16 + National Criteria, *Report of the Subject Working Party in History*, 1982, section 2.1.2.

41. ibid., section 2.3.2.

42. See, for example, Shemilt, op. cit.; *Explorations*; and Chapters 3 and 5 of this volume.

43. The International Baccalaureate, 2 Taviton St, London WC1H 0BT, requires examiners to send a report on each extended essay. It also publishes grade criteria and distributes a questionnaire inviting teachers to comment on the quality of examination papers. The Oxford Delegacy of Local Examinations is another Board that publishes grade criteria – see Lambert, op. cit.

44. Inter-GCE Board Working Party on Common Core in A level History, *Final Report*, 1983.

45. See DES, 1980, op. cit., sections 8.23 and 8.25. Of course there are many splendid exceptions and they are likely to include those teachers who bother to read a book like this!

46. Becher, Eraut, and Knight, op. cit., p. 154, provide evidence that recruitment to the teaching profession has become more competitive. Some important changes have been made in public examinations in history and experimental schemes are producing evidence of the feasibility of assessing a wider range of abilities than hitherto and providing all school leavers with some kind of useful certification – see Burgess, T., and Adams, E. (eds), *Outcomes of Education*, Macmillan, 1980. There has also been a considerable increase in the number of teachers involved in formal arrangements to investigate the effectiveness of their teaching as a result of the growth of teacher-based research groups, LEA monitoring schemes and curriculum development groups associated with the Schools Council Project *History 13–16*. (Nixon, J. (ed), *A Teachers' Guide to Action Research*, Grant McIntyre, 1981, provides some useful information on networks that seek to strengthen the links between teacher-based research groups.)

9. New History: An Historical Perspective

R. E. ALDRICH

The 1978 annual conference of the History of Education Society was devoted to the subject 'Post-War Curriculum Development: an Historical Appraisal',[1] the third annual conference sponsored by the Society in this field. The first, in 1971, had considered 'The Changing Curriculum',[2] the second, in 1975, 'The School Curriculum'.[3] In 1974 a group was formed to explore 'The History of the Curriculum'. It still flourishes.

Though many historians of education have shown interest in the curriculum – in conferences, teaching, research and publications – the influence of such work upon contemporary curriculum development is more difficult to identify. Indeed it would appear that much of the curriculum debate of the last twenty years, *even in relation to the teaching of history*, has taken place in an ahistorical or unhistorical context. In the former sense historical perspectives have simply been ignored. In the latter the past has been misused – raided, distorted and condemned – so that 'Attention is drawn to the past, not for its own sake, but as a means of sharpening a particular contemporary axe.'[4]

The purpose of this chapter is to offer, in a very modest way, some historical perspectives upon the teaching of history in secondary schools, and in particular upon the 'new' history of the last decade and more. This contemporary concept of new history I would take to be as outlined by R. Ben Jones in 1973.

The New History lays less emphasis on content and more on the process of learning . . . .

The New History emphasises that the basis of this selection (of content) is the educational objectives to be achieved and the historical skills to be acquired . . . .

. . . the approach of the New History is what is popularly called the Enquiry Method.[5]

The new history in schools is new in so far as each movement and event in historical time is new and unique in itself. It is new in so far as the new history is a response to the challenge and opportunities, and problems, of a particular age, an age characterized in secondary schools by, among other developments, the rapid application of the comprehensive principle from 1965, and the first CSE examinations in history taken in the same year. It is not correct, however, to suppose that inquiry methods, the use of sources, historical skills, educational objectives, and learning 'how' rather than learning 'what' are new in themselves. Such procedures have formed an essential part of writings on the aims and methods of history teaching in schools since the beginning of this century at least. Thus from 1911 *A History of England for Schools with Documents, Problems, and Exercises* supplied 'the apparatus for work which to some extent is analogous to that provided by the laboratory in the teaching of science'.[6] This book with its 'Nuffield' or heuristic approach was a response to the demand from inspectors and history teachers in schools and teacher-training establishments, who were seeking to implement the ideas put forward by Keatinge in *Studies in the Teaching of History*.

This seminal work, first published in January 1910 and reprinted in 1913, 1921 and 1927, was concerned with the teaching of pupils in the middle forms of secondary schools. It sought to establish history as an essential part of the curriculum by proving the subject's capacity for rigorous intellectual training. Keatinge wanted to introduce pupils to the methods of the modern scientific historian, to reduce part of the subject in schools to problem form, and to confront pupils with evidence. This, however, was not simply to reduce history to a set of mechanical exercises. Though *Studies in the Teaching of History* laid particular emphasis upon scientific methods and the use of contemporary documents, chapters on 'method and moral training' and 'history and poetry' were also included. Above all, Keatinge made no extravagant claims for source work. Pupils would not be constructing their own history, nor writing their own textbooks. 'The boy is no more placed in the position of the historian who weighs and estimates his raw material than the boy in the laboratory who is being put through a course of practical work is . . . being placed in the position of the scientific discoverer.'[7]

In 1929 H. Ann Drummond, Lecturer in Education at the University of Bristol and formerly for two years history mistress at Bedales, described the experiments and conversions of students on teaching practice to the Keatinge method.[8] She confidently declared that 'Most teachers would agree that "sources" should certainly be used in the history course in school, whether elementary or secondary.'[9]

The Learning of History in Elementary Schools appeared in the same year. It came from the pen of Catherine Firth, formerly Director of Studies in History at Newnham, and subsequently Lecturer at Furzedown Training College. A key chapter on historical method linked the worlds of research, teaching and learning.

> The search for evidence, the framing of hypotheses, their testing, their verification, modification or rejection, and the search again: this is in actual fact the process followed not only by the student in the Public Record Office, but by every teacher who works out a fresh lesson for a class, and by every child who writes his own answer to a 'thinking question'.[10]

Firth believed that though history was essentially chronological and bound up with the dimension of time, the history teacher's basic responsibility was to encourage the double question, ' "Is it true?" and "How do we know?" '.[11] Subsequent chapters on 'The activity of children towards historical material', 'The use of original authorities' and 'Independent work', continued the same theme.

F. C. Happold's experiments in history teaching were undertaken at the Perse School, Cambridge, and his methods were set out in an Historical Association pamphlet of 1927. For Happold historical study in schools meant:

> the ability to collect, examine and correlate facts and to express the result in clear and vivid form, freedom from bias and irrational prejudices, the ability to think and argue logically and to form an independent judgement supported by the evidence which is available, and, at the same time, the realisation that every conclusion must be regarded as a working hypothesis to be modified or rejected in the light of fresh evidence.[12]

The Approach to History, which appeared in the following year, was Happold's 'plea for the substitution of historical training for the mere teaching of history in schools'.[13] Happold emphasized the importance of pupil activity, projects and independent work. Though he declared himself less sanguine than Keatinge about the particular value of using original sources in the classroom, Happold also saw history as a means of acquiring the art of thinking, and as a sound mental discipline. A carefully structured and graded course in historical method was outlined in which 'emphasis is placed not so much on the acquisition of historical knowledge as of correct methods of work and of a capacity for historical thinking'.[14]

The wide-ranging aims and methods of history teaching in schools, as set out by such writers as Allen,[15] Drummond, Findlay,[16] Firth, Happold, Hasluck,[17] Jarvis[18] and Keatinge became the intellectual orthodoxy of their day. In a survey of fifty years of answers to the question 'Why teach history', Rogers concluded that by the later 1920s 'the value was seen to lie in the methods of study', '. . . it did not matter so much *what* the pupils learnt so long as they learned *how* to learn it'.[19]

Much of what is claimed as the new history of today, therefore, does not appear to be new at all. Emphases upon sources, historical skills, pupil involvement, inquiry methods and learning 'how', have a firm place in the tradition of history teaching in this country. They need not depend essentially upon Bloom, Bruner or Piaget, nor upon highly contentious notions of structure or doubtful taxonomies for the measurement of historical and other educational objectives and skills.[20]

To the historian of education, however, the most significant feature of the new history movement is its unhistorical, rather than its ahistorical basis. It is unhistorical in so far as its proponents imply that all previous history teaching in schools has been content-dominated, superficial and boring. It is unhistorical in so far as the word 'traditional' has been used simply as a term of abuse. For, on the contrary, there is considerable evidence both as to the achievements (as well as the failures) of history teachers of the first half of the twentieth century, and of the nature and quality of their debates about aims and methods.

By the beginning of the twentieth century history was an accepted subject at both university and secondary school levels. In the 1870s separate honours schools were established at Oxford and Cambridge. *The English Historical Review* was founded in 1886, the Historical Association some twenty years later. By 1890 more candidates had taken history in the Oxford Locals than in any other subject. In that year 68,000, some 91 per cent of the total entries for Oxford Locals, Oxford and Cambridge Schools Examination Board, and London Matriculation offered history.[21] Connections between a genuinely 'new' history at university and school levels were forged in this period. Thus essays on the aims and practice of history teaching in schools by W. H. Woodward, Principal of the University Training College, Liverpool, and C. H. K. Marten, history master at Eton and one time President of the Historical Association, were included in a collection of *Essays on the Teaching of History* published in 1901 by the Cambridge University Press.[22] Of the other contributions five were on aspects of history teaching in English universities, and one on university teaching in the USA. School teachers of history, particularly those who had relied on an uncritical use of such textbooks as Mangnall's *Historical Questions*, or Ince's *Outlines of English History*, might well have benefited from the guidance of their university mentors. Thus H. M. Gwatkin, Dixie Professor of Ecclesiastical History at Cambridge, established three chief aims in the practical teaching of history, 'to rouse interest, to give the guiding facts, and to teach the principles of research and criticism',[23] and briefly discussed their implications for school teaching. J. R. Tanner, in his essay on constitutional history, gave examples of good practice in the university teaching of the subject. Thus, he reported, one Cambridge lecturer supplied his class with two 32-page pamphlets which included 'a list of books recommended, a statement of the subject-matter of each lecture, and short paragraphs on points of special difficulty, with abundant references to the best sources of information'.[24]

Such connections were extended into the elementary school world. Between May 1909 and June 1911 a conference of some twenty-five teachers, headmasters, lecturers and inspectors, presided over by A. F. Pollard, Fellow of All Souls, Oxford, and Professor of English History in the University of London, was set up by the London County Council 'To consider and report as to the methods of teaching history in the public elementary schools of London.' The LCC was committed to a policy of Co-operation between elementary schools, secondary schools, training colleges and universities, and since 1909 had produced reports on the teaching of English, geography and arithmetic. The 72-page report on history was published in 1911. It began with a summary of the historical background to history teaching, and then proceeded to an examination of existing teaching methods in London elementary schools. Material for comparative study was provided by accounts of history teaching in the British Dominions, USA, Germany, Austria, Hungary, Norway, Holland, Belgium, France, Italy and Japan. Two central chapters on the aims of history teaching and suggestions as to the best methods of attaining them were summarized in seven recommendations including:

1. The whole teaching must be governed by the desire to stimulate the use of reasoning power on the part of the pupil rather than of the teacher.
2. Mere knowledge of historical facts is no guarantee of historical understanding.
3. Each school should be allowed at discretion to select for more detailed treatment such aspect or portion of the period as may suit its special circumstances or the character of its pupils.
4. To attain these ends each teacher must omit a considerable portion of what is now considered necessary in a history syllabus.[25]

A concluding chapter on the initial and in-service training of teachers advised that instruction in general principles of pedagogy was insufficient to secure these ends. Historical culture must become an essential element in the curriculum of every training college. The conference outlined five necessary ingredients in this historical culture: '(a) adequate range of historical knowledge, (b) some acquaintance with the means of ascertaining historical fact, (c) some conception of the nature and meaning of historical evidence, (d) some capacity to comprehend historical value and interpret historical truth, and (e) some facility in methods of expressing and presenting results'.[26]

For many years F. R. Worts, headmaster of the City of Leeds School, had nursed the strongest convictions that the 'academic' approach to history that resulted from the university connections was wrong.[27] The *Memorandum on the Teaching of History* of 1925, produced by the IAAM, encouraged Worts 'to continue what seemed to be a hopeless task. I no longer felt *contra mundum*'.[28] The *Memorandum* of 1925 that drew on the wisdom of a committee of seventy-four history teachers in grammar and public schools, was edited by a central co-ordinating committee of twelve. Within its pages was gathered together 'the accumulated experience of men who do the practical work of teaching'.[29] This included not only the what, why and how of history teaching, but also a protest against the control of school history by university professors, examiners and inspectors. The merits of history as a training of the intellect or a training in right living having been raised, the authors wondered whether they should even

concentrate on imparting a body of knowledge, leaving time and reflection to do the rest. Formerly this last was regarded as the sole purpose of history teaching; if the pupil knew certain facts and dates, the work was well done, and nothing more was expected. We have moved far since those days, and such knowledge is now regarded in its right perspective – as a means and not as an end in itself. Teachers at any rate think so, though the demands of examination boards and the questions of examiners leave them wondering if such a conception had made much progress beyond the schools.[30]

Worts's own book, *The Teaching of History in Schools. A New Approach*, first published in 1935, was a powerful attack on the 'old' methods foisted on schools by so-called ' "experts" viewing school-life from the fence or the rim of its true experience; they theorise rather than demonstrate'.[31] Worts did not discount the value of much that had been written about the teaching of history but now he argued that any theorizing could and should be based upon practical classroom experience. This would have been less possible in 1900 when the development of history teaching in schools was seen as a logical extension of the development of historical studies at university level, with the newly trained graduate history teacher as the agent for securing these advances. By the 1930s such graduates, and the secondary schools in which they taught, had more than come of age. Thus Drummond's book of 1929 was criticized for being based on an 'all-too-short teaching experience'[32] while, in Worts's view, the Perse School, where Happold had been senior history master, could not 'be accepted as a normal standard for the average Secondary school'.[33]

The relative merits of the moral and intellectual aims and dimensions of history teaching in schools had been a matter of concern since the days of Thomas Arnold, a century before. Worts sought to reverse the existing emphasis as he saw it, 'to give precedence to ethical over intellectual values'. He concluded:

(i) That we schoolmasters and mistresses are wrong in attempting to inculcate academic ideas of History into our pupils.

(ii) That we ought not to treat History as a science.

(iii) That the scientific 'historical method' ought to find much less favour in our 'methodology' and school practice.

(iv) That History in schools ought not primarily to be regarded as inducing a certain habit of mind or as an agent of mental discipline . . .

(vi) . . . that History in schools is the witnessing of the 'Pageant of Man' rather than the learning of a 'science' that is not a 'science' and never can be.[34]

On the use of sources, historical materials, and research methods below the sixth-form level Worts commented:

today, certainly the vain hope is held that from a knowledge of original documentary matter, juveniles and adolescents will perceive in 'elementary' fashion the principles underlying the true historian's work of knowing original authorities, of discriminating and adjudging their records, and of using the approved material for the making or the writing of History . . . . It is far better to leave this provision of 'sources', primary or secondary, to its first and simple task, namely, of supplying reading material capable of stimulating interest, adding colour to, and infusing the sense of action and reality into, dry and colourless texts.[35]

By 1935 Happold himself had acquired a new perspective, having moved to the headmastership of Bishop Wordsworth's School in Salisbury. *Citizens in the Making* was not concerned to train better historians but rather with the 'fundamental need of the training of better citizens'.[36] In the difficult days of the 1920s and 1930s many teachers were aware of the 'transition in this country from the old order to the new'[37] and saw schools in general, and history lessons in particular, as a key means of ensuring that this transition took place by evolutionary rather than revolutionary means.[38] There was, however, no simple dichotomy between the intellectual and moral approaches to history teaching. Thus in 1929 Firth's book had included a chapter on 'The teaching of local history and the preparation for political citizenship'.[39] A decade later, M. V. C. Jeffreys concluded a classic plea for the line of development approach with a short section on ' "social studies" and "education for citizenship" '.[40]

International citizenship was promoted in schools in the UK by the League of Nations Union, formed in 1918 under the presidency of Lord Grey, the former Foreign Secretary. History lessons, it was argued, should emphasize peace and not war, co-operation rather than antagonism, culture rather than destruction, international rather than national ideals. This theme reached a peak in 1927–8 and Drummond, in her publication of 1929, advocated the establishment of a branch of the Union in every secondary school. Similarly, the much travelled Fred Clarke, whose early writings included a *Social History of Hampshire* (1909), argued in *Foundations of History Teaching*, a book written in 1927 while on a voyage 'Off Finisterre', for the importance of the study of 'humanity' in history, an ideal that had 'come to expression in the form of a League of Nations'.[41]

Doubts, however, about the wisdom of using history lessons for propaganda purposes had been expressed in Historical Association meetings from 1921. In the 1930s, as the inadequacies of the League became more apparent, so the influence of the Union declined, as shown in the poor response to its pamphlet *History Teaching and World Citizenship* (1938).[42]

In the post-war period the several editions and reprints of *The Teaching of History*, first produced in 1950 by another IAAM committee of history teachers, were worthy successors to the *Memorandum* of a quarter of a century before. Multiple aims included 'the weighing of evidence, the detection of bias, the distinguishing of truth from falsehood, or at least the probable from the impossible',[43] Variety in method was encouraged and encompassed sections on sources, project work and 'research' methods. On the other hand undue lecturing, note-taking and reading aloud from textbooks was deplored. The two editions of the *Handbook for History Teachers*,[44] however, drew on the resources of the university world, both in articles on the teaching of history and in bibliographies for advanced work in schools.

For the first sixty years of this century school history teaching in this country relied heavily upon academic historical study and practical classroom experience. Little part was played either by general educational theory or by specific educational research. Thus Ian Steele concluded a recent article by suggesting that:

> the key problem which bedevilled the history teacher in the nineteenth century has still not been resolved: the lack of a coherent theory of history teaching in the context of which aims and objectives, content, learning experiences, evaluation techniques etc., will assume a more identifiable shape. The 'new' history of the 1960s points the way to the future but it seems we are still only at the starting gate![45]

In the past two decades it has become possible to remedy these omissions.

Some advocates of new history, however, by their fundamentally unhistorical approach, have sought to denigrate and destroy earlier foundations and to build anew. This destruction has been justified by such statements as 'Grammar school history teaching aimed principally to equip pupils with a body of factual knowledge',[46] or 'This tradition is now worn out, and must be replaced by one which bases its claims not upon a received corpus of emasculated academic knowledge, but upon the needs of children who will be adults in the twenty-first century'.[47] History teachers and teaching of the past having been summarily condemned and dismissed, school history is to be re-created in accordance with the writings of three educationists, not one of whom was primarily concerned with history as a subject.

Thus *The Teaching of History* of Dennis Gunning rests upon two premises: 'the primacy of concept-learning and the vital importance of skill-learning'.[48]

(a) From Bruner and Piaget we take the idea of the central importance of concept development.
(b) From Bloom we take the idea of the possibility of isolating and developing specific, named intellectual skills.[49]

These, however, are not even to be key concepts of the subject nor historical skills as such, for that would be 'too restricting an idea'.[50] Protests from 'traditionalists' are forestalled. 'There is an academic discipline called "History". There is also a school subject called "History". There is no self-evident reason why they have to be the same.'[51] New history in schools is thereby cut off from history as understood by academics, most schoolteachers and children, and the general public. Whereas the ahistorical dimension raises the question as to how much of the new history is genuinely new, the unhistorical dimension prompts the query as to how much of it is genuinely history.

Two preliminary conclusions may be offered at this point. First, the historian of education can point to evidence from the early twentieth century onwards of a number of well-informed works on the aims and methods of history teaching in schools. In the second place the authors of these works, whether university dons, teacher trainers, schoolteachers or inspectors, whether singly or in committee, whether motivated by a wish to inculcate historical skills, mental discipline, patriotism, peace or moral excellence, have, almost without exception, taken pains to condemn the practice of teaching history as a simple body of received fact. An official memorandum on the study of history produced by the Scottish Education Department in 1907 provides a typical example. Having outlined the value of interest in the life of the past, of training in the laws of evidence, of a philosophical understanding of the development of human civilization, and 'a clarified moral sense', it concluded that 'compared with these, the mere accumulation of a knowledge of historical facts is a matter of quite secondary importance'.[52]

It is not difficult, on the other hand, to furnish evidence that much history teaching in the twentieth century has fallen far short of these high ideals.[53] Emphasis upon such shortcomings, however, has fuelled the belief that inadequate history teachers have consigned the subject to a subordinate place in the secondary school, whence it can now be rescued by the thorough application of new history. For example, John Elliott characterized the years 1918–40 as a time of failure in curriculum reform, so that by the outbreak of the Second World War 'History had failed to become a dominant subject of the curriculum'.[54] This he attributed principally to insufficient and ineffective training in the teaching of the subject, concluding that 'With a less than half-trained and overworked teaching force available, the high hopes pinned on history in 1918 never rose off the ground'.[55] Whether the gap between theory and practice has been wider in history than in other subjects is difficult to determine. Latin, for example, has been advocated for the noblest of reasons – as giving access to a great culture and history, as an agent of mental discipline, as a source of moral example, as an essential basis for grammatical, literary and certain professional studies. Countless generations of schoolboys, and girls, however, have identified Latin in terms of incomprehensible gerund grinding.

The fate of Latin in twentieth-century schools is instructive. Classical study, the staple diet of grammar and public schools since their inception in the medieval period, maintained a pre-eminent position in the education of the upper and aspiring classes until very recent times. In 1914, 92 of 114 boys' public schools had headmasters with classical degrees.[56] All Oxbridge entrants, whether for arts or sciences, were required to have an O level pass in Latin until the 1960s. Latin, however, was never a popular subject. Its status in grammar, preparatory and public schools did not depend upon mass appeal, coherent theories of instruction, nor enlightened methods of presentation. It had little enough place in the curricula of elementary or primary schools. By the nineteenth century Latin had become essentially exclusive, a means of identification and selection, the hallmark of the gentleman or scholar, an elite curriculum device to distinguish the few from the many. Latin was the pivot of a literary, liberal arts, faculty psychology, transfer of training, concept of education. Its status, like that of any subject in the school curriculum, depended to a large extent upon factors quite outside the control of the classroom teacher.

History's position in the primary school curriculum has been much stronger than that of Latin. Indeed there is evidence of a significant history presence in nineteenth-century elementary schools prior to the introduction of the Revised Code in the 1860s with its emphasis upon the three Rs.

History's place in the secondary school curriculum was confirmed in the Secondary Regulations of 1904 which prescribed a broad humanistic as opposed to a particular vocational or technical curriculum. Thus 'Not less than $4\frac{1}{2}$ hours per week must be allotted to English, geography and history; not less than $3\frac{1}{2}$ hours to a language (other than English) where only one was taken, or less than 6 hours where two were taken; and not less than $7\frac{1}{2}$ to Science and Mathematics, of which at least three must be devoted to Science. The instruction in Science must be both theoretical and practical.'[57]

In the Oxford Local Examinations of 1908 both at junior and senior levels, history was taken by the third highest number of candidates, a total exceeded only by arithmetic and English. In the same year the Cambridge Local Examinations produced a virtually identical pattern, with history again in third place both at junior and senior levels. At this period history was a compulsory subject in the preliminary examinations of such professional bodies as the Institutes of Accountants, Architects, Auctioneers and Surveyors, the Law Society and the General Medical Council.[58] In the inter-war years history became a predominant university subject, particularly at Oxford. A history degree thus became a useful qualification for a secondary school headship. In the mid-1950s open awards in history at Oxford and Cambridge constituted some one-fifth of the total, more than in classics, and almost as many as in science as a whole. It was indeed an established status subject.[59]

Though the prestige of history as a university and a school subject may be lower today than it was fifty or even twenty-five years ago, in the second half of the twentieth century the secondary school curriculum, as shown by passes in GCE examinations in England and Wales, is broadly the same as that outlined in the regulations of 1904. In 1956 history was the fifth most popular subject at O level. Ten years later it had slipped to sixth place, and in 1976 to seventh (see Table 9.1).

Table 9.1 GCE O level passes: summer examination

	Eng. Lang.	Maths	Eng. Lit.	French	History	Geography	Biology
1956	100,960	77,419	69,313	59,337	51,496	50,215	30,508
1966	193,425	154,168	122,928	96,190	80,605	88,886	74,750
1976	269,252	191,300	146,241	90,892	85,091	102,802	118,193

Source: Annual Statistics of Education.

At A level history climbed from fifth place in 1956 to fourth in 1966. In 1976 it stood fifth again, having been overtaken by economics with 35,292 passes, a category, however, that included both economic history and British constitution (see Table 9.2).

Table 9.2 GCE A level passes: summer examination

	Maths	Physics	Chemistry	Eng. Lit.	History	French	Geography
1956	15,773	14,382	11,964	11,462	10,004	8,328	6,256
1966	40,772	28,556	21,582	31,850	23,103	18,497	17,645
1976	49,996	29,163	24,508	46,446	26,870	17,252	25,528

Source: Annual Statistics of Education.

In 1966 CSE passes at grade 5 or above showed history in fourth place. Ten years later it had been overtaken by both Art and Craft, and Biology with 138,136 passes (see Table 9.3).

In 1966 an inquiry was conducted into the attitudes of young school-leavers. Some 4,618 13–16-year-olds, their parents and teachers, and some 3,421 former pupils from the same schools, then aged 19–20, were interviewed. These findings were collected and summarized in Schools Council Enquiry I, *Young School Leavers*. This report has been widely and uncritically adduced by

Table 9.3   CSE passes at grade 5 or above, all modes

	English	Maths	Geography	History	Tech. Drawing	Art and Craft	Physics
1966	92,415	89,676	40,944	33,185	28,311	22,389	22,336
1976	447,126	347,106	150,996	131,841	75,677	143,185	91,192

Source: Annual Statistics of Education.

advocates of new history as fundamental proof of the failure of 'traditional' history teaching in secondary schools.[60]

In the history of education *Young School Leavers* occupies a position midway between the Newsom Report of 1963 entitled *Half Our Future*, which considered the education between the ages of 13 and 16 of pupils of average or less than average ability, and the proposed raising of the school leaving age to 16 in 1970–1. It concentrated upon 'what teachers, 15-year-old leavers and parents considered should be the main functions of secondary schools and the ways in which they thought that school curricula and school life in general should develop to meet the needs of the kind of pupils who would be affected by the raising of the school leaving age'.[61]

In general terms the report showed that 15-year-old leavers and their parents saw the most significant purpose of secondary schooling as being the provision of basic knowledge and skills that would enable the young school leaver to obtain immediate employment and the best possible career prospects. Thus boys in the 13–16-year-old group placed maths, English, metalwork, engineering, woodwork, science and technical drawing at the head of their list of useful school subjects. Girls in this group similarly chose English, maths, housecraft, commercial subjects, typing and needlework as the most useful subjects in the school curriculum. History, quite understandably, occupied a low place in their lists. Headteachers and teachers of these pupils, however, gave a very low priority both to vocational preparation and to examination achievements. In a list of twenty-four objectives headteachers assigned examination achievement and 'things of direct use in jobs' to the bottom two places. Examination achievement occupied the lowest place in teachers' objectives, with 'things of direct use in jobs' but three places higher. The educational objectives of headteachers and teachers centred rather around 'personality and character', 'speaking well', 'independence', 'confidence', 'knowing right from wrong', 'getting on well with others'. These reactions were understandable. In 1966 early school-leavers had little opportunity of taking, let alone of succeeding, in external examinations. Their teachers thus often had little experience either of teaching for external examinations or of the jobs to which their pupils would be going.

Significantly, however, the longer pupils intended to stay at school, or in the case of the 19–20-year-olds, had stayed at school, the more interested they had been in history. This was true of most academic subjects. On the other hand interest in the more practical subjects had declined. Thus boys in the older group who had left aged 17/18 thought that history had been more interesting than woodwork and carpentry. Girls in this category thought that history had been more interesting than housecraft, cookery and mothercraft (see Table 9.4).

Table 9.4   **Percentages saying subject was interesting, by age of leaving school and sex (percentages are of those taking the subject)**

Subjects	Age of leaving school	13–16-year-olds % saying subject is interesting		19–20-year-olds % saying subject is interesting	
		Boys	Girls	Boys	Girls
History	15	41	40	42	37
	16	58	53	46	53
	17/18	61	63	65	69
Maths	15	49	44	52	46
	16	60	49	59	47
	17/18	62	50	64	48
Woodwork,	15	75	—	72	—
Carpentry	16	65	—	71	—
	17/18	50	—	63	—
Housecraft,	15	—	87	—	80
Cookery,	16	—	82	—	83
Mothercraft	17/18	—	76	—	66
Bases		13–16 year-olds who were taking the subject		19–20-year-olds who took the subject in their fourth or fifth year at school	

There were similar discrepancies in attitudes towards the usefulness of history. For example, of the 19–20-year-olds who had taken the subject in their fourth and fifth years, only 22 per cent of the girls who left at 15, but 58 per cent of the girls who left aged 17–18, subsequently thought it had been a useful subject to have learned at school.

Table 9.5 shows that even the 15-year-old leavers among the 13–16-year-olds gave history a much higher rating for interest than for usefulness.

Evidence from the 8,039 pupils and ex-pupils interviewed in 1966 for Schools Council Enquiry I suggests that the longer they had stayed at school, the more they had appreciated, both in terms of interest and value, the history studied in fourth- and fifth-form years. Since that date comprehensive re-organization, the growth of CSE, the raising of the school leaving age and the problems of unemployment have brought about new dimensions to secondary schooling. These changes, in spite of the strong plea for vocationally oriented

Table 9.5 Percentages of those taking the subjects saying that various school subjects were interesting in excess of percentages saying they were useful (15-year-olds among the 13–16-year-olds)

		15-year-old leavers	
%	*Boys*	%	*Girls*
+ 25	Art and handicraft	+ 28	Art and handicraft
+ 12	History	+ 20	Physical education and games
+ 11	Physical education and games	+ 12	Music
+ 7	Woodwork	+ 11	History
+ 6	Music	+ 4	Science
+ 5	Metalwork, engineering	− 1	Religious instruction
+ 3	Geography	− 4	Housecraft
—	Science	− 6	Geography
− 2	Technical drawing	− 11	Foreign languages
− 4	Religious instruction	− 12	Current affairs, social studies
− 9	Current affairs, social studies	− 13	Commercial subjects and typing
− 14	Foreign languages	− 14	Needlework
− 37	English	− 24	English
− 44	Mathematics	− 48	Mathematics

courses by the sample of 15-year-old leavers and their parents, and the low priority given to examination achievement by their teachers, have not so far ousted history from its traditional position as a major subject in the secondary school curriculum. Thus whereas in the summer of 1966 there were 136,893 passes in history at GCE and CSE levels, by the summer of 1976 there were 243,802. The vast bulk of this increase was accounted for by CSE passes which roughly quadrupled in this period.

In conclusion, therefore, whatever the faults and failures of history teachers and teaching in the distant and immediate past, and much attention has been drawn to them by advocates of today's new history, it cannot be denied that the subject has achieved considerable prominence in our society. History has flourished as an independent area of academic inquiry, as a key component in programmes of liberal and professional education, as a favourite examination subject at secondary school level, and as an essentially popular interest and activity. This has not been the product of pure chance. It reflects, in part, a number of general social and political factors. It also reflects the fact that the new history of today is but the most recent in a series of new histories which in the last 100 years have enriched and enlarged the teaching and study of the subject.

NOTES

1. Marsden, W. E. (ed), *Post-war Curriculum Development: An Historical Appraisal*, History of Education Society, 1979.
2. History of Education Society, *The Changing Curriculum*, Methuen, 1971.
3. Individual papers from this conference were published in *History of Education*.
4. Marsden, W. E., 'Historical approaches to curriculum study', in Marsden, op. cit., p. 82. One notable exception is the introduction to Palmer, M., and Batho, G. R., *The Source Method in History Teaching*, Historical Association, 1981, pp. 5–7.

5. Jones R. Ben, 'Introduction: the new history', in Jones, R. Ben (ed.), *Practical Approaches to the New History*, Hutchinson Educational, 1973, p. 14.

6. Keatinge, M. W., and Frazer, N. L., *A History of England for Schools with Documents, Problems and Exercises*, 2nd edn, Black, 1920, p. iv.

7. Keatinge, M. W., *Studies in the Teaching of History*, Black, 1910, pp. 38-9.

8. Drummond, H. Ann, *History in Schools. A Study of some of Its Problems*, Harrap, 1929, pp. 140-1.

9. ibid., p. 138.

10. Firth, C. B., *The Learning of History in Elementary Schools*, Kegan Paul, Trench, Trubner and Co., 1929, pp. 10-11.

11. ibid., p. 12.

12. Happold, F. C., *The Study of History in Schools, as a Training in the Art of Thought*, Bell, 1927, p. 4.

13. Happold, F. C., *The Approach to History*, Christophers, 1928, p. xv.

14. ibid.

15. Allen, J. W., *The Place of History in Education*, Blackwood, 1909.

16. Findlay, J. J., *History and its Place in Education*, University of London Press, 1923.

17. Hasluck, E. L., *The Teaching of History*, Cambridge University Press, 1926.

18. Jarvis, C. H., *The Teaching of History*, Oxford University Press, 1917.

19. Rogers, A., 'Why teach history? The answer of 50 years', *Educational Review*, vol 14, 1962, pp. 153-4, 160. The latter comment in particular refers to Happold. For the nineteenth century see Batho, G. R., 'Sources for the history of history teaching in elementary schools 1833-1914', in Cook, T. G. (ed), *Local Studies and the History of Education*, Methuen, 1972, and Roach, J., 'History teaching and examining in secondary schools, 1850-1900', *History of Education*, vol. 5, no. 2, 1976.

20. For a recent comment on the state of play on this issue, see Gard, A., and Lee, P. J., 'Educational objectives for the study of history reconsidered', in Dickinson, A. K., and Lee, P. J. (eds), *History Teaching and Historical Understanding*, Heinemann Educational Books, 1978, pp. 21-38.

21. Figures quoted in IAAM, *The Teaching of History in Secondary Schools*, 3rd edn, Cambridge University Press, 1965, p. 2.

22. Maitland, F. W., *et al.*, *Essays on the Teaching of History*, Cambridge University Press, 1901.

23. ibid., p. 2.

24. ibid., p. 66.

25. LCC Education Committee, *Report of a Conference on the Teaching of History in London Elementary Schools*, 1911, p. 46.

26. ibid., p. 63.

27. Worts, F. R., *The Teaching of History in Schools. A New Approach*, Heinemann, 1935.

28. ibid., p. ix.

29. IAAM, *Memorandum on the Teaching of History*, Cambridge University Press, 1925, preface.

30. ibid., p. 9.

31. Worts, op. cit., p. 10.

32. ibid.

33. ibid., p. 12.

34. ibid., p. 3.

35. ibid., p. 48.

36. Happold, F. C., *Citizens in the Making*, Christophers, 1935, p. 15.

37. ibid., p. 14.

38. See, for example, Madeley, H. M., *History as a School of Citizenship*, Oxford University Press, 1920, and Showan, P. B., *Citizenship and the School*, Cambridge University Press, 1923, especially pt II, 'A scheme of civic instruction based on history', pp. 39-141.

39. Firth, op. cit., pp. 159–75.

40. Jeffreys, M. V. C., *History in Schools: The Study of Development*, Pitman, 1939, pp. 91–4.

41. Clarke, F., *Foundations of History Teaching*, Oxford University Press, 1929, p. 167.

42. Elliott, B. J., 'The League of Nations Union and history teaching in England: a study in benevolent bias', *History of Education*, vol. 6, no. 2, 1977, pp. 131–41.

43. IAAM, *The Teaching of History*, 2nd edn, Cambridge University Press, 1957, p. 3.

44. Burston, W. H., and Green, C. W. (eds), *Handbook for History Teachers*, Methuen, 1962, 1972.

45. Steele, I. J. D., 'The teaching of history in England: an historical perspective', *History Teaching Review*, vol. 12, no. 1, 1980, pp. 6, 11.

46. George, Peggy, 'New syllabus problems in the comprehensive school', in Jones, G. and Ward, L. (eds), *New History Old Problems: Studies in History Teaching*, University College of Swansea Faculty of Education, 1978, p. 8.

47. Steel, D. J., and Taylor, L., *Family History in Schools*, Phillimore, 1973, p. 3.

48. Gunning, Dennis, *The Teaching of History*, Croom Helm, 1978, p. 13.

49. ibid., p. 17.

50. ibid., p. 13.

51. ibid.

52. Scottish Education Department, *Memorandum on the Study of History in Schools* (Cd. 3843), HMSO, 1907, p. 18.

53. For example, Booth, M. B., *History Betrayed?*, Longmans, Green, 1969; and Duckworth, John, 'The evolution of the history syllabus in English schools in the first quarter of the 20th century', *History of Education Society Bulletin*, vol. 15, 1975, pp. 44–51.

54. Elliott, B. J., 'An early failure of curriculum reform: history teaching in England 1918–1940', *Journal of Educational Administration and History*, vol. 12, no. 2, 1980, p. 41.

55. ibid., p. 45.

56. Duckworth, op. cit., p. 44.

57. Quoted in Eaglesham, E. J. R., *The Foundations of 20th Century Education in England*, Routledge & Kegan Paul, 1967, p. 59.

58. *Report of the Consultative Committee on Examinations in Secondary Schools* (Cd. 6004), HMSO, 1911, pp. 164–6, 177–80, 357–8.

59. IAAM, *The Teaching of History*, 2nd. edn, Cambridge University Press, 1957, p. 117, quoting results published in the Press in 1955–6. Of a total of 990 awards, 196 were made in history, 176 in classics, 210 in science, and 408 in all other subjects combined.

60. Even by Steele, op. cit., p. 3.

61. Schools Council Enquiry I, *Young School Leavers*, HMSO, 1968, p. 3. Tables 9.4 and 9.5 have been compiled from statistics supplied in ch. 2 of the report.

Index